THE FAIR TRADING ACT 1973

By

BRUCE REYNOLDS, B.A., B.C.L.(Oxon.)

of the Inner Temple, Barrister

and

ALAN PARDOE, M.A., LL.B.(Cantab.)

of Lincoln's Inn, Barrister

LONDON

BUTTERWORTHS

1975

Annotated Legislation Service Volume 229

ENGLAND: Butterworth & Co. (Publishers) Ltd.
88 Kingsway, London WC2B 6AB

AUSTRALIA: Butterworth Pty. Ltd.
586 Pacific Highway, Chatswood, Sydney 2067
343 Little Collins Street, Melbourne 3000
240 Queen Street, Brisbane 4000

CANADA: Butterworth & Co. (Canada) Ltd.
2265 Midland Avenue, Scarborough, M1P 4S1

NEW ZEALAND: Butterworths of New Zealand Ltd.
26–28 Waring Taylor Street, Wellington 1

SOUTH AFRICA: Butterworth & Co. (South Africa) (Pty.) Ltd.
152–154 Gale Street, Durban

ISBN 0 406 54734 3

PRINTED IN GREAT BRITAIN BY OFFSET LITHOGRAPHY BY
BILLING & SONS LTD., GUILDFORD AND LONDON

PREFACE

The Fair Trading Act 1973 is a lengthy and, at first sight, formidable statute. As we say in our Introduction, the Act really has two quite distinct objects. One portion of the Act is concerned with the protection of consumers; the other reorganises and consolidates the law relating to monopolies, mergers and restrictive practices. The authors have therefore felt it appropriate to divide the work according to the divisions found in the Act. Mr. Alan Pardoe has undertaken the task of annotating the sections relating to monopolies, mergers and restrictive practices (*i.e.*, ss. 6–11 and 44–117). He has also written the portion of the Introduction dealing with these topics. Mr. Bruce Reynolds has taken responsibility for the portion of the Act concerned with the protection of consumers (ss. 1–5, 13–43 and 118–40, and all the Schedules to the Act). This author has also written the portion of the Introduction dealing with these matters and describing most of the statutory bodies and officers set up by the Act. The book however ultimately remains a work of joint authorship.

The book endeavours to give a short explanation of, and commentary on, each of the provisions of the Act. It is hoped that this detailed commentary on the statutory provisions will assist those who are, in practice, concerned with the operation of this Act. Neither in format, nor in content, is this book suitable as an academic or philosophical treatise and it is hoped that it will not be judged as such. Furthermore, we feel that, in the long term, it is unrealistic to consider the Act in isolation. The Act itself makes numerous provisions for the introduction of regulations under it. Only when these regulations have been made, and when a considerable body of case law has been built up will one be able to get a fair and accurate picture of the scope and importance of this legislation. We trust that we have described the basic anatomy of this legislation—the work of shading and colouring must await future developments.

Lastly, we would wish to express our appreciation and thank all those who have assisted in the preparation of this work. In particular we would like to thank Butterworths' editorial staff for their assistance and patience, all those who have assisted in the typing and printing of the book and Mr. Stephen Laws for his valuable research. The passage in the Introduction describing the work of the Monopolies and Mergers Commission owes much to the help of the Chairman of the Commission, Sir Ashton Roskill. For all errors and eccentricities we alone are responsible.

We hope that this book accurately states the law as at 1st May 1975.

Inner Temple,
London, E.C.4.
May 1975

BRUCE REYNOLDS
ALAN PARDOE

CONTENTS

TABLE OF CASES

In the following Table references are given to the English and Empire Digest where a digest of the case may be found.

PARA.

Broadbent *v.* Crisp, [1974] 1 All E.R. 1052; [1974] I.C.R. 248 . . . . . **[237]**

Brown *v.* London and North Western Rail. Co. (1863), 4 B. & S. 326; [1861–73] All E.R. Rep. 487; 2 New Rep. 447; 32 L.J.Q.B. 318; 8 L.T. 695; 27 J.P. 711; 10 Jur. N.S. 234; 11 W.R. 884; 13 Digest (Repl.) 417 . . . . . . **[190]**

C

Cabell *v.* Vaughan (1669), 1 Wms. Saund. 291; 2 Keb. 525; 1 Vent. 34; *sub. nom.* Chappel *v.* Vaughan, 1 Sid. 420; 12 Digest (Reissue) 42 . . . . . **[140]**

Cain *v.* Butler, [1916] 1 K.B. 795; 85 L.J.K.B. 804; 114 L.T. 698; 32 T.L.R. 310; 13 Digest (Repl.) 417 . . . . **[190]**

Cameron *v.* Tyler, [1899] 2 Q.B. 94; 68 L.J.Q.B. 759; 80 L.T. 764; 63 J.P. 567; 47 W.R. 559; 15 T.L.R. 369; 43 Sol. Jo. 498; 19 Cox C.C. 353; 47 Digest (Repl.) 792 **[129]**

Cassidy *v.* Engwirda Construction Co., [1967] Q.W.N. 16 . . . . . . **[219]**

Caughey, *Re, Ex parte* Ford (1876), 1 Ch. D. 521; 45 L.J. Bcy. 96; 34 L.T. 634; 24 W.R. 590, C.A.; 5 Digest (Repl.) 792 . . . . **[138]**, **[232]**

Cenlon Finance Co., Ltd. *v.* Elwood, [1962] A.C. 782; [1962] 1 All E.R. 854; [1962] 2 W.L.R. 871; 106 Sol. Jo. 280; 40 Tax Cas at p. 201; [1962] T.R. 1; 41 A.T.C. 11, H.L.; 28 (1) Digest (Reissue) 48 . . . . **[229]**

Chappell & Co., Ltd. *v.* Nestle Co., Ltd., [1958] Ch. 529; [1958] 2 All E.R. 155; [1958] 2 W.L.R. 657; 102 Sol. Jo. 270, C.A.; reversed, [1960] A.C. 87; [1959] 2 All E.R. 701; [1959] 3 W.L.R. 168; 103 Sol. Jo. 561, H.L.; Digest Cont. Vol. A 312 . . . . **[198]**

Chemists' Federation Agreement (No. 2), *Re*, [1958] 3 All E.R. 448; L.R. 1 R.P. 75; [1958] 1 W.L.R. 1192; 102 Sol. Jo. 861; 45 Digest (Repl.) 412 . . . . **[181]**

Chong *v.* Fairfield Municipal Council (1968), 89 W.N. (Pt. 1) N.S.W. 194 . . **[219]**

Christie *v.* Leachinsky, [1947] A.C. 573; [1947] 1 All E.R. 567; [1947] L.J.R. 757; 176 L.T. 443; 111 J.P. 224; 63 T.L.R. 231; 45 L.G.R. 201, H.L.; 14 Digest (Repl.) 204 . . . . **[129]**

Churchill *v.* Walton. *See* R. *v.* Churchill.

Churchman *v.* Churchman, [1945] P. 44; [1945] 2 All E.R. 190; 114 L.J.P. 17; 173 L.T. 108; 61 T.L.R. 464; 89 Sol. Jo. 508, C.A.; 27 (1) Digest (Reissue) 500 **[232]**

City of Plymouth (City Centre) Declaratory Order, 1946, *Re*, Robinson *v.* Minister of Town and Country Planning, [1947] K.B. 702; [1947] 1 All E.R. 851; [1947] L.J.R. 1285; 177 L.T. 375; 111 J.P. 378; 63 T.L.R. 374; 91 Sol. Jo. 294; 45 L.G.R. 497, C.A.; 45 Digest (Repl.) 366 . . . . **[129]**

Concentrated Foods, Ltd. *v.* Champ, [1944] K.B. 342; [1944] 1 All E.R. 272; 113 L.J.K.B. 417; 170 L.T. 302; 108 J.P. 119; 60 T.L.R. 194; 42 L.G.R. 82; 25 Digest (Repl.) 98 . . . . **[124]**

Cornelius *v.* Philips, [1918] A.C. 199; [1916–17] All E.R. Rep. 685; 87 L.J.K.B. 246; 118 L.T. 228; 34 T.L.R. 116; 62 Sol. Jo. 140, H.L.; 12 Digest (Reissue) 330 **[190]**

Coupe *v.* Guyett, [1973] 2 All E.R. 1058; [1973] 1 W.L.R. 669; 137 J.P. 694; 117 Sol. Jo. 415; 71 L.G.R. 355 . . . . **[124]**, **[125]**

Crompton (Alfred) Amusement Machines, Ltd. *v.* Customs and Excise Commissioners, [1971] 2 All E.R. 843; 115 Sol. Jo. 307; Digest Supp. . . . . **[129]**

Cunard's Trustees *v.* Inland Revenue Commissioners, [1946] 1 All E.R. 159; 174 L.T. 133; 27 Tax Cas. at p. 130, C.A.; 28 (1) Digest (Reissue) 263 . . . **[220]**

Curtis *v.* Chemical Cleansing and Dyeing Co., Ltd., [1951] 1 K.B. 805; [1951] 1 All E.R. 631; [1951] 1 T.L.R. 452; 95 Sol. Jo. 253, C.A.; 3 Digest (Repl.) 103 . **[130]**

D

Dale *v.* Smith, [1967] 2 All E.R. 1133; [1967] 1 W.L.R. 700; 131 J.P. 378; 111 Sol. Jo. 330; Digest Cont. Vol. C 252 . . . . **[134]**

Davies *v.* Winstanley (1930), 144 L.T. 433; 95 J.P. 21; 47 T.L.R. 104; 29 L.G.R. 94; 29 Cox C.C. 242; 33 Digest (Repl.) 553 . . . . **[129]**

Davis *v.* Carew-Pole, [1956] 2 All E.R. 524; [1956] 1 W.L.R. 833; 100 Sol. Jo. 510; 25 Digest (Repl.) 505 . . . . **[247]**

Davis *v.* Lisle, [1936] 2 K.B. 434; [1936] 2 All E.R. 213; 105 L.J.K.B. 593; 155 L.T. 23; 100 J.P. 280; 52 T.L.R. 475; 80 Sol. Jo. 409; 34 L.G.R. 253; 30 Cox C.C. 412; 15 Digest (Repl.) 852 . . . . **[130]**

Dean *v.* Hiesler, [1942] 2 All E.R. 340; 106 J.P. 282; 40 L.G.R. 262; 17 Digest (Reissue) 532 . . . . **232]**

Delany *v.* Delany (1885), 15 L.R. Ir. 55; 48 Digest (Repl.) 566 . . . . . **[233]**

Derry *v.* Peek (1889), 14 App. Cas. 337; [1886–90] All E.R. Rep. 1; 58 L.J. Ch. 864; 61 L.T. 265; 54 J.P. 148; 38 W.R. 33; 5 T.L.R. 625; 1 Meg. 292, H.L., 9 Digest (Repl.) 127 . . . . **[146]**

PARA.

H

I

J

K

L

PARA.

M

McDowell *v.* Standard Oil Co. (New Jersey), [1927] A.C. 632; 96 L.J. Ch. 386; 137 L.T. 734; 43 T.L.R. 592; 44 R.P.C. 335, H.L.; 46 Digest (Repl.) 59 . **[219]**

McGlennon's Application for Registration of Shamrock, *Re* (1908), 25 T.L.R. 23; 53 Sol. Jo. 14; 25 R.P.C. 797; 46 Digest (Repl.) 43 . . . . . . **[219]**

McHole *v.* Davies (1875), 1 Q.B. 59; 45 L.J.M.C. 30; 33 L.T. 502; 40 J.P. 548; 24 W.R. 343; 33 Digest (Repl.) 485 . . . . **[129]**

M'Intyre *v.* Laird, 1943 S.C.(J.) 96 . . . . **[125]**

MacMillan & Co., Ltd. *v.* Rees, [1946] 1 All E.R. 675; 175 L.T. 86; 62 T.L.R. 331, C.A.; 31 (2) Digest (Reissue) 999 . . . . **[129]**

Maddox *v.* Storer, [1963] 1 Q.B. 451; [1962] 1 All E.R. 831; [1962] 2 W.L.R. 958; 126 J.P. 263; 106 Sol. Jo. 372; 61 L.G.R. 41; 45 Digest (Repl.) 32 . . **[257]**

Mallon *v.* Allon, [1964] 1 Q.B. 385; [1963] 3 All E.R. 843; [1963] 3 W.L.R. 1053; 128 J.P. 81; 107 Sol. Jo. 892; 62 L.G.R. 58; Digest Cont. Vol. A 625 . **[130]**, **[232]**

Marshall *v.* Gotham Co., Ltd., [1954] A.C. 360; [1954] 1 All E.R. 937; [1954] 2 W.L.R. 812; 98 Sol. Jo. 268, H.L.; 33 Digest (Repl.) 910 . . . . **[181]**

Melbourne Corporation *v.* Commonwealth (1947), 74 C.L.R. 31, 61 . . . **[263]**

Mileage Conference Group of Tyre Manufacturers' Conference, Ltd.'s Agreement, *Re*, [1966] 2 All E.R. 849; [1966] 1 W.L.R. 1137; 110 Sol. Jo. 483; Digest Cont. Vol. B 712 . . . . **[238]**

Miller *v.* Ottilie (Owners), [1944] K.B. 188; [1944] 1 All E.R. 277; 113 L.J.K.B. 115; 170 L.T. 204; 60 T.L.R. 169; 36 B.W.C.C. 236, C.A.; 34 Digest (Repl.) 349 . **[157]**

Monk *v.* Warbey, [1935] 1 K.B. 75; [1934] All E.R. Rep. 373; 104 L.J.K.B. 153; 152 L.T. 194; 51 T.L.R. 77; 78 Sol. Jo. 783; 50 Ll. L. Rep. 33, C.A.; 29 Digest (Repl.) 537 . . . . **[134]**

N

Naish *v.* Gore, [1971] 3 All E.R. 737; 136 J.P. 1.; [1972] R.T.R. 102; Digest Supp. **[125]**

Nakkuda Ali *v.* Jayaratne, [1951] A.C. 66; 66 (pt. 2) T.L.R. 214; 94 Sol. Jo. 516, P.C.; 8 Digest (Repl.) 803 . . . . **[125]**, **[129]**

North Cheshire and Manchester Brewery Co. *v.* Manchester Brewery Co., [1899] A.C. 83; 68 L.J. Ch. 74; 79 L.T. 645, 15 T.L.R. 110, H.L.; 22 Digest (Reissue) 204 . . . . **[219]**

Noss Farm Products, Ltd. *v.* Lilico, [1945] 2 All E.R. 609; 173 L.T. 251; 109 J.P. 211; 61 T.L.R. 488; 89 Sol. Jo. 413; 43 L.G.R. 289; 25 Digest (Repl.) 87 . **[124]**

O

Oken *v.* Perraton, [1947] 2 All E.R. 286; 63 T.L.R. 537; 31 (1) Digest (Reissue) 391 **[129]**

Osborne *v.* Barclay, Curle & Co., [1901] A.C. 269; 85 L.T. 286, H.L. . . . . **[34]**

P

Paddington Burial Board *v.* Inland Revenue Commissioners (1884), 13 Q.B.D. 9; 53 L.J.Q.B. 224; 50 L.T. 211; 48 J.P. 311; 32 W.R. 551; 2 Tax Cas. 46; 28 (1) Digest (Reissue) 80 . . . . **[129]**

Padfield *v.* Minister of Agriculture, [1968] A.C. 997; [1968] 2 W.L.R. 924; 110 Sol. Jo. 604, C.A.; reversed, [1968] A.C. at p. 1016; [1968] 1 All E.R. 694; [1968] 2 W.L.R. at p. 936; 112 Sol. Jo. 171, H.L., Digest Cont. Vol. C389 . **[102]**, **[112]**, **[115]**, **[134]**, **[183]**

Panorama Developments (Guildford), Ltd. *v.* Fidelis Furnishing Fabrics, Ltd., [1971] 2 Q.B. 711; [1971] 3 All E.R. 16; [1971] 3 W.L.R. 440; 115 Sol. Jo. 483, C.A.; 12 Digest (Reissue) 101 . . . . **[232]**

Pauley *v.* Kenaldo, Ltd., [1953] 1 All E.R. 226; [1953] 1 W.L.R. 187; 97 Sol. Jo. 49; 34 Digest (Repl.) 105 . . . . **[237]**

Popperwell *v.* Cockerton, [1968] 1 All E.R. 1038; [1968] 1 W.L.R. 438; 132 J.P. 231; 112 Sol. Jo. 175; Digest Cont. Vol. C 915 . . . . **[257]**

Post Office *v.* Union of Post Office Workers, [1974] 1 All E.R. 229; [1974] 1 W.L.R. 89; 118 Sol. Jo. 183, H.L. . . . . **[263]**

Price *v.* Humphries, [1958] 2 Q.B. 353; [1958] 2 All E.R. 725; [1958] 3 W.L.R. 304; 122 J.P. 423; 102 Sol. Jo. 583; 35 Digest (Repl.) 801 . . . . . . **[229]**

R

R. *v.* Banks, [1916] 2 K.B. 621; [1916–17] All E.R. Rep. 356; 85 L.J.K.B. 1657; 115 L.T. 457; 80 J.P. 432; 25 Cox C.C. 535; 12 Cr. App. Rep. 74, C.C.A.; 14 Digest (Repl.) 304 . . . . **[129]**

PARA.

PARA.

Rumbelow *v.* Rumbelow and Hadden (or Hadder), [1965] p. 207; [1965] 2 All E.R. 767; [1965] 3 W.L.R. 242; 109 Sol. Jo. 454, C.A.; 27 (1) Digest (Reissue) 499 **[138]**

S

Schweppes, Ltd.'s Agreement (No. 2), *Re*, Registrar of Restrictive Trading Agreements *v.* Schweppes, Ltd., [1971] 2 All E.R. 1473; L.R. 7 R.P. 336; [1971] 1 W.L.R. 1148; 115 Sol. Jo. 263; Digest Supp. . . . . **[217]**

Secretary of State for Employment *v.* Associated Society of Locomotive Engineers and Firemen (No. 2), [1972] 2 Q.B. 455; [1972] 2 All E.R. 949; [1972] 2 W.L.R. 1370; 116 Sol. Jo. 434; affirmed, [1972] 2 Q.B. at p. 470; [1972] 2 All E.R. at p. 962; [1972] 2 W.L.R. at p. 1384; 116 Sol. Jo. 467, C.A.; Digest Supp. . **[102]**, **[112]**, **[115]**, **[129]**, **[134]**, **[141]**, **[183]**

Shawinigan, Ltd. *v.* Vokins & Co., Ltd., [1961] 3 All E.R. 396; [1961] 1 W.L.R. 1206; 105 Sol. Jo. 588; [1961] 2 Lloyd's Rep. 153; Digest Cont. Vol. A 81 . **[146]**

Sherratt *v.* Geralds, the American Jewellers, Ltd. (1970), 114 Sol. Jo. 147; 68 L.G.R. 256; Digest Cont. Vol. C 1024 . . . . **[125]**

Small *v.* Bickley (1875), 32 L.T. 726; 40 J.P. 119; 25 Digest (Repl.) 117 . . **[129]**

Smedley's Ltd. *v.* Breed, [1974] A.C. 839; [1974] 2 All E.R. 21; [1974] 2 W.L.R. 575; 138 J.P. 439; 118 Sol. Jo. 363, H.L. . . . . **[125]**

South Behar Rail. Co., Ltd. *v.* Inland Revenue Commissioners, [1925] A.C. 476; 94 L.J.K.B. 386; 132 L.T. 802; 69 Sol. Jo. 379; 41 T.L.R. 328, H.L. . . **[233]**

Southern Electricity Board *v.* Collins, [1970] 1 Q.B. 83; [1969] 2 All E.R. 1166; [1969] 3 W.L.R. 147; 113 Sol. Jo. 425; Digest Cont. Vol. C 691 . . . . **[237]**

Stevens and Steeds, Ltd. and Evans *v.* King, [1943] 1 All E.R. 314; 41 L.G.R. 108; 25 Digest (Repl.) 152 . . . . **[130]**

Stone *v.* Burn, [1911] 1 K.B. 927; [1908–10] All E.R. Rep. 477; 80 L.J. K.B. 560; 103 L.T. 540; 74 J.P. 456; 27 T.L.R. 6; 46 Digest (Repl.) 166 . . . **[125]**

Sunair Holidays, Ltd. *v.* Dodd, [1970] 2 All E.R. 410; [1970] 1 W.L.R. 1037; 134 J.P. 507; 114 Sol. Jo. 372; Digest Cont. Vol. C 1023 . . . . **[130]**

Swallow *v.* London County Council, [1916] 1 K.B. 224; [1914–15] All E.R. Rep. 403; 85 L.J. K.B. 234; 114 L.T. 368; 80 J.P. 164; 32 T.L.R. 181; 14 L.G.R. 301; 25 Cox C.C. 295; 47 Digest (Repl.) 791 . . . . . . **[130]**

Symonds *v.* Kurtz (1889), 61 L.T. 559; 53 J.P. 727; 5 T.L.R. 511; 16 Cox C.C. 726; 15 Digest (Repl.) 997 . . . . **[129]**

T

Tarleton Engineering, Ltd. *v.* Nattrass, [1973] 3 All E.R. 699; [1973] 1 W.L.R. 1261; 137 J.P. 837; 117 Sol. Jo. 745; 72 L.G.R. 56 . . . . . **[125]**

Taylor *v.* Mead, [1961] 1 All E.R. 626; [1961] 1 W.L.R. 435; 125 J.P. 286; 105 Sol. Jo. 159; 59 L.G.R. 202; 39 Digest (Repl.) 284 . . . . . **[257]**

Taylor's Central Garages (Exeter), Ltd. *v.* Roper (1951), 115 J.P. 445; *sub nom.* Roper *v.* Taylor's Central Garages (Exeter), Ltd., [1951] 2 T.L.R. 284; 45 Digest (Repl.) 134 . . . . **[130]**, **[232]**

Tendler *v.* Sproule, [1947] 1 All E.R. 193, C.A.; 31 (2) Digest (Reissue) 1083 . **[129]**

Terrell *v.* Mabie Todd & Co., [1952] 2 T.L.R. 574; 96 Sol. Jo. 596; 69 R.P.C. 234; affirmed, (1953), 70 R.P.C. 97, C.A.; 36 Digest (Repl.) 829 . . . . **[134]**

Tesco Supermarkets, Ltd. *v.* Nattrass, [1972] A.C. 153; [1971] 2 All E.R. 127; [1971] 2 W.L.R. 1166; 135 J.P. 289; 115 Sol. Jo. 285; 69 L.G.R. 403, H.L.; Digest Supp. . . . . **[123]**, **[124]**, **[125]**, **[138]**, **[232]**

Treacher & Co., Ltd. *v.* Treacher, [1874] W.N. 4; 45 Digest (Repl.) 491 . . **[190]**

Trickers (Confectioners), Ltd. *v.* Barnes, [1955] 1 All E.R. 803; [1955] 1 W.L.R. 372; 99 Sol. Jo. 239; 53 L.G.R. 366; 25 Digest (Repl.) 130 . . . . **[125]**

Trow *v.* Ind Coope (West Midlands), Ltd., [1967] 2 Q.B. at p. 909; [1967] 2 All E.R. 900; [1967] 3 W.L.R. 633; 111 Sol. Jo. 375, C.A.; Digest Cont. Vol. C 955 **[120]**

U

Union of Whippingham and East Cowes Benefices, *Re*, Derham *v.* Church Commissioners of England, [1954] A.C. 245; [1954] 2 All E.R. 22; [1954] 2 W.L.R. 804; 98 Sol. Jo. 268, P.C.; 19 Digest (Repl.) 433 . . . . . . **[120]**

W

Walkling (A.), Ltd. *v.* Robinson (1929), 99 L.J.K.B. 171; [1929] All E.R. Rep. 658; 143 L.T. 105; 94 J.P. 73; 46 T.L.R. 151; 28 L.G.R. 88; 29 Cox C.C. 131; 25 Digest (Repl.) 133 . . . . **[125]**

DIVISION I

COMMENTARY

1. INTRODUCTION

The Fair Trading Act 1973 has two quite distinct objects. First, it contains provisions designed to provide additional protection for consumers. Secondly, it reorganises, and to some extent consolidates, the law relating to monopolies, mergers and restrictive practices. [**1**]

Although the Act was passed on 25th July 1973 it did not immediately come into force. By s. 140 (3) of the Act, it was provided that the legislation would come into operation on such day or days as the Secretary of State may "by order made by statutory instrument appoint". The Act further provided that different dates could be appointed for the purpose of bringing different provisions of the Act into force from different dates. Two such commencement orders have been made—the Fair Trading Act 1973 (Commencement No. 1) Order 1973[1]; and the Fair Trading Act 1973 (Commencement No. 2) Order 1973[2]. (The dates upon which particular sections of the Act came into operation are to be found in the notes to the Act in Division 2, *post*.) [**2**]

The Act provides for the appointment of an important new officer—the Director General of Fair Trading.[3] In the field of consumer affairs the Director receives assistance from the Consumer Protection Advisory Committee, which is empowered to consider and report upon such "consumer trade practices" as are referred to it.[4] [**3**]

The provisions designed to protect consumers fall into 3 distinct categories. These are:—

(1) a "consumer trade practice" may be referred to the Consumer Protection Advisory Committee simply for the purpose of consideration and report. Such a practice may also be referred to the Advisory Committee together with recommendations that the Secretary of State exercise his powers by making an order upon receipt of the report of the Advisory Committee. If such an order is subsequently made, the Act contains provision for the enforcement of such order;

(2) the director is empowered to institute action, usually before the Restrictive Practices Court, against persons who persist in a course of conduct which is detrimental to the interests of consumers or is to be regarded as unfair to such consumers. If such proceedings are brought, the Restrictive Practices Court is empowered, if no undertaking is forthcoming from the defendant, to make orders requiring the defendant to refrain from that course of conduct;

---

[1] S.I. 1973 No. 1545, which brought the relevant portions of the Act into operation on 14th September 1973.

[2] S.I. 1973 No. 1652, which brought the relevant portions of the Act into operation on 2nd October 1973.

[3] See ss. 1 and 2 and the notes thereto, *post*.

[4] See s. 3 and the note thereto, *post*; for "consumer trade practice" see s. 13 and the note thereto, *post*.

(3) the Act provides for certain restrictions on the operation of "pyramid selling" and similar trading schemes. As a result these schemes are carefully controlled by regulations made under the Act. The Director also takes over the functions of the former Registrar of Restrictive Trading Agreements. The Restrictive Practices Court remains as before. There are however certain amendments to the jurisdiction of that Court. In particular the Act makes provision for the application of Part I of the Restrictive Practices Act 1956 to agreements and arrangements between suppliers of services which involve restrictions upon the supply or acquisition of those services. The extension of the jurisdiction does not however apply to services of a professional nature. [**4**]

The Monopolies Commission, basically, continues in existence. It is however renamed the Monopolies and Mergers Commission. This Commission is empowered to investigate and report on monopoly situations, general mergers and mergers of newspapers. Although, in this context, the Act makes some important changes of substance, which are considered in more detail later, this aspect of the Act can quite properly be regarded as consolidating, rather than innovating, legislation. [**5**]

One cannot read this Act in isolation. The Act contains numerous provisions permitting the making of orders or regulations.[5] The full effect and importance of the Act will only become apparent when a sufficient number of these orders and regulations have been made. Only then will it be possible to assess the significance of this Act in the field of consumer protection. [**6**]

[5] See ss. 22, 39, 50, 56, 73, 107, 108, 119, 127 and 140, together with the notes thereto, *post*.

2. THE STATUTORY BODIES AND OFFICERS

DIRECTOR GENERAL OF FAIR TRADING

The Director General of Fair Trading is the most important new officer established by the Act. General provisions defining the powers and duties of the Director are to be found in ss. 2 and 3 of the Act. The Director is generally charged with the duty of keeping commercial activities in the United Kingdom under review with a view to "becoming aware of and ascertaining" circumstances relating to practices which may adversely affect the economic interests of consumers in the United Kingdom. The Director is also obliged to receive and collate evidence of commercial activities in the United Kingdom which may adversely affect the interest of consumers in the United Kingdom. In this regard the Director is not confined to receiving and collating evidence of practices adversely affecting economic interests; he is entitled to receive and collate evidence concerning health, safety or other matters – see s. 2 of the Act. The general duties of the Director in the field of consumer protection also require him to have regard to any evidence becoming available to him "with respect to any course of conduct on the part of a person carrying on a business which appears to be conduct detrimental to the interests of consumers in the United Kingdom". A curious provision of s. 2 (5) imposes a duty on the Director to have regard to the needs of regional development and the dispersal of offices, and office accommodation, from London. [**7**]

This last provision is an anomaly which is unrelated to any policy specifically enshrined in the Act. With this exception, however, the general duties imposed on the Director are intended to facilitate the exercise of the powers and duties conferred by the more specific sections of the Act. The general duties are clearly intended to confer a wide ranging duty of scrutiny upon the Director. Section 124 of the Act empowers the Director, from time to time, to publish such information and advice as it may appear to him to be expedient to give to consumers in the United Kingdom. He is also required to make an Annual Report to the Secretary of State in which he includes a general survey of matters falling within his jurisdiction—see s. 125. This Report is then required to be laid before each House of Parliament for the purpose of publication. In addition to the duty of making an Annual Report the Director is also empowered to devise and publish such other reports as he may, from time to time, consider appropriate—see s. 125 of the Act. [**8**]

In addition to his general duties the Director is also required to carry out certain specific obligations and exercise particular powers. The Director is empowered to refer to the Consumer Protection Advisory Committee the question whether any "consumer trade practice" adversely affects the economic interests of consumers in the United Kingdom. This power is shared amongst the Director, the Secretary of State and any other Minister. The Director may make such a reference solely for the purpose of obtaining a report on the practice or may couple the reference with a recommendation that the Secretary of State should exercise his powers under s. 22 of the Act to prohibit or modify that practice.[6] The Director is also empowered to require assurances from persons who persist in a course of conduct which is detrimental to the interests of consumers in the United Kingdom; if the Director is unable to obtain such assurances he is empowered to bring proceedings against those persons before the Restrictive Practices Court.[7] The Director is also entrusted with numerous powers and duties in the field of monopolies, restrictive practices and mergers. These include the power to require information as to monopoly situations; the right to make monopoly references; the duty of collecting information and making recommendations in relation to mergers; the right to receive the reports of the Monopolies and Mergers Commission; the duty to take action in the light of such Reports; and the obligation of discharging the functions of the former Registrar of Restrictive Trading Agreements.[8] It is thus apparent from these particular functions and from the more general rights and obligations under the Act that the Director occupies a most important place in the scheme of this legislation. **[9]**

The Director is an "officer" appointed by the Secretary of State. The Director is appointed for a term not exceeding 5 years and may at any time resign his office by notice in writing to the Secretary of State. Conversely the Secretary of State may at any time remove the Director on the ground of incapacity or misbehaviour.[9] The detailed provisions governing the remuneration, tenure and terms of service of the Director are to be found in Schedule 1 to the Act. Although it is apparent from the previous provisions of s. 1 that the Secretary of State's power to remove the Director should be severely limited, it is difficult to conceive of the remedies available to a Director in the event of unjustified removal by the Secretary of State.[10] The Director would appear primarily to be left to rely upon the power of political argument and the forces of publicity in the event of any unjustified removal. **[10]**

CONSUMER PROTECTION ADVISORY COMMITTEE

The Act also provides for the establishment of the Consumer Protection Advisory Committee. This Advisory Committee is to be a body consisting of between 10 and 15 members appointed by the Secretary of State. Although these members may be either full or part-time, the Secretary of State is under some duty to ensure that this Advisory Committee includes persons in each of the following categories:—

(1) those qualified to advise on practices relating to the supply of goods or services by reason of their experience or knowledge in the supply of such services. Since such experience is not required to have been

[6] See ss. 14 and 17 and the notes thereto, *post*.
[7] See ss. 34 and 35, *post*.
[8] See ss. 14, 17, 34, 47 *et seq*., 50, 76, 88, and 94, together with the notes thereto, *post*; see also the note to s. 1, *post*.
[9] See s. 1 and the note thereto, *post*.
[10] See the note to s. 1, *post*, and also para. 3 of Schedule 1 (and the notes thereto), *post*. The Schedule contains some provision for the payment of compensation in the event of loss of office.

gained directly from supplying such goods or services to consumers, it is clear that this category can potentially include either manufacturers or retailers;

(2) persons qualified by reason of their knowledge of or experience in the enforcement of the Weights and Measures Act 1963 or the Trade Descriptions Act 1968 (or other such Acts). Although this category of persons is primarily intended to include weights and measures officers and former officers; the wording of the Act is, it is suggested, sufficiently wide to include those with legal qualifications, whether practical or academic;

(3) persons qualified to advise on these practices by reason of their knowledge of or experience in organisations established or carried on for the protection of consumers. This third category is clearly desgined to permit the inclusion of persons who have played an official or unofficial part in what is now known as the "Consumer Movement".[11]

[11]

Although the members of the Advisory Committee are not to be regarded as servants or agents of the Crown, or as enjoying any status, immunity or privilege in that regard, they are entitled to remuneration and to the payment of other expenses. The members of the Advisory Committee are permitted to resign their office by notice in writing and may be removed by the Secretary of State on the ground of incapacity or misbehaviour. Although it is obviously contemplated that there should be some restriction upon the removal of members of the Advisory Committee it is again difficult to conceive of a direct legal remedy available to a member of the Advisory Committee in the event of a wrongful removal from office. Some suggestions as to a possible cause of action are however made in the notes to Schedule 2 to the Act. That Schedule also lays down provisions governing the procedure of the Advisory Committee.[12]

[12]

The duties of the Advisory Committee lie solely in the field of consumer protection. As previously indicated the Advisory Committee is empowered to consider and report upon the effect of a "consumer trade practice" referred to them in accordance with the provisions of s. 14 of the Act. When a reference is made to the Advisory Committee under this section the Committee is simply required to state whether or not the "consumer trade practice" adversely affects the economic interests of consumers in the United Kingdom. If however the Director wishes to recommend that the Secretary of State exercise his powers under s. 22 by introducing orders prohibiting or regulating such "consumer trade practices", the Director is required to refer the matter to the Advisory Committee under s. 17 of the Act. Under such circumstances the Advisory Committee is required to advise the Secretary of State both upon the effect or adverse effect of that "consumer trade practice" and upon the form and extent of any orders to be introduced in consequence thereof. If such a reference is made the Advisory Committee is not confined to accepting or rejecting the

---

[11] For the Consumer Protection Advisory Committee see s. 3 and the notes thereto, *post*.

[12] For general provisions governing the Consumer Protection Advisory Committee, see Schedule 2 and the notes thereto, *post*.

recommendations made by the Secretary of State but has itself a power of modifying those recommendations.[13] [**13**]

In carrying out an investigation under s. 17 of the Act the Advisory Committee is required to follow the procedure laid down by s. 81. In general the Advisory Committee is required to take into consideration any representations made to them by "persons appearing to them to have a substantial interest in the subject-matter of the reference" or by bodies "appearing to them to represent substantial numbers of persons who have such an interest". In general the Advisory Committee is required to permit such persons or bodies to make oral representations. The general procedure to be followed by the Advisory Committee is similarly regulated by s. 81 of the Act and the contents and publication of the reports of that Committee are likewise regulated by statutory provisions contained in ss. 82 and 83. [**14**]

MONOPOLIES AND MERGERS COMMISSION

Under the Monopolies and Restrictive Practices (Inquiry and Control) Act 1948 a body called the Monopolies and Restrictive Practices Commission was set up as an independent statutory authority. By the Monopolies and Restrictive Practices Act 1953 its constitution and membership were expanded and it was empowered to operate in groups. [**15**]

Until 1956 this Commission was for the most part engaged actively in reporting on price rings affecting the supply of goods both in the United Kingdom and for export and by the end of that year 21 Reports of the Commission had been published. [**16**]

In 1955 the Commission produced a general report on collective discrimination which led directly to the enactment of the Restrictive Trade Practices Act 1956 under which the Restrictive Practices Court was established. The former Monopolies and Restrictive Practices Commission was renamed the Monopolies Commission and its membership was reduced and it was no longer empowered to sit in groups. [**17**]

By 1965 public concern over take-overs and mergers and over the possibility of monopoly situations in the supply of services had been aroused and under the Monopolies and Mergers Act 1965 provision was made for the reference to the Monopolies Commission of mergers, with special provision being made for newspaper mergers and also for the reference of monopolies in the supply of services. The Commission was enlarged and once again empowered to work in groups. [**18**]

Under the Fair Trading Act 1973, the Monopolies Commission is renamed the Monopolies and Mergers Commission but its structure and size remains largely unchanged. Its jurisdiction over mergers as well as monopolies which has existed since 1965 continues. [**19**]

The Commission's Procedure on a Reference

Parts VII and VIII of the Fair Trading Act contain statutory provisions relating to the Commission's proceedings and these are considered in the notes to ss. 81–93 of the Act, *post*. [**20**]

[13] For references to the Advisory Committee, see ss. 14 and 22 and the notes thereto, *post*.

Subject to these provisions, the Commission is master of its own proceedings[14] and its practice on a reference has now fallen into a settled pattern which is the same for a merger reference as in a monopoly reference. On a reference being made the Chairman appoints a group, hitherto about seven in number, to consider it. Apart from the Chairman all the members of the Commission are part-time, covering a range of expertise including accountancy, business, law, trade union affairs, economics and finance. [**21**]

As soon as possible after the group has been formed a questionnaire is sent to the party or parties concerned in the reference covering what appear to be the material facts. Information is also obtained from other concerns, sometimes as the result of answers to announcements in the national or local press, sometimes by direct approach. Specific invitations are usually sent to trade unions concerned. They and others concerned may ask to be heard or may be invited to be heard. [**22**]

The Commission's hearings have hitherto been in private. [**23**]

After the questionnaire is answered the replies are closely considered and, when all material facts have been obtained, the Commission sends to the parties concerned a document by tradition called "the public interest letter". Before sending this letter the Commission will have satisfied itself that a *prima facie* case has been made for concluding that the necessary monopoly or merger situation in fact exists—*i.e.*, that the statutory criteria for a reference are satisfied.[15] If the relevant criteria are not satisfied the Commission will at once so report to the person or persons making the reference. [**24**]

The public interest letter usually has three Annexes. The first contains a fairly full factual statement. The second sets out the public interest issues (on which s. 84, *post*, sets out some of the criteria to be used by the Commission if considered relevant) which are thought to arise for consideration from the facts. The third sets out complaints and criticisms of the party concerned which have been brought to the notice of the Commission. If, as in the case of a complex monopoly situation[16] or a merger there is more than one party concerned each will receive a separate public interest letter. [**25**]

The letter will invite the party to an oral hearing and also, prior to such hearing, to submit in writing any further arguments if it so wishes. The hearing, called "the public interest hearing" is usually taken very seriously by all parties although the Commission's proceedings are conducted with as much informality as is consistent with the preservation of order. Thus there is no dais, Counsel are not robed and smoking is allowed. [**26**]

The party concerned is usually represented by Counsel and, since the necessary fact-finding has already been done, the hearing, including speeches of Counsel, rarely lasts more than two days and often lasts less. The shortness of the hearing is owed to the fact that a Commission inquiry is not conducted by "adversary" procedures. In a Commission inquiry there is no plaintiff or prosecutor since nobody is making any claim or alleging any offence. The inquiry is an administrative inquiry directed to ascertaining the effect on the public interest of certain facts. Because the facts have been elicited in advance

[14] See s. 87 (2) and the note thereto, *post*.
[15] See ss. 6–11 on monopoly situations and ss. 58 and 64 on merger situations, *post*.
[16] See s. 11 and the note thereto, *post*.

they do not have to be ascertained as in most legal proceedings by the exhaustive process of examination, cross-examination and re-examination of witnesses. What happens is that the Chairman of the group (in most references the Chairman of the Commission) asks questions in a predetermined order as arranged in a fully considered brief. Such questions are answered by any witness selected by the party or by Counsel or by a combination of witness and Counsel. Members of the group may ask supplementary questions arising out of the answers received. The Commission is empowered under s. 85, *post*, to take evidence on oath but it is not its practice to do so. [**27**]

A full shorthand note of the proceedings is always taken and those who have given evidence have full opportunity of making any amendments to the transcript. [**28**]

After the conclusion of the public interest hearing the group will, on a day or days appointed, meet to consider its conclusions. This consideration is usually very detailed. The conclusions together with any recommendations are then embodied in the final chapter of the Commission's report on the reference. [**29**]

The earlier chapters of the report are factual. Those parts of the factual chapter which relate to a party or to a witness will, so far as possible, be put back to the party or witness for any comments as to accuracy or otherwise. If objection is raised to the inclusion of a particular passage careful consideration will be given to each objection before the passage is included in the report. [**30**]

When the report is finally agreed it will be signed by those members of the Commission who form the group and will be sent to the Secretary of State and also, in most cases of monopoly reference and all merger references other than newspaper mergers, to the Director General of Fair Trading.[17] [**31**]

Any member of the group who dissents from the conclusions of the group is entitled to add a dissenting note. [**32**]

Every reference to the Commission of a monopoly or merger situation under the Fair Trading Act 1973 must contain a time-limit for report by the Commission (see s. 55, *post*, on monopoly references, s. 60 for newspaper mergers and s. 70 for other merger references). In all cases however the time-limit may be extended although only once in the case of merger references for which the criteria for extension are rigorous. [**33**]

RESTRICTIVE PRACTICES COURT

The Restrictive Practices Court was set up under the Restrictive Trade Practices Act 1956 as a superior court of record. It is not a division of the High Court of Justice. It consists of a number of judicial members and of a larger number of lay members.[18] The judicial members are appointed from judges of the High Court of Justice, the Court of Session and the Supreme Court of Northern Ireland.[19] One of them acts as president of the Court. Lay members are appointed by the Queen on the recommendation of the Lord Chancellor, and appointment is based on experience of industry, commerce or

---

[17] See s. 86, *post*.
[18] See the Restrictive Trade Practices Act 1956, s. 2.
[19] See the Restrictive Trade Practices Act 1956, s. 3.

public affairs.[20] Matters of law are decided by the judicial members alone[21] and their decisions can be appealed, in the case of proceedings in England and Wales, to the Court of Appeal[22] and thence to the House of Lords.[23] In Scotland appeal lies to the Court of Session and thence probably to the House of Lords.[24] Matters of fact are decided by the majority of members, lay and judicial, hearing the case[25] and no appeal lies from decision on such matters.[26] [**34**]

SECRETARY OF STATE

The Secretary of State is entrusted with wide-ranging powers and duties under the Act. Under s. 12 the Secretary of State may give general directions to the Director, particularly regarding the order of priority in which matters are to be brought under review by him under s. 2 of the Act and regarding the classes of goods or services to be brought under review for the purpose of considering whether a monopoly situation exists or may exist in relation to those goods or services. The Secretary of State may also give general directions indicating considerations to which the Director should pay particular regard in determining whether or not to make a recommendation to the Secretary of State with a view to obtaining an order under s. 22 of the Act. The Secretary of State may also give general directions to the Director as to considerations to be taken into account in determining whether "consumer trade practices" adversely affect the interests of consumers and considerations to be taken into account in determining whether a monopoly situation exists or whether a monopoly reference should be made. [**35**]

The Secretary of State is also empowered to make a reference to the Consumer Protection Advisory Committee under s. 14 of the Act—*i.e.*, referring the question whether a "consumer trade practice" adversely affects the economic interests of consumers in the United Kingdom. The Secretary of State is not however empowered to make any reference to the Advisory Committee which is coupled with a recommendation under s. 17 of the Act. Where however a reference has been previously made to that Committee under s. 17 of the Act the Secretary of State is empowered, if he considers fit, to introduce an order under s. 22 as a result of the report of the Advisory Committee. [**36**]

The Secretary of State is also empowered to make monopoly references to the Monopolies and Mergers Commission on his own initiative—see s. 51. Whenever a reference is made to that Commission a copy of the Report is required to be sent to the Secretary of State (or the appropriate Minister)[27] and in the light of that Report the Secretary of State is empowered to introduce orders under s. 56 of the Act.[28] The Secretary of State is also entrusted with powers to consent to newspaper mergers or, alternatively, to make a "newspaper

---

20 See the Restrictive Trade Practices Act 1956, s. 4.
21 See the Restrictive Trade Practices Act 1956, Schedule, para. 5.
22 See the Restrictive Trade Practices Act 1956, Schedule, para. 7.
23 See the Appellate Jurisdiction Act 1876 (39 & 40 Vict. c. 59), s. 4.
24 Contrast *Osborne* v. *Barclay Curle & Co.*, [1901] A.C. 269.
25 See the Restrictive Trade Practices Act 1956, Schedule, para. 5.
26 See the Restrictive Trade Practices Act 1956, Schedule, para. 7.
27 See s. 86 and the notes thereto, *post*.
28 This power also extends to any appropriate Minister.

merger reference" to the Commission.[29] The power of the Secretary of State to refer mergers to the Commission is not confined to "newspaper mergers" but extends to all mergers falling within the provisions of the Act.[30] The Secretary of State is also entitled to receive copies of the report of the Commission made in consequence of any merger or newspaper merger.[31] The power of introducing legislation in consequence of any merger reference likewise falls upon the Secretary of State.[32] **[37]**

The powers of the Secretary of State in the context of monopolies and mergers do extend somewhat beyond the particular functions previously outlined. The Secretary of State is empowered to require the Commission to submit a report to him on the general effect on the public interest of practices of a specified class which are, in the view of the Secretary, commonly adopted as a result of or for the purpose of preserving monopoly situations. The Secretary is also empowered to require a Report on any specified practices which appear to him to be uncompetitive.[33] The Secretary of State is similarly empowered to refer the possible existence and effect of any "restrictive labour practices" to the Commission for the purpose of examination and report.[34] The Secretary of State is also empowered to extend the operation of the Restrictive Practices Act 1956 to agreements relating to the supply of services and information agreements relating to the supply of such services.[35] **[38]**

Lastly the Secretary of State was entrusted with the power of introducing regulations designed to control pyramid selling and other such schemes.[36] The powers conferred by this section have now been exercised by the Secretary of State and the consequent regulations are contained in the Pyramid Selling Schemes Regulations 1973, which came into operation on 15th November 1973.[37] **[39]**

As has been seen, the Restrictive Practices Court survived the introduction of the Fair Trading Act 1973. This Court retains its functions under the Restrictive Practices Act 1956. As previously stated the powers of this Court under that Act can now be extended to cover agreements or arrangements relating to services to which the Fair Trading Act 1973 has been extended and to information agreements existing in relation to such services.[38] If the Director is unable to obtain the necessary assurance from a person persisting in a course of conduct which is detrimental to the interests of consumers in the United Kingdom and which is to be regarded as unfair,[39] the Director is empowered to bring proceedings against that person before the Restrictive Practices Court. If such proceedings are brought the Restrictive Practices Court may then make an order against the person concerned directing that person to refrain from continuing that course of conduct and to refrain from carrying on any similar course of conduct in the course of his business.[40] **[40]**

---

[29] See s. 59 and the notes thereto, *post*.
[30] See s. 63 and the notes thereto, *post*.
[31] See s. 86 and the notes thereto, *post*.
[32] See ss. 73–75 and the notes thereto, *post*.
[33] See, generally, s. 78 and the notes thereto, *post*.
[34] See s. 79 and the notes thereto, *post*.
[35] See ss. 107, 108 and the notes thereto, *post*.
[36] See s. 119 and the notes thereto, *post*.
[37] S.I. 1973 No. 1740, set out in Division 3, *post*.
[38] See ss. 107 and 108 and the notes thereto, *post*.
[39] See s. 34 and the notes thereto, *post*.
[40] See ss. 34–43 and the notes thereto, *post*.

LOCAL WEIGHTS AND MEASURES AUTHORITIES

The enforcement of orders made by the Secretary of State in consequence of a reference to the Advisory Committee under s. 17 of the Act is entrusted to the local weights and measures authority.[41] The various powers of entry and seizure and of making test purchases are entrusted to the officers of such local weights and measures authorities. To this extent the Fair Trading Act 1973 follows the models of the Weights and Measures Acts and the Trade Descriptions Act 1968. The sections of the Act which confer these powers upon those officers are, almost entirely, drafted in the same terms as the powers conferred by those earlier Acts. [**41**]

[41] See s. 27 and the notes thereto, *post*.

3. REFERENCES TO CONSUMER PROTECTION ADVISORY COMMITTEE

The Secretary of State, the Director or any other Minister may generally refer to the Consumer Protection Advisory Committee the question whether a "consumer trade practice" adversely affects the economic interests of consumers in the United Kingdom.[42] Those persons are not however entitled to make such a reference if it appears to the person who might otherwise make such a reference that the consumer trade practice in question is carried on in connection only with the supply of services of a description specified in Schedule 4 to the Act and that a monopoly situation exists or may exist in relation to the supply of services of that description. The services are itemised in the Schedule and are almost entirely "professional" services. One can therefore reasonably surmise that these services were excluded from the jurisdiction of the Consumer Protection Advisory Committee because it was felt that, under such circumstances, an investigation by the Monopolies and Mergers Commission would afford a better method of remedying any abuses that might exist. Secondly, the Director (but not the other persons previously referred to) may not make a reference to the Advisory Committee without the consent of the Minister concerned, if it appears to the Director that the practice in question is carried on only in connection with the supply, by a body corporate to which s. 16 applies, of goods or services of a description specified in Parts I and II of Schedule 5 to the Act.[43] Since the goods and services itemised in that Schedule are those supplied by the nationalised industries, it is apparent that these have been excluded from the ambit of the Advisory Committee because it was thought that an adequate statutory framework already existed before the introduction of the Fair Trading Act 1973. [**42**]

As has been previously indicated a reference of a "consumer trade practice" may be made to the Advisory Committee under either s. 14 or 17 of the Act. Under s. 14 the question whether a "consumer trade practice" adversely affects the economic interests of consumers in the United Kingdom may be referred to the Advisory Committee for the purpose of obtaining a Report from that Committee. In preparing that Report that Committee is required to consider whether the practice in question "adversely affects the economic interests of consumers in the United Kingdom". The expression "economic interests" remains undefined in the Act and is of uncertain scope. In the future there will undoubtedly be problems of deciding when some practice merely affects the health or safety of the consumers, rather than the economic interests of those consumers. This is a problem which will, doubtless, receive a detailed exposition in cases to be decided under the Act. [**43**]

The expression "consumer trade practice" is defined in s. 13 of the Act.[44] This expression means any practice which is for the time being carried on in

[42] See ss. 14 and 17 and the notes thereto, *post*.
[43] For these provisions see s. 16 and Schedule 5, together with the notes thereto, *post*.
[44] See s. 13 and the notes thereto, *post*.

connection with the supply of goods (whether by way of sale or otherwise) to consumers or in connection with the supply of services for consumers and which relates to the matters specified in s. 13 of the Act. The requirement that there be some "practice" suggests that a "consumer trade practice" will not exist unless the person concerned has acted in accordance with some settled rule or course of conduct. This practice must be "carried on in connection with" the supply of such goods or services to or for consumers. It seems likely that this requirement will be satisfied if the practice relates either directly or indirectly to the supply of such goods or services to or for the consumers. Again this requirement would appear to be satisfied by a practice adopted by wholesalers or manufacturers which indirectly affected consumers (as defined in s.137 (1) (vi)). The definition further requires that the practice in question relates to one of the matters specified in s. 13. By s. 13 the practice must relate:—

(*a*) to the terms or conditions (whether as to price or otherwise) on or subject to which goods or services are or are sought to be supplied, or
(*b*) to the manner in which those terms or conditions are communicated to persons to whom goods are or are sought to be supplied or for whom services are or are sought to be supplied, or,
(*c*) to promotion (by advertising, labelling or marking of goods, canvassing or otherwise) of the supply of goods or of the supply of services, or
(*d*) to methods of salesmanship employed in dealing with consumers, or
(*e*) to the way in which goods are packed or otherwise got up for the purpose of being supplied, or
(*f*) to methods of demanding or securing payment for goods or services supplied.

The general effect of this definition is obvious. There are however some detailed problems of exposition which are more fully considered in the note to s. 13 of the Act in Division 2, *post*. [**44**]

A reference to the Advisory Committee may also be made under s. 17 of the Act. A reference under that section can however only be made if it appears to the Director that the consumer trade practice in question has the effect, or is likely to have the effect—

(*a*) of misleading consumers as to, or withholding from them adequate information as to, or an adequate record of, their rights and obligations under relevant consumer transactions,[45] or
(*b*) of otherwise misleading or confusing consumers with respect to any matter in connection with relevant consumer transactions, or
(*c*) of subjecting consumers to undue pressure to enter into relevant consumer transactions, or
(*d*) of causing the terms or conditions, on or subject to which consumers enter into relevant consumer transactions, to be so adverse to them as to be inequitable.

Again the general effect of this requirement is clear, although there are detailed points of interpretation which are considered in the Notes to s. 17 in Division 2, *post*. [**45**]

---

[45] As defined in s. 17 (5), *post*.

A reference may also be made by the Director to the Advisory Committee under s. 17 of the Act. If he elects to make such a reference the Director will inform the Advisory Committee which of the effects previously set out the "consumer trade practice" has or is likely to have. The Director may also, if he thinks fit, include proposals for recommending to the Secretary of State that he exercise his powers, in particular under s. 22 of the Act, by making an order. **[46]**

A report made by the Advisory Committee in consequence of a reference under s. 17 must state whether the "consumer trade practice" adversely affects the economic interests of consumers in the United Kingdom and, if so, whether it does so by reason (or partly by reason) that it has or is likely to have one or more of the effects previously set out.[46] If the Advisory Committee does find that the "consumer trade practice" does adversely affect the economic interests of consumers in the United Kingdom and does so, wholly or partly, for the reasons specified in s. 17 (2), the Committee is then required to state whether they agree or disagree with the proposals set out in the reference to the Committee. The Committee is empowered to state whether it agrees wholeheartedly with those proposals, whether it would agree with those proposals if they were modified in a manner specified by the Committee in its Report or whether they disagree entirely with those proposals.[47] **[47]**

If the report of the Advisory Committee states that it agrees with the recommendations, or that it would agree with those recommendations if they were modified, a copy of the report is then to be laid before Parliament.[48] When such a Report has been laid before Parliament the Secretary of State may then, if he thinks fit, by an order made by statutory instrument give effect either to the proposals as originally set out in the reference or to the proposals as modified by the Advisory Committee.[49] **[48]**

Once such an order has been made it has the effect of delegated legislation. Subject to the defences set out in ss. 24 and 25 of the Act it then becomes an offence, punishable by fine or imprisonment, to contravene that order.[50] The existence of such an order will not however affect the enforceability in the civil courts of a contract contravening an order made in accordance with these provisions; nor will the contravention of such an order give rise to any civil remedy.[51] **[49]**

The provisions establishing the defences to a prosecution brought as a result of the contravention of an order made under s. 22 are taken, almost exactly, from the provisions of the Trade Descriptions Act 1968. The cases decided under that Act are presumably therefore to be regarded as, at least, of persuasive importance in relation to the equivalent provisions of this Act. Furthermore, the provisions empowering the local weights and measures authorities to enforce these orders by way of test purchases, seizures, etc. (and the offences existing in relation to such seizures, test purchases, etc.) are similarly in the same form as the powers conferred under the Trade Descriptions Act 1968.[52] **[50]**

---

[46] See s. 21 and the notes thereto, *post*.
[47] See s. 83 and the notes thereto, *post*.
[48] See s. 22 and the notes thereto, *post*.
[49] See s. 23 and the notes thereto, *post*.
[50] See s. 26 and the notes thereto, *post*
[51] The various powers are set out in ss. 27–33 of the Act, for which see the notes, *post*.
[52] See s. 34 and the notes thereto, *post*.

4. ADDITIONAL FUNCTIONS OF DIRECTOR FOR PROTECTION OF CONSUMERS

If it appears to the Director that a person carrying on business has, in the course of that business, persisted in a course of conduct which satisfies the conditions set out in s. 34 of the Act, the Director will use his best endeavours to obtain a satisfactory written assurance from that person that the person will, in future, refrain from continuing with that course of conduct or from any similar course of conduct. This provision is however available only if the person concerned has "persisted" in a "course of conduct". It has been decided that one cannot "persist" in doing something unless it has been repeated on more than one occasion.[53] Furthermore the cases strongly suggest that, although the existence or non-existence of a course of conduct is largely a question of fact and degree, 3 or 4 transactions over a period of 4 years do not constitute a course of conduct.[54] [**51**]

The conditions set out in s. 34 of the Act are that it should appear to the Director that the person in question has persisted in a course of conduct which—

(*a*) is detrimental to the interests of consumers in the United Kingdom, whether those interests are economic interests or interests in respect of health, safety or other matters, and

(*b*) in accordance with the provisions of the remainder of s. 34 of the Act are to be regarded as unfair to consumers. [**52**]

For the purpose of determining whether a person has persisted in a course of conduct satisfying these conditions the Director is obliged to have regard to complaints received by him (whether from consumers or elsewhere) and to any other information collected by or furnished to him. This provision clearly empowers the Director to take account of matters coming to his notice in the exercise of the duties imposed on him by s. 2 of the Act. The expression "detrimental to the interests of consumers" is not defined in the Act; the expression "unfair to consumers" is defined in s. 34. In deciding whether a course of conduct is detrimental to the interests of consumers it is expressly said to be permissible to consider economic interests and interests in respect of health, safety or other matters. The scope of this provision is thus extremely wide and undoubtedly requires the Director to exercise a value judgement in deciding whether the effect on consumers is or is not "detrimental". [**53**]

A course of conduct is to be regarded as unfair to consumers if it consists of contraventions of one or more enactments which impose duties, prohibitions or restrictions enforceable by criminal proceedings—irrespective of whether the person concerned has ever been convicted of any such offence. A course of conduct is also to be regarded as unfair to consumers if it consists of breaches

---

[53] See s. 34 and the notes thereto, *post*.

[54] See s. 34 and the notes thereto, *post*.

of contract or of duty, whether such duty is imposed by statute or by the general law, provided that such breach of statute or the general law is enforceable by civil proceedings. Again the course of conduct is to be regarded as "unfair to consumers" whether or not civil proceedings have been brought as a result of that breach of contract or duty. **[54]**

If the Director considers that the requirements of s. 34, as previously set out, are satisfied, he will, first, use his best endeavours to obtain an assurance that the person will refrain from that course of conduct in the future.[55] If the Director is unable to obtain such an assurance, or if such an assurance has been given and is not observed, the Director may bring proceedings against that person in the Restrictive Practices Court. If, on such a hearing, the Court finds that the person had, in the course of a business, persisted in a course of conduct as specified in s. 34 (1) of the Act and it appears to the Court that the person is likely to continue that course of conduct (or to carry on a similar course of conduct)[56] the Court will invite the person to give an undertaking to refrain from continuing that course of conduct or any conduct to a like effect.[57] The Court may then accept the undertaking provided. **[55]**

If however that person is not willing to furnish such an undertaking, or if the Court is unwilling to accept such an undertaking, the Court may make an order directing the person to refrain from that course of conduct or any similar conduct. The order then becomes an order of the Court and is enforceable by the normal remedies available in the event of a contempt of court. **[56]**

The provisions permitting proceedings to be brought before the Restrictive Practices Court are further extended to include persons who "consent to or connive at" a course of conduct such as that specified in s. 34 of the Act.[58] The Act further makes express provision for extending the scope of orders made under Part III of the Act to bind "interconnected bodies corporate".[59] The provisions regarding such bodies corporate and persons consenting to or conniving at practices falling within s. 34 similarly contain provisions entitling the Court to ask for, and accept, undertakings or, alternatively, enabling the Court to make orders backed by the normal sanctions.[60] **[57]**

If the proceedings are uncomplicated, and the person against whom the proceedings would have to be brought (and any associated person against whom proceedings had been brought or were intended) is comparatively small, the Director is empowered to bring the relevant proceedings in the county court rather than the Restrictive Practices Court.[61] Lastly, appeals, both on fact and law, will lie from a decision or order of any court made in relation to a course of conduct falling within s. 34 of the Act .[62] **[58]**

---

[55] See s. 35 and the note thereto, *post*.
[56] See s. 37 and the note thereto, *post*.
[57] See s. 37 and the note thereto, *post*.
[58] See s. 38 and the note thereto, *post*.
[59] See s. 40 and the note thereto, *post*.
[60] See ss. 39 and 40 and the notes thereto, *post*.
[61] For the detailed provisions see s. 41 and the note thereto, *post*.
[62] See s. 42 and the note thereto, *post*.

5. PYRAMID SELLING AND SIMILAR TRADING SCHEMES

The Act provides for the detailed regulation and restriction of a "trading scheme" which *includes* the following elements:—

(*a*) goods or services or both are to be provided by the person promoting the scheme (who is known as "the promoter") or in the case of a scheme promoted by two or more persons acting in concert (who are known as "the promoters") are to be provided by one or more of those persons;

(*b*) the goods or services so provided are to be supplied to or for other persons under transactions effected by persons (other than the promoter or any of the promoters) who participate in the scheme (these persons are each referred to as "participants");

(*c*) those transactions, or most of them, are to be effected elsewhere than at premises at which the promoter or any of the promoters or the participant effecting the transaction carries on business; and

(*d*) the prospect is held out to participants of receiving payments or other benefits in respect of: the introduction of other persons who become participants; the promotion, transfer or other change of status of participants within the trading scheme; the supply of goods to other participants; the supply of training facilities or other services for other participants; or transactions effected by other participants under which goods are to be supplied to or services are to be supplied for, other persons. [**59**]

It must be observed that these provisions are extremely wide and that they certainly extend beyond "pyramid selling" as that expression is colloquially used. The section (together with the related provisions) does not however apply unless a "trading scheme" is in existence. This is defined in s. 118 of the Act to include any arrangements made in connection with the carrying on of a business (whether recorded in writing or not). The use of the expression "arrangements"[63] indicates that a "trading scheme" is not required to be legally binding as between the promoters and the participants or even as between the participants themselves. Although the matters previously set out are expressly mentioned in the section, a "trading scheme" falls within the provisions of s. 118 even though it is not confined to the matters expressly set out. Detailed points arising on the interpretation of this section are set out in the notes to these sections. [**60**]

A "trading scheme" does not become illegal merely because it falls within

[63] See s. 118 which indicates that the "arrangements" are not required to be legally enforceable as between any of the parties.

the ambit of s. 118. Regulations have been made by the Secretary of State, in accordance with s. 119, for the purpose of defining the rights of participants in such trading schemes and for imposing controls on such schemes.[64] [**61**]

These regulations apply to all "trading schemes" other than schemes under which the prospect of payments or benefits is held out to only one participant in the United Kingdom or, alternatively, schemes in which the only prospect of benefit is the receipt of a sum not exceeding £10 in respect of the introduction of another participant. It is thus apparent that the regulations will govern most of the schemes which were formerly in use. These regulations prescribe the contents of advertisements relating to "trading schemes". They also define, in considerable detail, the rights of participants under such schemes, define the contractual rights of such participants; and limit the fiscal liability which can be imposed under such schemes. They also make provision for the civil liabilities of participants and promoters in such schemes and expressly establish the legal consequences of a contravention of the regulations.[65] [**62**]

Section 120 of the Act imposes criminal liability on persons who issue, circulate or distribute (or cause another person to issue, circulate or distribute) a document which contravenes any of the provisions of those regulations. This section also imposes criminal liability on persons to whom or for whose benefit payments are made by participants in trading schemes who are induced to make those payments by reason that the prospect of receiving payment or other benefits in respect of the introduction of other persons who become participants in the trading scheme is held out to that other participant. Likewise a person who induces another to make any payments to or for the benefit of a promoter of a trading scheme is likewise rendered guilty of an offence.[66] A defence is however provided by s. 121 of the Act to persons who "prove that they are persons whose business it is to publish or arrange for publication of advertisements and who receive the advertisement for publication in the ordinary course of business and who did not know and had no reason to suspect that its publication would amount to an offence under section 120 of the Act". It is also a defence under that section to prove that the relevant trading scheme was in operation before the commencement of this Act and that the act constituting the offence was committed without the connivance or consent of the person charged. [**63**]

---

[64] See the Pyramid Selling Schemes Regulations 1973, S.I. 1973 No. 1740, and the notes thereto, set out in Division 3, *post*.

[65] See the notes to the Pyramid Selling Schemes Regulations 1973, S.I. 1973 No. 1740, set out in Division 3, *post*.

[66] See s. 120 and the notes thereto, *post*.

6. MONOPOLIES AND MERGERS

Statutory provision for the review of monopoly and merger situations is, when the Fair Trading Act 1973 comes fully into operation, to be found wholly within that Act, since the Monopolies and Restrictive Practices (Inquiry and Control) Act 1948 and the Monopolies and Mergers Act 1965 are repealed in their entirety under s. 139 and Sch. 13, *post*. [**64**]

The scheme of the Act with regard to monopolies is that the Monopolies and Mergers Commission can be requested to consider whether a monopoly situation, as defined under ss. 6–11 of the Act, exists and can be further requested to consider the effect on the public interest if such a situation does exist and to make appropriate recommendations on which various persons such as the Secretary of State and the Director General of Fair Trading can then act. [**65**]

Details of this scheme are given in the notes to ss. 6–11 and to Parts IV, VII and VIII of the Act, *post*. [**66**]

As for mergers, the Act provides in Parts V, VII and VIII, *post*, for the reference of merger situations for the Commission's consideration, report and recommendation. [**67**]

7. RESTRICTIVE PRACTICES

The Fair Trading Act 1973 contains additions and amendments to the law on restrictive trade practices which continues to be contained also in the Restrictive Trade Practices Acts 1956 and 1968. The principal addition made is the regulation of restrictive trade agreements and arrangements affecting services. [**68**]

Detailed consideration of these changes is contained in the notes to Parts IX and X of the Act, *post*. [**69**]

In addition, under Part VI of the Act, *post*, references may be made to the Commission for the consideration of uncompetitive practices as defined in s. 78, *post*, and of restrictive labour practices as defined in s. 79. Both provisions are new. [**70–100**]

DIVISION 2

THE FAIR TRADING ACT 1973

THE FAIR TRADING ACT 1973

(1973 c. 41)

ARRANGEMENT OF SECTIONS

PART I

INTRODUCTORY

PART XI

PYRAMID SELLING AND SIMILAR TRADING SCHEMES

PART XII

MISCELLANEOUS AND SUPPLEMENTARY PROVISIONS

SCHEDULES:

An Act to provide for the appointment of a Director General of Fair Trading and of a Consumer Protection Advisory Committee, and to confer on the Director General and the Committee so appointed, on the Secretary of State, on the Restrictive Practices Court and on certain other courts new functions for the protection of consumers; to make provisions, in substitution for the Monopolies and Restrictive Practices (Inquiry and Control) Act 1948 *and the Monopolies and Mergers Act* 1965, *for the matters dealt with in those Acts and related matters, including restrictive labour practices; to amend the Restrictive Trade Practices Act* 1956 *and the Restrictive Trade Practices Act* 1968, *to make provision for extending the said Act of* 1956 *to agreements relating to services, and to transfer to the Director General of Fair Trading the functions of the Registrar of Restrictive Trading Agreements; to make provision with respect to pyramid selling and similar trading schemes; to make new provision in place of section* 30(2) *to* (4) *of the Trade Descriptions Act* 1968; *and for purposes connected with those matters* [25th July 1973]

PART I

INTRODUCTORY

1. Director General of Fair Trading

(1) The Secretary of State shall appoint an officer to be known as the Director General of Fair Trading (in this Act referred to as "the Director") for the purpose of performing the functions assigned or transferred to the Director by or under this Act.

(2) An appointment of a person to hold office as the Director shall not be for a term exceeding five years; but previous appointment to that office shall not affect eligibility for re-appointment.

(3) The Director may at any time resign his office as the Director by notice in writing addressed to the Secretary of State; and the Secretary of State may remove any person from that office on the ground of incapacity or misbehaviour.

(4) Subject to subsections (2) and (3) of this section, the Director shall hold and vacate office as such in accordance with the terms of his appointment.

(5) The Director may appoint such staff as he may think fit, subject to the approval of the Minister for the Civil Service as to numbers and as to terms and conditions of service.

(6) The provisions of Schedule 1 to this Act shall have effect with respect to the Director. [**101**]

COMMENCEMENT

See s. 140 (3), *post*, and the Fair Trading Act 1973 (Commencement No. 2) Order 1973, S.I. 1973 No. 1652, which brought this section into force on 1st November 1973.

DEFINITION

"The Director": *I.e.*, the Director General of Fair Trading; see s. 137 (2), *post*.

GENERAL NOTE

Sub-s. (1): *"Officer"*. Probably therefore the Director cannot be considered as a Crown employee—see, *e.g.*, *Ridge* v. *Baldwin*, [1964] A.C. 40; see also the Trade Union and Labour Relations Act 1974, s. 30 (1), Sch. 1, para. 33.

"Functions of Director". General functions (s. 2); assistance to Commission (s. 5 (2));

references to CPAC (ss. 14, 17); assurances from and proceedings against those that persist in conduct unfair and detrimental to the interests of consumers (s. 34); informa-Trading Agreements (s. 94); publicity and Reports (ss. 124, 125); notices of intended prosecution and conviction (ss. 130, 131).

"*Shall appoint*". The Secretary of State is therefore under a mandatory obligation to appoint such an officer. As no time limit is laid down, this must presumably be within a reasonable time.

Sub-s. (2): "*Shall not be for a term exceeding five years*". The appointment may however be for such shorter period as the Secretary of State may determine.

Sub-s. (3): "*Notice in Writing*". See Interpretation Act 1889, s. 20.

"*Secretary of State*". See Interpretation Act s. 12 (3).

"*May remove etc.*". Although the power of removal appears to be limited, it is hard to see what legal remedies would be available to the Director in the event of removal: the principles of natural justice would not appear to be relevant (see *e.g.*, *Ridge* v. *Baldwin*, [1964] A.C. 40); nor the principles of unfair dismissal (see the Trade Union and Labour Relations Act 1974, s. 30 (1), Sch. 1, para. 33). Furthermore compensation would appear to be payable only in so far as provided by Sch. 1, para. 3, *post*; see however *Reilly* v. *R.*, [1934] A.C. 176.

Sub-s. (5): "*The Director may appoint etc.*" This appears to confer a discretion on the Director.

"*Staff.*" A word of no certain legal meaning which seems equivalent to the more common "officers and servants".

Sub-s. (6): "*Schedule* 1." This provides for the detailed requirements of the office of Director.

2. General functions of Director

(1) Without prejudice to any other functions assigned or transferred to him by or under this Act, it shall be the duty of the Director, so far as appears to him to be practicable from time to time,—

(*a*) to keep under review the carrying on of commercial activities in the United Kingdom which relate to goods supplied to consumers in the United Kingdom or produced with a view to their being so supplied, or which relate to services supplied for consumers in the United Kingdom, and to collect information with respect to such activities, and the persons by whom they are carried on, with a view to his becoming aware of, and ascertaining the circumstances relating to, practices which may adversely affect the economic interests of consumers in the United Kingdom, and

(*b*) to receive and collate evidence becoming available to him with respect to such activities as are mentioned in the preceding paragraph and which appears to him to be evidence of practices which may adversely affect the interests (whether they are economic interests or interests with respect to health, safety or other matters) of consumers in the United Kingdom.

(2) It shall also be the duty of the Director, so far as appears to him to be practicable from time to time, to keep under review the carrying on of commercial activities in the United Kingdom, and to collect information with respect to those activities, and the persons by whom they are carried on, with a view to his becoming aware of, and ascertaining the circumstances relating to, monopoly situations or uncompetitive practices.

(3) It shall be the duty of the Director, where either he considers it expedient or he is requested by the Secretary of State to do so,—

(*a*) to give information and assistance to the Secretary of State with respect to any of the matters in respect of which the Director has any duties under subsections (1) and (2) of this section, or (*b*) subject to the provisions of Part II of this Act in relation to recommendations under that Part of this Act, to make recommendations to the Secretary of State as to any action which in the opinion of the Director it would be expedient for the Secretary of State or any other Minister to take in relation to any of the matters in respect of which the Director has any such duties.

(4) It shall also be the duty of the Director to have regard to evidence becoming available to him with respect to any course of conduct on the part of a person carrying on a business which appears to be conduct detrimental to the interests of consumers in the United Kingdom and (in accordance with the provisions of Part III of this Act) to be regarded as unfair to them, with a view to considering what action (if any) he should take under Part III of this Act.

(5) It shall be the duty of the Director to have regard to the needs of regional development and to the desirability of dispersing administrative offices from London in making decisions on the location of offices for his staff. [**102**]

COMMENCEMENT

See s. 140 (3), *post*, and the note to s. 1, *ante*.

DEFINITIONS

"The Director": s. 137 (2).
"monopoly situation": s. 5 (3).
"commercial activities in the United Kingdom": s. 137 (2).
"consumer", "goods", "Minister", "practice", "supply" and "uncompetitive practices": s. 137 (2); for "consumer"—see also s. 137 (6).
"services supplied": s. 137 (3).
"services": s. 137 (4) (as regards "consumer", also s. 138).

GENERAL NOTE

Sub-s. (1) (*a*): "*Duty of the Director*". Although some duty appears to be imposed on the Director, it seems probable that, so long as he acts reasonably, he remains judge of the extent of that duty—see, *e.g.*, *Padfield* v. *Minister of Agriculture*, [1968] A.C. 997, and *Secretary of State for Employment* v. *Associated Society of Locomotive Engineers and Firemen* (*No.* 2), [1972] 2 Q.B. 455.

"*Keep under review.*" This subsection therefore imposes an active obligation on the Director in relation to commercial activities which may adversely affect the economic interests of such consumers.

"*Collect information.*" This likewise imposes an active obligation on the Director.

"*Becoming aware of and ascertaining the circumstances.*" The duty imposed by this subsection is therefore in two parts.

"*May adversely affect.*" This is ambiguous: it may suggest that practices which are likely to have adverse effects in the future are included; or, alternatively, it may mean that such practices are likely to have adverse effects, although on the available evidence it is impossible to be sure.

"*United Kingdom.*" See the Royal and Parliamentary Titles Act 1927, s. 2 (2).

"*Economic interests.*" This is undefined and of uncertain scope. For example, if the practice threatens health or safety, and seems likely to cause physical injury and consequent financial loss, does it affect the economic interests of consumers? Although it seems probable that this question should receive a negative answer, the position is not clear.

Sub-s. (1) (*b*): "*Receive and collate.*" This indicates that the duty imposed on the Director under this paragraph is passive.

"*Such activities.*" *I.e.*, commercial activities in the United Kingdom.

"*Or other matters.*" This should probably be construed *eiusdem generis* with health and safety.

Sub-s. (2): "*Monopoly situations.*" These may exist in relation to the supply of goods (s. 6 (1)); the supply of services (s. 7 (1)); and exports from the United Kingdom (s. 8 (1)).

"*Uncompetitive Practices.*" See s. 137, *post*, and the definition therein contained which is similar to the wording used in Article 85 of the Treaty of Rome.

Sub-s. (3): "*It shall be the duty of the Director.*" The duty to give information and assistance or to make recommendations exists if (1) On his own initiative he considers it expendient *or* (2) If the Secretary of State so requests.

"Secretary of State." See note to s. 1, *ante.*

"Subject to the provisions of Part II." The Director shall not recommend the Secretary of State to make an order under s. 22, *post*, except by way of making a reference to the Advisory Committee under s. 17, *post.*

Sub-s. (4): *"It shall also be the duty of the Director to have regard."* The Director is obliged to have regard only to evidence which satisfies the following four conditions:— It must be evidence with respect to a course of conduct; that conduct must be on the part of a person carrying on a business; it must appear (probably reasonably) to the Director to be detrimental to the interests of consumers in the United Kingdom and that conduct must be regarded as unfair within s. 34 (2)—see also s. 138, *post.*

Sub-s. (5): *"Regional Development etc."* Although this subsection imposes a duty, it is not easy to see whether anyone, apart from the Attorney-General, would have sufficient *locus standi* to enforce it. However, see *A.-G.* v. *Independent Broadcasting Authority*, [1973] Q.B. 629.

3. Consumer Protection Advisory Committee

(1) There shall be established an advisory committee to be called the Consumer Protection Advisory Committee (in this Act referred to as "the Advisory Committee") for the purpose of performing the functions assigned to that Committee by Part II of this Act.

(2) Subject to subsection (6) of this section, the Advisory Committee shall consist of not less than ten and not more than fifteen members, who shall be appointed by the Secretary of State.

(3) The Secretary of State may appoint persons to the Advisory Committee either as full-time members or as part-time members.

(4) Of the members of the Advisory Committee, the Secretary of State shall appoint one to be chairman and one to be deputy chairman of the Advisory Committee.

(5) In appointing persons to be members of the Advisory Committee, the Secretary of State shall have regard to the need for securing that the Advisory Committee will include—

(*a*) one or more persons appearing to him to be qualified to advise on practices relating to goods supplied to consumers in the United Kingdom or produced with a view to their being so supplied, or relating to services supplied for consumers in the United Kingdom, by virtue of their knowledge of or experience in the supply (whether to consumers or not) of such goods or by virtue of their knowledge of or experience in the supply of such services;

(*b*) one or more persons appearing to him to be qualified to advise on such practices as are mentioned in the preceding paragraph by virtue of their knowledge of or experience in the enforcement of the Weights and Measures Act 1963 or the Trade Descriptions Act 1968 or other similar enactments; and

(*c*) one or more persons appearing to him to be qualified to advise on such practices by virtue of their knowledge of or experience in organisations established, or activities carried on for the protection of consumers.

(6) The Secretary of State may by order made by statutory instrument increase the maximum number of members of the Advisory Committee to such number as he may think fit.

(7) The provisions of Schedule 2 to this Act shall have effect with respect to the Advisory Committee. [**103**]

COMMENCEMENT

See s. 140 (3), *post*, and the note to s. 1, *ante*.

DEFINITIONS

"Consumer", "enactment", "goods", "practice" and "supply": s. 137 (2) (for "consumer" also s. 137 (6)).

"services supplied": s. 137 (3).

"services": s. 137 (4).

"Advisory Committee": s. 137 (2).

GENERAL NOTE

Sub-s. (1): *"The functions assigned."* The functions assigned to the Advisory Committee under Part II of the Act are the duty to consider and report on a consumer trade practice referred to it under s. 14; and the duty to consider and report on a consumer trade practice coupled with a recommendation under s. 17.

Sub-s. (2): *"Secretary of State."* See note to s. 1, *ante*.

Sub-s. (3): *"Full time members or as part time members."* The relative proportions of full time and part time members lie entirely within the discretion of the Secretary of State: there are no fixed or minimum proportions.

Sub-s. (5): *"Have regard to the need."* Although this appears to impose some form of duty, and the test of such need seems to be objective, the whole requirement is qualified by the later use of the word "include"—see below.

"Will include." Although three categories are expressly outlined in paras. (*a*), (*b*) and (*c*) there is no fixed or minimum requirement for such members.

Composition of the Advisory Committee. The Committee will (probably) comprise members from each of the categories outlined in paras. (*a*), (*b*) and (*c*) together with such other members with experience in this field as are appointed by the Secretary of State.

"United Kingdom." See note to s. 2, *ante*.

"Whether to consumers or not." Those members falling within category (*a*) may include manufacturers and wholesalers.

"By order." See s. 134, *post*. No order has yet been made under this subsection.

"Statutory instrument." See generally Statutory Instruments Act 1946.

Schedule 2. This regulates the status, tenure, remuneration and procedure of the Advisory Committee.

4. The Monopolies and Mergers Commission

(1) The Commission established under section 1 of the Monopolies and Restrictive Practices (Inquiry and Control) Act 1948 by the name of the Monopolies and Restrictive Practices Commission, and subsequently renamed the Monopolies Commission, shall as from the commencement of this Act be known as the Monopolies and Mergers Commission, and shall continue to exist by that name for the purpose of performing the functions assigned to that Commission (in this Act referred to as "the Commission") by or under this Act.

(2) There shall be not less than ten and (subject to the next following subsection) not more than twenty-five regular members of the Commission, who shall be appointed by the Secretary of State.

(3) The Secretary of State may by order made by statutory instrument increase the maximum number of regular members of the Commission to such number as he may think fit.

(4) The provisions of Schedule 3 to this Act shall have effect with respect to the Commission. [**104**]

COMMENCEMENT

See s. 140 (3), *post*, and the note to s. 1, *ante*.

DEFINITION

"Commission": s. 137 (2).

GENERAL NOTE

"Subsequently renamed." By the Restrictive Trade Practices Act 1956, s. 28 (1) (repealed).

"Commencement of this Act." I.e., the day appointed for the coming into operation of this provision; see 150 (3), (4), *post.*

"The functions assigned." Under s. 5, *post,* the Commission is principally required to investigate and report on monopoly situations, merger situations and newspaper mergers; the Commission is also required to report on general references of matters concerning the adverse effects of monopoly situations—s. 78; and on restrictive labour practices—s. 79.

"Regular members." All members of the Commission are regular members except for the additional members which the Secretary of State is empowered to appoint for the purposes of a newspaper merger reference—Sch. 3, para. 22.

"Secretary of State." See note to s. 1, *ante.*

"By order." See s. 134, *post*; no order has yet been made under this subsection.

"Statutory instrument." See note to s. 3, *ante.*

"Schedule 3." This regulates the status, staff and terms of remuneration of the Commission. It also lays down the procedure.

Transitional provisions. See s. 139 (2) and Sch. 11, para. 1 (2), *post.*

5. Principal functions of Commission

(1) Without prejudice to any other functions assigned to the Commission by or under this Act, it shall be the duty of the Commission, subject to and in accordance with the following provisions of this Act, to investigate and report on any question which may be referred to the Commission under this Act—

(*a*) with respect to the existence, or possible existence, of a monopoly situation, or

(*b*) with respect to a transfer of a newspaper or of newspaper assets (within the meaning of Part V of this Act), or

(*c*) with respect to the creation, or possible creation, of a merger situation qualifying for investigation (within the meaning of Part V of this Act).

(2) It shall be the duty of the Director, for the purpose of assisting the Commission in carrying out an investigation on a reference made to them under this Act, to give to the Commission—

(*a*) any information which is in his possession and which relates to matters falling within the scope of the investigation, and which is either requested by the Commission for that purpose or is information which in his opinion it would be appropriate for that purpose to give to the Commission without any such request, and

(*b*) any other assistance which the Commission may require, and which it is within his power to give, in relation to any such matters,

and the Commission, for the purpose of carrying out any such investigation, shall take account of any information given to them for that purpose under this subsection.

(3) In this Act "monopoly reference" means any reference to the Commission under this Act which falls within paragraph (*a*) of subsection (1) of this section; "merger reference" (subject to section 63 of this Act) means any reference to the Commission under this Act which falls within paragraph (*b*) or paragraph (*c*) of that subsection; and "monopoly situation" (except in sections 6 to 8 of this Act) means circumstances in which, in accordance with the following provisions of this Part of this Act, a monopoly situation is for the purposes of this Act to be taken to exist in relation to any matters specified in section 6(1), section 7(1) or secion 8 of this Act. [**105**]

COMMENCEMENT

See s. 140 (3), *post,* and the note to s. 1, *ante.*

DEFINITIONS

"Director", "Commission": s. 137 (2).

"newspaper", "transfer of a newspaper or newspaper assets": s. 57 (2) and 57 (1) (*a*).
"merger situation qualifying for investigation": s. 64 (8).
For other relevant definitions: s. 5 (3).

GENERAL NOTE

"Other functions assigned." See ss. 78 and 79, *post*, and the note to s. 4, *ante*.

"Subject to . . . the following provisions of this Act." See ss. 47 *et seq*; Part V (ss. 57–77); Part VI (ss. 78–80); Part VII (ss. 81–83); and Part VIII (ss. 84–93).

"May be referred." The Commission therefore has no power to initiate an investigation or to collect information. It may only act upon a reference from the Director, the Secretary of State or a Minister.

"Duty of the Director." This therefore imposes a mandatory obligation.

"For the purpose of assisting." The words "from time to time" do not appear in this section. It is not therefore clear whether the duty persists throughout the investigation or only at the outset.

"To give to the Commission." The Director is obliged to provide the Commission with information and other assistance, provided that the information is requested *or* he considers it appropriate for the purpose of the reference; and provided that the assistance is requested *and* it is within the power of the Director to give it.

"Shall take account." The Commission is therefore under a duty to take account of the information. It therefore seems probable that, in an appropriate case, the Commission could be compelled to do so by an order of mandamus; and that any action taken in consequence of a report which failed to take account of such information would be ultra vires and void—see *e.g.*, s. 56.

6. Monopoly situation in relation to supply of goods

(1) For the purposes of this Act a monopoly situation shall be taken to exist in relation to the supply of goods of any description in the following cases, that is to say, if—

(*a*) at least one-quarter of all the goods of that description which are supplied in the United Kingdom are supplied by one and the same person, or are supplied to one and the same person, or

(*b*) at least one-quarter of all the goods of that description which are supplied in the United Kingdom are supplied by members of one and the same group of interconnected bodies corporate, or are supplied to members of one and the same group of interconnected bodies corporate, or

(*c*) at least one-quarter of all the goods of that description which are supplied in the United Kingdom are supplied by members of one and the same group consisting of two or more such persons as are mentioned in subsection (2) of this section, or are supplied to members of one and the same group consisting of two or more such persons, or

(*d*) one or more agreements are in operation, the result or collective result of which is that goods of that description are not supplied in the United Kingdom at all.

(2) The two or more persons referred to in subsection (1)(*c*) of this section, in relation to goods of any description, are any two or more persons (not being a group of interconnected bodies corporate) who whether voluntarily or not, and whether by agreement or not, so conduct their respective affairs as in any way to prevent, restrict or distort competition in connection with the production or supply of goods of that description, whether or not they themselves are affected by the competition and whether the competition is between persons interested as producers or suppliers or between persons interested as customers of producers or suppliers. **[106]**

COMMENCEMENT

See s. 140 (3), *post*, and notes to s. 1, *ante*.

DEFINITIONS

"United Kingdom": see notes to s. 2, *ante*.

"person": includes any body of persons corporate or unincorporate. See the Interpretation Act 1889, s. 19.

"interconnected bodies corporate": s. 137 (5).

"supply": s. 137 (2).

"goods": s. 137 (2).

"agreement": s. 137 (2).

"produce": s. 137 (2).

"group": s. 137 (2).

There is no exemption of nationalised industries from s. 6.

GENERAL NOTE

Monopoly situations in respect of supply of goods have hitherto been regulated by s. 3 of the Monopolies and Restrictive Practices (Inquiry and Control) Act 1948. Only the supply of goods can qualify as a monopoly situation under s. 6. Production of goods qualifies in itself as a monopoly situation solely in relation to exports of goods by virtue of s. 8.

Sub-s. (1) (*a*), (*b*), (*c*): For a supply to qualify—

(i) it must account for one quarter (a reduction from one-third in the 1948 Act) of the supply in the U.K. of those goods and

(ii) the supply must be *to* or *by* a qualifying entity (see below). Monopoly buyers are thus covered as well as monopoly suppliers. If a monopoly buyer is being considered provided the buyer is in the U.K. the supplier need not be. If a monopoly supplier is under review the supplier must be in the U.K.

Entities capable of making or taking monopoly supplies:

(*a*) a single person, whether natural or corporate or an unincorporated body;

(*b*) members of one and the same group of interconnected bodies corporate (see s. 137 (5));

(*c*) persons not within (*b*) who, whether or not by agreement conduct their affairs in the way and with the results described in s. 6 (2). This may be done by persons acting independently of one another and without intending any result within s. 6 (2). Provided the proportion of one-quarter is attained there will be a monopoly situation.

Sub-s. (1) (*d*): The result of no supply of goods in the U.K. at all may be achieved voluntarily by agreement or agreements or may be the unintended result. Either way it will qualify as a monopoly situation.

Supplementary provisions. See ss. 9 and 10 and notes thereto, *post*.

7. Monopoly situation in relation to supply of services

(1) For the purposes of this Act a monopoly situation shall be taken to exist in relation to the supply of services of any description in the following cases, that is to say, if—

(*a*) the supply of services of that description in the United Kingdom is, to the extent of at least one-quarter, supply by one and the same person, or supply for one and the same person, or

(*b*) the supply of services of that description in the United Kingdom is, to the extent of at least one-quarter, supply by members of one and the same group of interconnected bodies corporate, or supply for members of one and the same group of interconnected bodies corporate, or

(*c*) the supply of services of that description in the United Kingdom is, to the extent of at least one-quarter, supply by members of one and the same group consisting of two or more such persons as are mentioned in subsection (2) of this section, or supply for members of one and the same group consisting of two or more such persons, or

(*d*) one or more agreements are in operation, the result or collective result of which is that services of that description are not supplied in the United Kingdom at all.

(2) The two or more persons referred to in subsection (1)(*c*) of this section, in relation to services of any description, are any two or more persons (not being a

group of interconnected bodies corporate) who whether voluntarily or not, and whether by agreement or not, so conduct their respective affairs as in any way to prevent, restrict or distort competition in connection with the supply of services of that description, whether or not they themselves are affected by the competition, and whether the competition is between persons interested as persons by whom, or as persons for whom, services are supplied.

(3) In the application of this section for the purposes of a monopoly reference, the Commission, or the person or persons making the reference, may, to such extent as the Commission, or that person or those persons, think appropriate in the circumstances, treat services as supplied in the United Kingdom if the person supplying the services—

(*a*) has a place of business in the United Kingdom, or
(*b*) controls the relevant activities from the United Kingdom, or
(*c*) being a body corporate, is incorporated under the law of Great Britain or of Northern Ireland,

and may do so whether or not those services would otherwise be regarded as supplied in the United Kingdom. **[107]**

COMMENCEMENT

See s. 140 (3), *post*, and notes to s. 1, *ante*.

DEFINITIONS

"United Kingdom": see notes to s. 2, *ante*.
"person": see notes to s. 6, *ante*.
"interconnected bodies corporate": s. 137 (5).
"supply": s. 137 (2).
"services": s. 137 (3) and (4).
"agreement": s. 137 (2).
"produce": s. 137 (2).
"group": s. 137 (2).

There is no exemption of nationalised industries from s. 7.

GENERAL NOTE

Monopoly situations in relation to supply of services have hitherto been regulated by s. 2 of the Monopolies and Mergers Act 1965. S. 7 introduces the change in qualifying market-share noted for s. 6, *ante*, from one third to one quarter.

With the substitution of "services" for "goods" all the comments on s. 6, *ante*, apply to s. 7. There are, in addition, provisions in s. 7 (3) under which persons are deemed to be supplying services in the United Kingdom whether or not those services would otherwise be regarded as supplied in the United Kingdom.

Supplementary provisions. See ss. 9 and 10, *post*.

8. Monopoly situation in relation to exports

(1) For the purposes of this Act a monopoly situation shall be taken to exist in relation to exports of goods of any description from the United Kingdom in the following cases, that is to say, if—

(*a*) at least one-quarter of all the goods of that description which are produced in the United Kingdom are produced by one and the same person, or
(*b*) at least one-quarter of all the goods of that description which are produced in the United Kingdom are produced by members of one and the same group of interconnected bodies corporate;

and in those cases a monopoly situation shall for the purposes of this Act be taken to exist both in relation to exports of goods of that description from the United Kingdom generally and in relation to exports of goods of that description from the United Kingdom to each market taken separately.

(2) In relation to exports of goods of any description from the United Kingdom generally, a monopoly situation shall for the purposes of this Act be taken to exist if—

(*a*) one or more agreements are in operation which in any way prevent or restrict, or prevent, restrict or distort competition in relation to, the export of goods of that description from the United Kingdom, and

(*b*) that agreement is or (as the case may be) those agreements collectively are operative with respect to at least one-quarter of all the goods of that description which are produced in the United Kingdom.

(3) In relation to exports of goods of any description from the United Kingdom to any particular market, a monopoly situation shall for the purposes of this Act be taken to exist if—

(*a*) one or more agreements are in operation which in any way prevent or restrict, or prevent, restrict or distort competition in relation to, the supply of goods of that description (whether from the United Kingdom or not) to that market, and

(*b*) that agreement is or (as the case may be) those agreements collectively are operative with respect to at least one-quarter of all the goods of that description which are produced in the United Kingdom. [**108**]

COMMENCEMENT

See s. 140 (3), *post*, and notes to s. 1, *ante*.

DEFINITIONS

"export" is not defined.
"market" is not defined.
"goods": s. 137 (2).
"United Kingdom": see notes to s. 2, *ante*.
"person": see notes to s. 6, *ante*.
"interconnected bodies corporate": s. 137 (5).
"agreement": s. 137 (2).

GENERAL NOTE

Monopoly situations in respect of export of goods have hitherto been regulated by s. 5 of the Monopolies and Restrictive Practices (Inquiry and Control) Act 1948. There is no provision relating to the export of services in this Act.

S. 8 (1) provides that a monopoly situation can exist in relation to a single producer's production of goods which are then exported. Whether or not the producer is also the exporter is irrelevant, provided that the producer, which may be a group of interconnected bodies corporate, produces at least one quarter of all the goods of that description which are produced in the United Kingdom.

S. 8 (2) provides that a monopoly situation exists when competition in relation to the export of goods to any or no particular market is distorted by one or more agreements operative with respect to at least a quarter of those goods which are produced in the United Kingdom.

S. 8 (3) covers the situation where agreements are operative with respect to at least a quarter of all the goods of a particular description that are produced in the United Kingdom and those agreements distort the supply of those goods (whether the supply originates from the United Kingdom or not) to a particular market outside the United Kingdom. Thus if a multinational company producing cars in the United Kingdom accounts for more than a quarter of United Kingdom production of cars any agreement that a particular foreign market shall be supplied mainly by German-made cars would create a monopoly situation. In contrast to s. 8 (2) competition between exporters of goods from the United Kingdom need not be distorted, though it may be, for s. 8 (3) to apply. The focus of attention in s. 8 (3) is a particular market outside the United Kingdom and distortions in competition over supplying that market.

Supplementary provision. See s. 10, *post*.

9. Monopoly situation limited to part of United Kingdom

(1) For the purposes of a monopoly reference, other than a reference relating to exports of goods from the United Kingdom, the person or persons making the

reference may, if it appears to him or them to be appropriate in the circumstances to do so, determine that consideration shall be limited to a part of the United Kingdom.

(2) Where such a determination is made, then for the purposes of that monopoly reference the provisions of sections 6 and 7 of this Act, or such of those provisions are as applicable for those purposes, shall have effect as if, wherever those provisions refer to the United Kingdom, they referred to that part of the United Kingdom to which, in accordance with that determination, consideration is to be limited.

(3) The preceding provisions of this section shall have effect subject to subsection (4) of section 50 of this Act in cases to which that subsection applies. **[109]**

COMMENCEMENT

See s. 140 (3), *post*, and the note to s. 1, *ante*.

DEFINITIONS

"United Kingdom": see notes to s. 2, *ante*.

Northern Ireland as a part of the United Kingdom: see sub-s. (3) above and s. 50 (4), *post*.

"agreement", "goods" and "produce": s. 137 (2).

"interconnected bodies corporate" and "group of interconnected bodies corporate": s. 137 (5).

GENERAL NOTE

This section allows a reference of a monopoly situation within s. 6 or s. 7 to be for the investigation of possible localised monopoly conditions in a part of the United Kingdom. Thus where even a single firm supplies, albeit only in a part, and possibly a small part, of the United Kingdom a quarter of any particular goods or services, a monopoly reference will now be possible.

Supplementary provisions. See s. 5 (3), *ante*, and s. 10, *post*.

10. Supplementary provisions relating to ss. 6 to 9

(1) In the application of any of the provisions of sections 6 to 9 of this Act for the purposes of a monopoly reference, those provisions shall have effect subject to the following provisions of this section.

(2) No account shall for those purposes to be taken of any provisions of an agreement in so far as they are provisions by virtue of which it is an agreement to which Part I of the Act of 1956 applies.

(3) In relation to goods or services of any description which are the subject of different forms of supply—

(*a*) references in paragraphs (*a*) to (*d*) of subsection (1), and in subsection (2), of section 6 or in section 8(3) of this Act to the supply of goods, or

(*b*) references in paragraphs (*a*) to (*d*) of subsection (1), and in subsection (2), of section 7 of this Act to the supply of services,

shall for those purposes be construed in whichever of the following ways the Commission, or the person or persons making the monopoly reference, think appropriate in all the circumstances, that is to say, as references to any of those forms of supply taken separately, to all those forms of supply taken together, or to any of those forms of supply taken in groups.

(4) For the purposes of subsection (3) of this section the Commission, or the person or persons making the monopoly reference in question, may treat goods or services as being the subject of different forms of supply whenever the transactions in question differ as to their nature, their parties, their terms or their surrounding circumstances, and the difference is one which, in the opinion

of the Commission, or the person or persons making the reference, ought for the purposes of that subsection to be treated as a material difference.

(5) For the purposes of a monopoly reference made by the Director, subsections (3) and (4) of this section shall have effect subject to section 50(3) and (4) of this Act.

(6) In determining, for the purposes of a monopoly reference, whether the proportion of one-quarter mentioned in any provision of section 6, section 7 or section 8 of this Act is fulfilled with respect to goods or services of any description, the Commission, or the person or persons making the reference, shall apply such criterion (whether it be value or cost or price or quantity or capacity or number of workers employed or some other criterion, of whatever nature) or such combination of criteria as may appear to them or him to be most suitable in all the circumstances.

(7) The criteria for determining when goods or services can be treated, for the purposes of a monopoly reference, as goods or services of a separate description shall be such as the person or persons making the reference may think most suitable in the circumstances.

(8) In construing the provisions of section 7(3) and section 9 of this Act and the provisions of subsections (1) to (7) of this section, the purposes of a monopoly reference shall be taken to include the purpose of enabling the Director, or the Secretary of State or any other Minister, to determine in any particular circumstances—

(*a*) whether a monopoly reference could be made under Part IV of this Act, and

(*b*) if so, whether in those circumstances such a reference could be made by the Director,

and references in those provisions to the person or persons making a monopoly reference shall be construed accordingly. [**110**]

COMMENCEMENT

See s. 140 (3), *post,* and the note to s. 1, *ante.*

DEFINITIONS

Secretary of State: see notes to s. 1, *ante.*
Part IV of this Act: *I.e.,* ss. 44–56, *post.*
"The Director": see s. 1 (1), *ante,* or s. 137 (2), *post.*
"The Commission": see s. 4 (1), *ante,* or s. 137 (2), *post.*
"monopoly reference": s. 5 (3).
"agreement", "goods", "Minister", "price", "supply" and "worker": see s. 137 (2), *post,* and see also as to "worker", s. 137 (9), *post.*
"supply of services": s. 137 (3).
"services": s. 137 (4).
"Act of 1956": *I.e.,* Restrictive Trade Practices Act 1956—see s. 137 (1), *post.*

GENERAL NOTE

Ss. 6 to 9 define various types of monopoly situation capable of being referred as a monopoly reference to the Monopolies and Mergers Commission.

S. 10 provides definitions and elaborations which, in applying any of the provisions of ss. 6 to 9 for the purposes of a monopoly reference must be taken into account: s. 10 (1).

As seen in the discussion of ss. 6, 7 and 11, *ante,* some monopoly situations are *prima facie* constituted by certain types of agreement. S. 10 (2) provides that, for the purposes of a monopoly reference, if there are provisions in any agreement or arrangement which render it subject to Part I of the Restrictive Trade Practices Act 1956 those provisions must be left out of account in assessing whether a monopoly situation capable of reference to the Commission exists.

Agreements subject to Part I of the Restrictive Trade Practices Act 1956 are described in s. 6 of that Act and they were formerly registrable with the Registrar of Restrictive Trading Agreements. By virtue of s. 94 of this Act (*post*) the functions of the Registrar have been transferred to the Director-General of Fair Trading who under s. 50 also has power to make monopoly references.

Nevertheless, s. 10 (2) clearly defines mutually exclusive classes of provision in agreements:

(*a*) provisions taking an agreement within s. 6 of the Restrictive Trade Practices Act 1956. If nothing else exists to constitute a monopoly situation then no monopoly situation capable of reference exists though the agreements are registrable with the Director as restrictive trade agreements;

(*b*) provisions not capable of such registration and which constitute a monopoly situation. These are capable of being the subject of a monopoly reference. An example of this type of agreement is one between a United Kingdom firm and an overseas firm: s. 6 of the Restrictive Trade Practices Act 1956 applies only to agreements "between two or more persons carrying on business within the United Kingdom" whereas ss. 6 (1) (*d*), 7 (1) (*d*), 8 (2) and 8 (3) (*ante*) of this Act also catch agreements between persons carrying on business in the United Kingdom and elsewhere.

S. 10 also defines three elements in the definitions contained in ss. 6–9: "supply," "one-quarter", and "goods or services of any description".

"*Supply*". This concept is amplified in s. 10 (3), (4) and (5). The supply of goods or services can take many forms. S. 10 (4) leaves it to the discretion of the person making the reference or the Commission in considering it whether to treat the different forms of supply of a commodity together or singly and if together, in what combination. For example there might be a reference of the wholesale or the retail supply of, for example, beer, or both. S. 10 (4) describes how differences in the forms of supply are to be assessed and gives a discretion.

S. 50 (2) debars the Director from referring certain forms of the supply of certain, goods set out in Schedules 5 and 7. For example the Director would be debarred from referring any forms of supply of refined sugar other than retail supply. S. 10 (5) accordingly indicates that the Director's general discretion under s. 10 (3) and 10 (4) is limited by s. 50 (2), (3) and (4) which are overriding.

"*One-quarter.*" This concept is amplified in s. 10 (6), which replaces s. 20 (3) of the Monopolies and Restrictive Practices (Inquiry and Control) Act 1948 as to goods and s. 2 (3) of the Monopolies and Mergers Act 1965 as to services.

These provisions with their extremely wide and vague criteria have been used but rarely and the use of s. 10 (6) will vary from industry to industry depending partly on the availability of information and statistics and partly on the nature of a product. Examples of use are the Commission's investigation of the colour film industry where it considered the Kodak share of the supply partly on a value basis and partly on a square footage basis. In considering men's hairdressing services the Commission found it most practical to try to ascertain the numbers of people engaged in supplying the service.

"*goods or services of any description.*" S. 10 (7) gives to the person or persons making the monopoly reference a discretion as to how to assess whether goods or services can be treated as being of separate descriptions.

S. 10 also amplifies the words "*the purposes of a monopoly reference*" to include the consideration of the question whether a monopoly reference can be made and whether a proposed reference is one that can be made by the Director having regard to the provisions of s. 50. Thus the purposes of a monopoly reference includes work done before a reference is made so that the provisions of ss. 8 (3), 9 and the other provisions of s. 10 can be used in such work. In all those sections the phrase "for the purposes of a monopoly reference" occurs.

11. Meaning of "complex monopoly situation"

(1) In this Act "complex monopoly situation" means circumstances in which, in accordance with the preceding provisions of this Act, a monopoly situation is for the purposes of this Act to be taken to exist in relation to the supply of goods or services of any description, or in relation to exports of goods of any description from the United Kingdom, by reason that the condition specified in paragraph (*c*) or in paragraph (*d*) of section 6(1) or of section 7(1) of this Act is fulfilled, or that the conditions specified in subsection (2) or in subsection (3) of section 8 of this Act are fulfilled.

(2) Any reference in the preceding subsection to paragraph (*c*) or paragraph (*d*) of section 6(1) or of section 7(1) of this Act shall be construed as including a reference to that paragraph as modified by section 9(2) of this Act. [**111**]

COMMENCEMENT

See s. 140 (3), *post*, and notes to s. 1, *ante*.

DEFINITIONS

"'United Kingdom": see notes to s. 2, *ante*.
"monopoly situation": s. 5 (3).
"goods", "supply": s. 137 (2).
"supply of services": s. 137 (3).
"services": s. 137 (4).
"preceding provisions of this Act": *I.e.*, ss. 6–10, *ante*.

GENERAL NOTE

S. 11 (1) provides that a monopoly situation which exists because of the existence of agreements or arrangements between firms in the particular market is a complex monopoly situation. It has a significance for the powers of the Director to gather information (see s. 45, *post*) and also allows refinement of a monopoly reference by virtue of s. 47 (2), *post*.

Under s. 11 (2) a complex monopoly situation may be constituted by agreements covering a relevant supply in even a part of the United Kingdom.

Every complex monopoly situation must satisfy the one quarter share of the market criterion which is contained in ss. 6, 7 and 8, *ante*—*i.e.*, the agreements in question must relate to one quarter of the supply of the particular goods, services or exports.

12. Powers of Secretary of State in relation to functions of Director

(1) The Secretary of State may give general directions indicating considerations to which the Director should have particular regard in determining the order of priority in which—

(*a*) matters are to be brought under review in the performance of his duty under section 2(1) of this Act, or

(*b*) classes of goods or services are to be brought under review by him for the purpose of considering whether a monopoly situation exists or may exist in relation to them.

(2) The Secretary of State may also give general directions indicating—

(*a*) considerations to which in cases where it appears to the Director that a practice may adversely affect the interests of consumers in the United Kingdom, he should have particular regard in determining whether to make a recommendation to the Secretary of State under section 2(3)(*b*) of this Act, or

(*b*) considerations to which, in cases where it appears to the Director that a consumer trade practice may adversely affect the economic interests of consumers in the United Kingdom, he should have particular regard in determining whether to make a reference to the Advisory Committee under Part II of this Act, or

(*c*) considerations to which, in cases where it appears to the Director that a monopoly situation exists or may exist, he should have particular regard in determining whether to make a monopoly reference to the Commission under Part IV of this Act.

(3) The Secretary of State, on giving any directions under this section, shall arrange for those directions to be published in such manner as the Secretary of State thinks most suitable in the circumstances. [**112**]

COMMENCEMENT

See s. 140 (3), *post*, and the note to s. 1, *ante*.

DEFINITIONS

"the Director", "the Advisory Committee", "the Commission": s. 137 (2).
"monopoly reference", "monopoly situation": s. 5 (3).
"consumer trade practice": s. 13.
"consumer", "goods": s. 137 (2); and for "consumer" also s. 137 (6).
"services": s. 137 (4).

GENERAL NOTE

"Secretary of State." See note to s. 1, *ante*.

"May give." This is purely permissive. Thus the Secretary of State is not obliged to give general directions under this section.

"General directions." Thus the Secretary of State is given power to lay down general guidelines for the exercise of the functions of the Director.

"Should have particular regard." Although this form of wording is not as emphatic as the mandatory, "shall", it is suggested that this section imposes a duty on the Director.

"Duty under section 2 (1)." See note to s. 2, *ante*.

"United Kingdom." See note to s. 2, *ante*.

"Reference to the Advisory Committee." This may either be a general reference under s. 14, *post*, or a reference proposing a recommendation under s. 17, *post*.

"Shall arrange." This therefore imposes a clear duty on the Secretary of State.

"Thinks most suitable." The Secretary of State therefore has a discretion as to the manner of publication. This is probably subject to the duty to act reasonably—*Padfield* v. *Minister of Agriculture*, [1968] A.C. 997, and *Secretary of State for Employment* v. *Associated Society of Locomotive Engineers and Firemen* (*No.* 2), [1972] 2 Q.B. 455.

PART II

REFERENCES TO CONSUMER PROTECTION ADVISORY COMMITTEE

General provisions

13. Meaning of "consumer trade practice"

In this Act "consumer trade practice" means any practice which is for the time being carried on in connection with the supply of goods (whether by way of sale or otherwise) to consumers or in connection with the supply of services for consumers and which relates—

(*a*) to the terms or conditions (whether as to price or otherwise) on or subject to which goods or services are or are sought to be supplied, or

(*b*) to the manner in which those terms or conditions are communicated to persons to whom goods are or are sought to be supplied or for whom services are or are sought to be supplied, or,

(*c*) to promotion (by advertising, labelling or marking of goods, canvassing or otherwise) of the supply of goods or of the supply of services, or

(*d*) to methods of salesmanship employed in dealing with consumers, or

(*e*) to the way in which goods are packed or otherwise got up for the purpose of being supplied, or

(*f*) to methods of demanding or securing payment for goods or services supplied. **[113]**

COMMENCEMENT

See s. 140 (3), *post*, and the note to s. 1, *ante*.

DEFINITIONS

"consumer", "goods", "practice", "price" and "supply": s. 137 (2); see also for "consumer", s. 137 (6).
"supply of services": s. 137 (3).
"services": s. 137 (4).
For relevant supplementary definitions, see also s. 138.

[113]

GENERAL NOTE

"*Any practice.*" Although the word practice is defined in s. 137 (2), *post*, the definition, which includes the word "practice", is circular and unhelpful. It seems to suggest some settled rule or course of conduct.

"*In connection with.*" This includes practices which relate directly or indirectly to the supply of goods or services for or to consumers. Therefore practices adopted by wholesalers or manufacturers appear to be included. Furthermore practices which operate as between third parties (*e.g.*, finance houses) and retailers but which indirectly affect consumers likewise appear to be included.

"*Terms or conditions, etc.*" The general meaning of this familiar expression is clear. It is not however clear whether the later expression "sought to be supplied" qualifies "terms or conditions" or only "goods or services". If it governs the former, then clauses included in written standard contracts could be referred even though void at law, *e.g.*, under the Supply of Goods (Implied Terms) Act 1973. In view of the potential difference in sanction this could be significant.

"*Price or otherwise.*" Therefore issues relating to prices and profit margins would fall within the definition of consumer practice.

"*Sought to be supplied.*" Therefore the terms upon which goods are offered or (probably) exposed for sale are included.

"*Manner in which.*" Therefore all forms of contractual document are included.

"*By advertising . . . or otherwise.*" There does not appear to be a *genus* here and the *eiusdem generis* rule is not therefore applicable.

"*Packed or otherwise got up.*" The expression "get up" is familiar in the field of passing-off—see, *e.g.*, *J. P. Williams & Co.* v. *Bronnley* (1909), 26 R.P.C. at p. 773.

"*For goods or services supplied.*" The words "sought to be" are omitted. Therefore methods of demanding or securing payment in advance do not seem to be included.

14. General provisions as to references to Advisory Committee

(1) Subject to sections 15 and 16 of this Act, the Secretary of State or any other Minister or the Director may refer to the Advisory Committee the question whether a consumer trade practice specified in the reference adversely affects the economic interests of consumers in the United Kingdom.

(2) The Secretary of State or any other Minister by whom a reference is made under this section shall transmit a copy of the reference to the Director.

(3) On any reference made to the Advisory Committee under this section the Advisory Committee shall consider the question so referred to them and shall prepare a report on that question and (except as otherwise provided by section 21(3) of this Act) submit that report to the person by whom the reference was made.

(4) Subject to the provisions of section 133 of this Act, it shall be the duty of the Director, where he is requested by the Advisory Committee to do so for the purpose of assisting the Committee in carrying out an investigation on a reference made to them under this section, to give to the Committee—

(*a*) any information which is in his possession and which relates to matters falling within the scope of the investigation, and

(*b*) any other assistance which the Committee may require, and which it is within his power to give, in relation to any such matters.

(5) The Advisory Committee shall transmit to the Secretary of State a copy of every report which is made by them under this section to a person other than the Secretary of State, and shall transmit to the Director a copy of every report which is made by them under this section to a person other than the Director.

COMMENCEMENT [114]

See s. 140 (3), *post*, and the note to s. 1, *ante*.

DEFINITIONS

"Director", "Advisory Committee", "Minister": s. 137 (1).
"monopoly situation": s. 5 (3).

"consumer trade practice": s. 13.
"consumer": s. 137 (2) and also s. 137 (*b*).
For supplementary interpretation, see s. 138.

GENERAL NOTE

"*Sections* 15 *and* 16." These, broadly, exclude references of the professions set out in Schedule 4 and restrict references of the nationalised industries set out in Schedule 5.

"*Secretary of State.*" See note to s. 1, *ante.*

"*Adversely affects.*" This wording should be contrasted with that included in s. 2 (1) (*a*), *ante*, and see the note thereon.

"*Economic interests.*" See s. 2 (1) (*a*) and the note thereon, *ante.*

"*Prepare report.*" For general provisions as to Reports of the Advisory Commission see s. 82 and the note thereon, *post.*

"*Section 21 (3).*" This provides that every Report under s. 17, *post*, is to be made to the Secretary of State. See also the note to s. 21, *post.*

"*Section 133.*" That section appears to prevent the Director from making information relating to a particular business available to the Advisory Committee if the Director obtained that information by virtue of the provisions of this Act—*e.g.*, s. 2, *ante.*

"*Duty.*" Thus a mandatory obligation is imposed on the Director.

"*Where he is requested.*" Although the Director is under a duty to provide information and assistance to the Advisory Committee if requested to do so, he is under no obligation to provide such information and assistance on his own initiative.

15. Exclusion from s. 14 in respect of certain services

No reference under section 14 of this Act shall be made to the Advisory Committee by the Secretary of State or by any other Minister or by the Director if it appears to him—

(*a*) that the consumer trade practice in question is carried on in connection only with the supply of services of a description specified in Schedule 4 to this Act, and

(*b*) that a monopoly situation exists or may exist in relation to the supply of services of that description. [**115**]

COMMENCEMENT

See s. 140 (3), *post*, and the note to s. 1, *ante.*

DEFINITIONS

"Director", Advisory Committee" and "Minister": s. 137 (2).
"monopoly situation": s. 5 (3).
"consumer trade practice": s. 13.
For supplementary interpretation, see s. 138.

GENERAL NOTE

"*No reference under section 14.*" For a further restriction on such references see s. 16, *post.*

"*Shall be made.*" The provision is therefore both mandatory and negative. It is therefore (likely) to be enforceable by way of injunction or prohibition and almost certainly by declaration.

"*Secretary of State.*" See note to s. 1, *ante.*

"*If it appears to him.*" Although the test is therefore made subjective, the decision must probably be based on reasonable grounds—see *Padfield* v. *Minister of Agriculture*, [1968] A.C. 997 and *Secretary of State for Employment* v. *Associated Society of Locomotive Engineers and Firemen* (*No. 2*), [1972] 2 Q.B. 455.

"*Of a description.*" For various authorities on the meaning of this expression see Sale of Goods Act 1893, s. 13, and Restrictive Trade Practices Act 1956, s. 6 (1) (*c*) and (*d*).

"*And.*" Thus the conditions set out in (*a*) and (*b*) are cumulative: there must be both the existence or possible existence of a monopoly situation and the practice must be in connection with a service falling within Schedule 4 to the Act.

"*Monopoly situation exists . . . etc.*" If such a situation exists it is possible to make a monopoly reference under Part IV of the Act. The exclusion contained in this section is therefore presumably justified on the ground that such a monopoly reference provides more appropriate machinery for the examination of services within Schedule 4.

16. Restriction on references under s. 14 in respect of certain goods and services

(1) No reference under section 14 of this Act shall be made to the Advisory Committee by the Director except with the consent of the appropriate Minister, if it appears to the Director that the consumer trade practice in question—

(*a*) is carried on in connection only with the supply, by a body corporate to which this section applies, of goods or services of a description specified in Part I of Schedule 5 to this Act, or

(*b*) is carried on in connection only with the supply by such a body corporate of goods or services of a description specified in the first column of Part II of that Schedule, in so far as that supply falls within the entry relating to it in the second column of that Part of that Schedule.

(2) This section applies to any body corporate which fulfils the following conditions, that is to say—

(*a*) that the affairs of the body corporate are managed by its members, and

(*b*) that by virtue of an enactment those members are appointed by a Minister;

and in this section "Minister" includes a Minister of the Government of Northern Ireland, and "the appropriate Minister", in relation to a body corporate, means the Minister by whom members of that body corporate are appointed.

(3) The Secretary of State may by order made by statutory instrument vary any of the provisions of Schedule 5 to this Act, either by adding one or more further entries or by altering or deleting any entry for the time being contained in it; and any reference in this Act to that Schedule shall be construed as a reference to that Schedule as for the time being in force. [**116**]

COMMENCEMENT

See s. 140 (3), *post*, and the note to s. 1, *ante*.

DEFINITIONS

"the Director"; "the Advisory Committee", "Minister" and "supply": s. 137 (2); also for "Minister" and "appropriate Minister", note sub-s. (2) above.

"consumer trade practice": s. 13.

For supplementary interpretation, see 138, *post*.

GENERAL NOTE

"*No reference under section 14.*" For a further restriction on such references see s. 15, *ante*.

"*Shall be made.*" The provision is therefore both negative and mandatory. For further note, see General Note to s. 15, *ante*.

"*The consent.*" There is no restriction on the manner or form of such consent.

"*Appropriate Minister.*" Note sub-s. (2) above.

"*If it appears to the Director.*" The test is therefore made subjective, but see also General Note to s. 15, *ante*.

"*Of a description.*" For indications as to meaning, see General Note to s. 15, *ante*.

"*Part I of Schedule 5.*" This lists nationalised industries and services, which are partially excluded on the ground that such are already regulated by a statutory framework.

"*Secretary of State.*" See the note to s. 1, *ante*.

"*By order.*" See s. 134; no order has yet been made under this subsection.

"*Statutory instrument.*" See note to s. 3, *ante*.

"*Vary etc.*" Although the Secretary of State appears to be given an unrestricted power to alter or delete the entries in Schedule 5, this power must be restricted in some way. Presumably the power to introduce further exclusions must be limited to nationalised industries and public corporations. As a matter of construction this result can be achieved by reference to the well known distinction in contract law between a variation and a total rescission—see e.g. *British and Beningtons, Ltd.* v. *North Western Cachar Tea Co., Ltd.*, [1923] A.C. 48 at p. 68.

17. Reference to Advisory Committee proposing recommendation to Secretary of State to make an order

(1) This section applies to any reference made to the Advisory Committee by the Director under section 14 of this Act which includes proposals in accordance with the following provisions of this section.

(2) Where it appears to the Director that a consumer trade practice has the effect, or is likely to have the effect,—

(*a*) of misleading consumers as to, or withholding from them adequate information as to, or an adequate record of, their rights and obligations under relevant consumer transactions, or

(*b*) of otherwise misleading or confusing consumers with respect to any matter in connection with relevant consumer transactions, or

(*c*) of subjecting consumers to undue pressure to enter into relevant consumer transactions, or

(*d*) of causing the terms or conditions, on or subject to which consumers enter into relevant consumer transactions, to be so adverse to them as to be inequitable,

any reference made by the Director under section 14 of this Act with respect to that consumer trade practice may, if the Director thinks fit, include proposals for recommending to the Secretary of State that he should exercise his powers under the following provisions of this Part of this Act with respect to that consumer trade practice.

(3) A reference to which this section applies shall state which of the effects specified in subsection (2) of this section it appears to the Director that the consumer trade practice in question has or is likely to have.

(4) Where the Director makes a reference to which this section applies, he shall arrange for it to be published in full in the London, Edinburgh and Belfast Gazettes.

(5) In this Part of this Act "relevant consumer transaction", in relation to a consumer trade practice, means any transaction to which a person is, or may be invited to become, a party in his capacity as a consumer in relation to that practice. [**117**]

COMMENCEMENT

See s. 140 (3), *post*, and the note to s. 1, *ante*.

DEFINITIONS

"Director", "Advisory Committee" and "Consumer": s. 137 (2); for supplementary definitions see also s. 137 (*b*), s. 138.

"consumer trade practice": s. 13.

"relevant consumer transaction": sub-s. (5) above.

GENERAL NOTE

"*Reference . . . under section 14.*" References under this section therefore constitute a sub-category of references under s. 14, and the exclusions and restrictions contained in ss. 15 and 16 are similarly applicable.

"*Appears to the Director.*" The test is therefore primarily subjective. However see the note to s. 15, *ante*.

"*Or is likely to have.*" There must therefore be a high probability that the practice has one of the effects set out at headings (*a*)–(*d*) of this section; cf., "may adversely affect" in s. 2 (1) (*a*), *ante*, and see the note thereto.

"*Misleading . . . withholding.*" This section therefore covers both the situation in which the information supplied was insufficient, and where it is sufficient but misleading.

"*Information . . . record.*" Information is presumably supplied before the relevant transaction is concluded; a record is supplied afterwards.

"Otherwise misleading." Headings (*a*) and (*b*) are therefore mutually exclusive. For the significance of this, see sub-s. (3) above.

"Subjecting consumers." This heading is primarily directed at methods of salesmanship; see s. 13 (*d*), *ante*.

"Causing the terms." The use of this expression suggests that the stated effect is an indirect consequence of the consumer trade practice: in all other cases it is direct.

"Terms or conditions." This probably refers only to contractual terms or conditions.

"If the Director thinks fit." The test is therefore primarily subjective—see however the note to s. 15, *ante*.

"For recommending." The Secretary of State has a discretion whether or not to accept a Report of the Advisory Committee—see s. 22, *post*.

"Secretary of State." See the note to s. 1, *ante*.

Casus Omissus? Although a consumer trade practice can exist in relation to "methods of securing or demanding payment for goods or services" (s. 13 (*f*), *ante*), the right to use such methods will not always, or usually, depend upon a contractual term. Accordingly such a practice may fall outside heading (*d*): it is difficult to find another heading of s. 17 which could cover such a practice. It may not therefore be possible to make a recommendation in relation to such practices.

"Shall state which, etc." This therefore imposes a duty on the Director. It is however unlikely that a failure to comply with this duty would render a Report under s. 21 void, or an Order under s. 22 void.

"Shall arrange for it." See the note immediately preceding.

18. No such recommendation to be made except in pursuance of reference to which s. 17 applies

The Director shall not make any recommendation to the Secretary of State to exercise his powers under the following provisions of this Part of this act except by way of making a reference to the Advisory Committee to which section 17 of this Act applies. **[118]**

COMMENCEMENT

See s. 140 (3), *post*, and the note to s. 1, *ante*.

DEFINITIONS

"Director", "Advisory Committee": s. 137 (2).

GENERAL NOTE

"Shall not make." This provision is both negative and mandatory—see also note to s. 15, *ante*.

"Secretary of State." See note to s. 1, *ante*.

"Exercise his powers." The powers of the Secretary of State are set out at s. 22, *post*.

"By way of making." Although the general effect of this provision is clear, the precise significance is not: it is probable that the Secretary of State may only exercise his powers upon the receipt of a Report from the Advisory Committee, and then subject to the conditions set out at s. 22 (2), *post*.

19. Scope of recommendation proposed in reference to which s. 17 applies

(1) In formulating any proposals which, in accordance with the provisions of section 17 of this Act, are included in a reference to which that section applies, the Director shall have regard—

(*a*) to the particular respects in which it appears to him that the consumer trade practice specified in the reference may adversely affect the economic interests of consumers in the United Kingdom, and

(*b*) to the class of relevant consumer transactions, or the classes (whether being some or all classes) of such transactions in relation to which it appears to him that the practice may so affect those consumers;

and the proposed recommendation shall be for an order making, in relation to relevant consumer transactions of that class or of those classes, as the case may be, such provision specified in the proposals as the Director may consider requisite for the purpose of preventing the continuance of that practice, or causing it to be modified, in so far as it may so affect those consumers in those respects.

(2) Without prejudice to the generality of the preceding subsection, for the purpose mentioned in that subsection any such proposals may in particular recommend the imposition by such an order of prohibitions or requirements of any description specified in Schedule 6 to this Act.

(3) In that Schedule, in its application to any such proposals, "the specified consumer trade practice" means the consumer trade practice specified in the reference in which the proposals are made, "specified consumer transactions" means transactions which are relevant consumer transactions in relation to that consumer trade practice and are of a description specified in the proposals, and "specified" (elsewhere than in those expressions) means specified in the proposals. [**119**]

COMMENCEMENT

See s. 140 (3), *post*, and the note to s. 1, *ante*.

DEFINITIONS

"Director", "consumer": s. 137 (2).
"consumer trade practice": s. 13.
"relevant consumer transaction": s. 17 (5).
For supplementary interpretation, see s. 138, *post*.

GENERAL NOTE

"*Shall have regard.*" This imposes a mandatory and positive obligation on the Director. This obligation could in an appropriate case, be imposed by mandamus. However it is unlikely that a failure to comply with this obligation would render a Report under s. 21 or Order under s. 22 void.

"*May adversely affect.*" This suggests a lower order of probability than is found under s. 17, *ante*—see the note "or is likely to have" thereto.

"*Economic interests.*" Consumer trade practices concern only economic interests—see also s. 2, *ante*, and the distinctions drawn in s. 2 (1) (*a*) and s. 2 (1), (6).

"*United Kingdom.*" See the note to s. 2, *ante*.

"*Those consumers.*" *I.e.*, consumers in the United Kingdom.

"*An order.*" *I.e.*, an order under s. 22; see the note thereto, *post*.

"*The Director may consider requisite.*" This provision therefore allows the Director a discretion, which must presumably be exercised reasonably.

"*Those respects.*" *I.e.*, those set out under heading (*a*) above.

"*Imposition by such an order, etc.*" Various forms of prohibition and requirement are listed in Schedule 6. In view of the wording of sub-s. (1) above those forms are not exclusive.

"*Schedule 6.*" See the note thereto, *post*.

20. Time-limit and quorum for report on reference to which s. 17 applies

(1) A report of the Advisory Committee on a reference to which section 17 of this Act applies shall not have effect, and no action shall be taken in relation to it under the following provisions of this Part of this Act, unless the report is made before the end of the period of three months beginning with the date of the reference or of such further period or periods (if any) as may be allowed by the Secretary of State.

(2) The Secretary of State shall not allow any further period for such a report except after consulting the Advisory Committee and considering any representations made by them with respect to the proposal to allow a further period.

(3) No such further period shall be longer than three months; but (subject to subsection (2) of this section) two or more further periods may be allowed in respect of the same reference.

(4) The quorum necessary for a meeting of the Advisory Committee held for the final settling of a report of the Committee on a reference to which section 17 of this Act applies shall be not less than two-thirds of the members of the Committee. [**120**]

COMMENCEMENT

See s. 140 (3), *post*, and the note to s. 1, *ante*.

DEFINITION

"Advisory Committee": s. 137 (2).

GENERAL NOTE

"*A report etc.*" See s. 21, *post*, for such a report.

"*Shall not have effect.*" Such a report would not therefore appear to satisfy the Director's obligations under s. 18 to exercise his powers only by way of making a reference under s. 17.

"*And no action shall be taken.*" This, and the previous provision are cumulative: the Report shall not have effect and the Director shall take no action. This latter requirement is accordingly both mandatory and negative. It can therefore (likely) be enforceable by way of injunction and prohibition and, almost certainly by declaration.

"*The following provisions.*" *I.e.*, action under s. 22, *post*.

"*Three months beginning, etc.*" Month means "calendar month", see Interpretation Act 1887, s. 3. In calculating this period the *dies a quo* is to be included; see *Hare* v. *Gocher*, [1962] 2 Q.B. 641, and *Trow* v. *Ind Coope (West Midlands), Ltd.*, [1967] 2 Q.B. 909.

"*Secretary of State.*" See the note to s. 1, *ante*.

"*After consulting.*" For the meaning of consultation, see *Rollo* v. *Minister of Town and Country Planning*, [1948] 1 All E.R. 13; *Re Union of Whippingham and East Cowes Benefices, Derham* v. *Church Commissioners of England*, [1954] A.C. 245; and *Agricultural, Horticultural and Forestry Industry Training Board* v. *Aylesbury Mushrooms, Ltd.*, [1972] 1 All E.R. 180.

"*And considering any representations, etc.*" This, and the previous provisions are cumulative: the Secretary of State must accordingly consult the Advisory Committee and consider any representations. The Secretary of State should not approach the representations with a "mind that was so foreclosed that he gave no genuine consideration to them"; see, *e.g.*, *Franklin* v. *Minister of Town and Country Planning*, [1948] A.C. 87. A similar duty to consider is imposed by various provisions governing the compulsory acquisition of land.

"*Two or more further periods.*" As long as the Secretary of State allows extensions every 3 months, the time which the Advisory Committee is permitted is theoretically unlimited.

"*Quorum necessary.*" For a judicial definition of quorum see *Faure Electric Accumulators Co., Ltd.* v. *Phillpart* (1888), 58 L.T. at p. 527, per Hawkins, J.

21. Report of Advisory Committee on reference to which s. 17 applies

(1) A report of the Advisory Committee on a reference to which section 17 of this Act applies shall state the conclusions of the Committee on the questions—

(*a*) whether the consumer trade practice specified in the reference adversely affects the economic interests of consumers in the United Kingdom, and

(*b*) if so, whether it does so by reason, or partly by reason, that it has or is likely to have such one or more of the effects specified in section 17(2) of this Act as are specified in the report.

(2) If, in their conclusions set out in such a report, the Advisory Committee find that the consumer trade practice specified in the reference does adversely affect the economic interests of consumers in the United Kingdom, and does so

wholly or partly for the reason mentioned in subsection (1)(*b*) of this section, the report shall state whether the Committee—

(*a*) agree with the proposals set out in the reference, or

(*b*) would agree with those proposals if they were modified in a manner specified in the report, or

(*c*) disagree with the proposals and do not desire to suggest any such modifications.

(3) Every report of the Advisory Committee on a reference to which section 17 of this Act applies shall be made to the Secretary of State, and shall set out in full the reference on which it is made. **[121]**

COMMENCEMENT

See s. 140 (3), *post*, and the note to s. 1, *ante*.

DEFINITIONS

"Advisory Committee", "consumer": s. 137 (2) (6).
"consumer trade practice": s. 13.
For supplementary definitions, see s. 138.

GENERAL NOTE

"*A report.*" See s. 82, *post*, and the note thereto for general provisions as to such reports.

"*Shall state the conclusions, etc.*" These need not be unanimous; for provision for the statement of the views of dissenting members, see s. 82 (2), *post*.

"*Or partly by reason.*" This provision would apply even though the adverse effect on the economic interest of such consumers was mainly a result of factors falling outside s. 17 (2), or outside those specified in the report.

"*United Kingdom.*" See the note to s. 2, *ante*.

"*Secretary of State.*" See the note to s. 1, *ante*.

"*Shall set out.*" This therefore imposes a duty (possibility of a directory nature) on the Advisory Committee.

Order in pursuance of report of Advisory Committee

22. Order of Secretary of State in pursuance of report on reference to which s. 17 applies

(1) The provisions of this section shall have effect where a report of the Advisory Committee on a reference to which section 17 of this Act applies has been laid before Parliament in accordance with the provisions of Part VII of this Act, and the report states that the Committee—

(*a*) agree with the proposals set out in the reference, or

(*b*) would agree with those proposals if they were modified in a manner specified in the report.

(2) In the circumstances mentioned in the preceding subsection, the Secretary of State may, if he thinks fit, by an order made by statutory instrument make such provision as—

(*a*) in a case falling within paragraph (*a*) of the preceding subsection, is in his opinion appropriate for giving effect to the proposals set out in the reference, or

(*b*) in a case falling within paragraph (*b*) of that subsection, is in his opinion appropriate for giving effect either to the proposals as set out in the reference or to those proposals as modified in the manner specified in the report, as the Secretary of State may in his discretion determine.

(3) Any such order may contain such supplementary or incidental provisions as the Secretary of State may consider appropriate in the circumstances; and (without prejudice to the generality of this subsection) any such order may restrict the prosecution of offences under the next following section in respect of contraventions of the order where those contraventions also constitute offences under another enactment.

(4) No such order, and no order varying or revoking any such order, shall be made under this section unless a draft of the order has been laid before Parliament and approved by a resolution of each House of Parliament. [**122**]

COMMENCEMENT

See s. 140 (3), *post*, and the note to s. 1, *ante*.

DEFINITION

"Advisory Committee": s. 137 (2).

GENERAL NOTE

"Reference to which section 17 of this Act applies." For such references see note to s. 17, *ante*.

"Laid before Parliament." See the Laying of Documents before Parliament (Interpretation) Act 1948, s. (1) and the provision of s. 83, *post*.

"Provisions of Part VII." *I.e.*, ss. 81–83.

"And the report states." For the form of conclusion which may be stated in the report, see s. 21 (2), *ante*.

"Secretary of State." See the note to s. 1, *ante*.

"May, if he thinks fit." The Secretary of State therefore has a discretion whether or not to make an order under this section. This discretion must presumably be exercised reasonably.

"By an order." For provision as to orders, see s. 134, *post*. No orders have yet been made under this section.

"Statutory instrument." See note to s. 3, *ante*.

"Is in his opinion appropriate." The Secretary of State therefore has a discretion as to the scope and form of the order. This must presumably be exercised reasonably.

"Either . . . or." Where the Advisory Committee has stated that it would agree to the proposals if modified in a manner specified in the report the Secretary of State may give effect either to the proposal in its original form or to the proposal as modified.

"May in his discretion." This confers a discretion in particularly emphatic terms. It may be therefore that the discretion is entirely unfettered.

"May consider appropriate." This too confers a discretion on the Secretary of State, which must, presumably, be exercised reasonably.

"Restrict the prosecution." It is not clear whether the power conferred by this provision extends only to complete prohibition, or whether it also permits the Secretary of State to restrict the time-limit for prosecutions or reduce or alter the penalties.

23. Penalties for contravention of order under s. 22

Subject to the following provisions of this Part of this Act, any person who contravenes a prohibition imposed by an order under section 22 of this Act, or who does not comply with a requirement imposed by such an order which applies to him, shall be guilty of an offence and shall be liable—

(*a*) on summary conviction, to a fine not exceeding £400;

(*b*) on conviction on indictment, to a fine or to imprisonment for a term not exceeding two years or both. [**123**]

COMMENCEMENT

See s. 140 (3), *post*, and the note to s. 1, *ante*.

GENERAL NOTE

"Subject to the following provisions." See in particular ss. 24 and 25, *post*.

"Any person." As to offences by bodies corporate, see s. 132, *post*, and the note thereto. See also on the liability of a person who aids, abets, counsels or procures the Magistrates Courts Act 1952, s. 35.

"*Contravenes a prohibition . . . or who does not comply with a requirement.*" The offence under this section is one of strict liability, subject to the defence allowed by s. 25 and the provisions of s. 24. For detailed analysis of a similar provision in the Trade Descriptions Act 1968, see *Tesco Supermarkets, Ltd.* v. *Nattrass*, [1972] A.C. 153. For a provision relating to goods or services supplied outside the United Kingdom, see s. 138 (3), *post*.

"*Should be guilty or an offence.*" For provisions as to enforcement, see ss. 27–33, *post*; for time limit for prosecutions, see s. 129, *post*; for notice of intended prosecution, s. 130, *post*.

"*Summary conviction.*" For jurisdiction and procedure, see Magistrates Courts Acts 1952 and 1957 and certain provisions of the Criminal Justice Act 1967.

"*Conviction on indictment.*" All proceedings on indictment are brought before the Crown Court; see the Courts Act 1971, s. 6 (1).

"*Fine.*" There is no limit to the amount of the fine which may be imposed on convict on indictment. The fine should however be within the offender's capacity to pay; see, in particular, *R.* v. *Churchill* (*No. 2*), [1967] 1 Q.B. 190 (reversed on other grounds at [1967] 2 A.C. 224), see also Bill of Rights 1688.

"*Not exceeding two years.*" An extended term may be imposed under the Criminal Justice Act 1967, s. 37.

24. Offences due to default of other person

Where the commission by any person of an offence under section 23 of this Act is due to the act or default of some other person, that other person shall be guilty of the offence, and a person may be charged with and convicted of the offence by virtue of this section whether or not proceedings are taken against the first-mentioned person. **[124]**

COMMENCEMENT

See s. 140 (3), *post*, and the note to s. 1, *ante*.

GENERAL NOTE

"*Where the commission by any person.*" Where the person first referred to in this section has no defence to a charge under s. 23 other than the defence expressly provided by s. 25 he can properly be regarded as "having committed the offence" for the purpose of this section. On the other hand if that person has a defence on the merits (*i.e.*, apart from s. 25) the person charged under this section could not properly be convicted of the offence—*Coupe* v. *Guyett*, [1973] 2 All E.R. 1058.

"*Act or default.*" "The word 'act' is wide enough to include any physical act of the other person which is causative of the offence. But the use of 'default' instead of the neutral expression 'omission' connotes a failure to act which constitutes a breach of a legal duty to act"; *Tesco* v. *Nattrass*, [1972] A.C. 153, [1971] 2 All E.R. 127, per Lord Diplock at pp. 196, 153. For further illustrations, see *Noss Farm Products, Ltd.* v. *Lilico*, [1945] 2 All E.R. 609; *Lamb* v. *Sunderland and District Creamery, Ltd.*, [1951] 1 All E.R. 923; *Lindley* v. *George W. Horner & Co., Ltd.*, [1950] 1 All E.R. 234; *Lester* v. *Balfour Williamson Merchant Shippers, Ltd.*, [1953] 2 Q.B. 168; *Fisher* v. *Barrett and Pomeroy* (*Bakers*), *Ltd.*, [1954] 1 All E.R. 249.

"*Some other person.*" Where the person first referred to in this section is a natural person, there is no reason for construing this expression as excluding a servant or agent of that person. However, where the person first referred to is a corporation, the other person must not be a director, manager, secretary or other similar officer of that corporation carrying out functions in that capacity; see *Tesco Supermarkets, Ltd.* v. *Nattrass*, [1972] A.C. 153; [1971] 2 All E.R. 127.

"*That other person.*" This section does not allow a complete defence in respect of the contravention or non-compliance. The other person can be prosecuted and convicted: indeed concurrent proceedings may be brought both against the person first mentioned in this section and "that other person"—contrast the former position under the Food and Drugs Act 1938, s. 83; see *Fisher* v. *Santovin, Ltd.*, [1953] 2 Q.B. 266.

"*Of the offence.*" The charge against the other person under this section is based upon the original offence. The time limit from the commencement of a prosecution (for which see s. 129) therefore runs from the date of that offence—*Concentrated Foods, Ltd.* v. *Champ*, [1944] K.B. 342. See also the authorities on s. 23 of the Trade Descriptions Act 1968 which is identically worded.

25. Defences in proceedings under s. 23

(1) In any proceedings for an offence under section 23 of this Act it shall, subject to subsection (2) of this section, be a defence for the person charged to prove—

(*a*) that the commission of the offence was due to a mistake, or to reliance on information supplied to him, or to the act or default of another person, an accident or some other cause beyond his control, and

(*b*) that he took all reasonable precautions and exercised all due diligence to avoid the commission of such an offence by himself or any person under his control.

(2) If in any case the defence provided by the preceding subsection involves the allegation that the commission of the offence was due to the act or default of another person or to reliance on information supplied by another person, the person charged shall not, without leave of the court, be entitled to rely on that defence unless, within a period ending seven clear days before the hearing, he has served on the prosecutor a notice in writing, giving such information identifying or assisting in the identification of that other person as was then in his possession.

(3) In proceedings for an offence under section 23 of this Act committed by the publication of an advertisement, it shall be a defence for the person charged to prove that he is a person whose business it is to publish or arrange for the publication of advertisements, and that he received the advertisement for publication in the ordinary course of business and did not know and had no reason to suspect that its publication would amount to an offence under section 23 of this Act. [**125**]

COMMENCEMENT

See s. 140 (3), *post* and the note to s. 1, *ante*.

DEFINITION

"Business": s. 137 (2).

GENERAL NOTE

Sub-s. (1) (*a*), (*b*): *"Be a defence"*. The burden of proving the defence is therefore placed on the defendant. This burden is however less onerous than the burden laid on the prosecutor and may be discharged by evidence which satisfies the jury on balance of probabilities of that which the defendant is called upon to prove; see *R.* v. *Carr-Briant*, [1943] K.B. 607, and *R.* v. *Dunbar*, [1958] 1 Q.B. 1.

"The person charged." This includes a person who is a defendant by reason of the Magistrates Courts Act 1952, s. 35, or a defendant brought in under s. 24.

"The commission of the offence." See the note to s. 24, *ante*, and *Coupe* v. *Guyett*, [1973] 2 All E.R. 1058.

"Mistake." This must be a mistake of fact not of law; *Stone* v. *Burn*, [1911] 1 K.B. 927. The mistake must be a mistake by the person charged and not by some other person or servant or agent; *Birkenhead and District Co-operative Society* v. *Roberts*, [1970] 3 All E.R. 391. See also for the application of this latter restriction in relation to corporations, *Tesco Supermarkets, Ltd.* v. *Nattrass*, [1972] A.C. 153; [1971] 2 All E.R. 127.

"Reliance upon information supplied to him." Presumably the defendant must establish that it was reasonable for him to rely on such information.

"Act or default of another person." See the note to s. 24, *ante*.

"An accident." Such as an unforeseeable breakdown in machinery; *Wolfenden* v. *Oliver* (1932), 147 L.T. 80. See however for an indication of something which would not be an accident, *Smedleys, Ltd.* v. *Breed*, [1974] A.C. 839.

"Some other cause beyond his control." The act or default of a servant or agent would not be beyond the control of the defendant; *Hall* v. *Farmer*, [1970] 1 All E.R. 729, and *A. Walkling, Ltd.* v. *Robinson* (1929), 99 L.J.K.B. 171. However the act of default of a wholesaler would probably be beyond the control of a retailer; *Whittaker* v. *Collings* (unreported, cited in O'Keefe, *Trade Descriptions*, at 59 [1]), *M'Intyre* v.

Laird, 1943 S.C.(J) 96, and *Trickers (Confectioners), Ltd.* v. *Barnes*, [1955] 1 All E.R. 803. For the application of this proposition to corporations, see *Tesco Supermarkets Ltd.* v. *Nattrass*, [1972] A.C. 153; [1971] 2 All E.R. 127.

"He took all reasonable precautions." This requires the person to establish a system designed to ensure that wrongful conduct does not take place; see *Sherratt* v. *Geralds, The American Jewellers, Ltd.* (1970), 114 Sol. Jo. 147; *Richmond London Borough Council* v. *Motor Sales (Hounslow), Ltd.* (1971), 115 Sol. Jo. 156; *Naish* v. *Cove*, [1971] 3 All E.R. 737, and *Tarleton Engineering, Ltd.* v. *Nattrass*, [1973] 3 All E.R. 699.

"Exercised due diligence." This requires the person who establishes a system to ensure that it works property. Whether or not due diligence was used is primarily a question of fact but the High Court will intervene if there was no evidence to support a finding on the point; *R. C. Hammett, Ltd.* v. *Crabb*, [1931] All E.R. Rep. 70. For the meaning of due diligence, see *Riverstone Meat Co., Pty., Ltd.* v. *Lancashire Shipping Co., Ltd.*, [1961] A.C. 807, and C.A. [1960] 1 Q.B. 536 at page 581. For the application of this doctrine to a corporation, see *Tesco Supermarkets Ltd.* v. *Nattrass* ,[1972] A.C. 153; [1971] 2 All E.R. 127.

"Any person under his control." See note entitled "some other cause beyond his control" above.

"And . . . and." The requirements of paras. (*a*) and (*b*) are cumulative; so are the requirements of reasonable precautions and due diligence.

Sub-ss. (2), (3): *"Due to the act or default of another person."* See note to sub-s. (1) above.

"Or to reliance of an information." See note to sub-s. (1) above.

"Shall not without the leave of the Court." Provided that the court does not take into account matters which it should not, or fail to take into account matters which it ought to consider, an appellate court will not interfere with the exercise of this discretion; *Birkenhead and District Co-operative Society* v. *Roberts*, [1970] 3 All E.R. 391.

"Seven clear days." I.e., 7 complete days before the giving of notice and the hearing; *R.* v. *Herefordshire Justices* (1823), 3 B. & Ald. 581.

"In writing." See note to s. 1, *ante*.

"By the publication"—this probably means "made public"—see *Boucicault* v. *Chatterton* (1876) 5 Ch. Div. 267. The requirement of publication is central to the law of defamation and there are many authorities to be found in that context.

"Advertisement." The verb to advertise is defined in *Breen* v. *Berliner*, [1936] 2 K.B. 477, at p. 496, as "to call attention to something by a public announcement".

"Whose business it is, etc." This defence would appear to include a publisher and printer; it would also appear appropriate to cover an advertising agent; cf., however, O'Keefe, *Trade Descriptions*, at [1] 62 B.

"Ordinary course of business." This and similar expressions are found in many statutes. There appear to be two separate requirements: that the defendant carries on a business; and that publication was in the ordinary course of that business. The word business is defined in s. 137 (2); the best definition of ordinary course of business is to be found in *Downs Distributing Co., Pty., Ltd.* v. *Associated Blue Star Stores Pty., Ltd.*, (1948), 76 C.L.R. 463—"part of the undistinguished flow of business done, calling for no remark and arising out of no special or particular situation."

"Did not know and had no reason to suspect." The defendant must prove that he did not actually know and that there were no grounds from which he reasonably should have reached that conclusion, see, *e.g.*, *Nakkuda Ali* v. *Jayaratne*, [1951] A.C. 66.

"Would amount." This must be read as "would otherwise amount."

26. Limitation of effect of orders under s. 22

A contract for the supply of goods or services shall not be void or unenforceable by reason only of a contravention of an order made under section 22 of this Act; and, subject to the provisions of section 33 of the Interpretation Act 1889 (which relates to offences under two or more laws), the provisions of this Part of this Act shall not be construed as—

(*a*) conferring a right of action in any civil proceedings (other than proceedings for the recovery of a fine) in respect of any contravention of such an order, or

(*b*) affecting any restriction imposed by or under any other enactment, whether public, local or private, or (*c*) derogating from any right of action or other remedy (whether civil or criminal) in proceedings instituted otherwise than under this Part of this Act. [**126**]

COMMENCEMENT

See s. 140 (3), *post,* and the note to s. 1, *ante.*

DEFINITIONS

"goods", "supply": s. 137 (2).
"supply of services": s. 137 (3).
"services": s. 137 (4).

GENERAL NOTE

"By reason only." However the fact that such an order has been contravened may be evidence that such a contract is void, voidable, unenforceable or has been broken in some way. A conviction under this Act could be used in such proceedings as evidence of the facts upon which the 1968 conviction was based; Civil Evidence Act 1968, s. 17.

"Contravention of an order." This presumably includes contravention of a prohibition and non-compliance with a requirement; see s. 23, *ante.*

"Section 33 of the Interpretation Act 1889." Where an act or omission constitutes an offence under two or more Acts, or both under an Act and at common law, the offender is liable to be punished under either or any of those Acts or at common law, but shall not be liable to be punished twice for the same offence.

Enforcement of orders

27. Enforcing authorities

(1) It shall be the duty of every local weights and measures authority to enforce within their area the provisions of any order made under section 22 of this Act; and section 37 of the Weights and Measures Act 1963 (power of local authorities to combine) shall apply with respect to the functions of such authorities under this Part of this Act as it applies with respect to their functions under that Act.

(2) Nothing in subsection (1) shall be taken as authorising a local weights and measures authority in Scotland to institute proceedings for an offence. [**127**]

COMMENCEMENT

See s. 140 (3), *post,* and the note to s. 1, *ante.*

GENERAL NOTE

"It shall be the duty." This therefore imposes a mandatory obligation which can be enforced by mandamus.

"Local weights and measures authority." See the the Local Government Act 1972, s. 201.

"Functions . . . under this Part." See especially ss. 28–32, *post.*

"Weights and Measures Act 1963, s. 37." See Local Government Act 1972, s. 201 (5), which provides that the Act of 1963 shall cease to apply except for an agreement entered into before 1st April 1974 by any two or more weights and measures authorities for areas within Greater London.

28. Power to make test purchases

A local weights and measures authority may make, or may authorise any of their officers to make on their behalf, such purchases of goods, and may authorise any of their officers to obtain such services, as may be expedient for the purpose of determining whether or not the provisions of any order made under section 22 of this Act are being complied with. [**128**]

COMMENCEMENT

See s. 140 (3), *post,* and the note to s. 1, *ante.*

DEFINITIONS

"goods": s. 137 (2).
"services": s. 137 (4).

GENERAL NOTE

"Purchases of goods." There appears to be no power under this section to obtain goods otherwise than by purchase. See also s. 31, *post*.

"May be expedient." That the authority has a discretion. This must however be exercised reasonably and in a manner compatible with the duty imposed by s. 27.

29. Power to enter premises and inspect and seize goods and documents

(1) A duly authorised officer of a local weights and measures authority, or a person duly authorised in writing by the Secretary of State, may at all reasonable hours, and on production, if required, of his credentials, exercise the following powers, that is to say—

(*a*) he may, for the purpose of ascertaining whether any offence under section 23 of this Act has been committed, inspect any goods and enter any premises other than premises used only as a dwelling;

(*b*) if he has reasonable cause to suspect that an offence under that section has been committed, he may, for the purpose of ascertaining whether it has been committed, require any person carrying on a business or employed in connection with a business to produce any books or documents relating to the business and may take copies of, or of any entry in, any such book or document;

(*c*) if he has reasonable cause to believe that such an offence has been committed, he may seize and detain any goods for the purpose of ascertaining, by testing or otherwise, whether the offence has been committed;

(*d*) he may seize and detain any goods or documents which he has reason to believe may be required as evidence in proceedings for such an offence;

(*e*) he may, for the purpose of exercising his powers under this subsection to seize goods, but only if and to the extent that it is reasonably necessary in order to secure that the provisions of an order made under section 22 of this Act are duly observed, require any person having authority to do so to break open any container or open any vending machine and, if that person does not comply with the requirement, he may do so himself.

(2) A person seizing any goods or documents in the exercise of his powers under this section shall inform the person from whom they are seized and, in the case of goods seized from a vending machine, the person whose name and address are stated on the machine as being the proprietor's or, if no name and address are so stated, the occupier of the premises on which the machine stands or to which it is affixed.

(3) If a justice of the peace, on sworn information in writing,—

(*a*) is satisfied that there is reasonable ground to believe either—

(i) that any goods, books or documents which a person has power under this section to inspect are on any premises and that their inspection is likely to disclose evidence of the commission of an offence under section 23 of this Act, or

(ii) that any offence under section 23 has been, is being or is about to be committed on any premises, and

(*b*) is also satisfied either—

(i) that admission to the premises has been or is likely to be refused and that notice of intention to apply for a warrant under this subsection has been given to the occupier, or

(ii) that an application for admission, or the giving of such a notice, would defeat the object of the entry or that the premises are unoccupied or that the occupier is temporarily absent, and it might defeat the object of the entry to await his return,

the justice may by warrant under his hand, which shall continue in force for a period of one month, authorise any such officer or other person as is mentioned in subsection (1) of this section to enter the premises, if need be by force.

In the application of this subsection to Scotland, "justice of the peace" shall be construed as including a sheriff and a magistrate.

(4) A person entering any premises by virtue of this section may take with him such other persons and such equipment as may appear to him necessary; and on leaving any premises which he has entered by virtue of a warrant under subsection (3) of this section he shall, if the premises are unoccupied or the occupier is temporarily absent, leave them as effectively secured against trespassers as he found them.

(5) Nothing in this section shall be taken to compel the production by a barrister, advocate or solicitor of a document containing a privileged communication made by or to him in that capacity or to authorise the taking of possession of any such document which is in his possession. [**129**]

COMMENCEMENT

See s. 140 (3), *post*, and the Fair Trading Act 1973 (Commencement No. 1) Order 1973 which brought this section into force on 14th September 1973.

DEFINITIONS

"Business" and "goods": s. 137 (2).

GENERAL NOTE

"*Local weights and measures authority.*" See note to s. 27, *ante*.

"*Writing*": "*Secretary of State.*" See note to s. 1, *ante*.

"*At all reasonable hours.*" This is basically a question of fact which the court will answer according to the circumstances of the particular case. The judgment of the individual officer will not necessarily be treated as final, *Small* v. *Bickley* (1875), 32 L.T. 726. See also *Davies* v. *Winstanley* (1930), 95 J.P. 21.

"*On production if required.*" This does not mean that the powers conferred by this section can only be exercised if there is somebody to whom the credentials may be produced; *Grove* v. *Eastern Gas Board*, [1952] 1 K.B. 77.

"*Exercise the following powers.*" All the powers conferred by sub-s. (1) are therefore subject to the conditions already mentioned.

"*For the purpose of ascertaining.*" The powers conferred by this paragraph are not, apparently, subject to the requirement of reasonable belief or cause to suspect.

"*Offence under section 23.*" See note to that section, *ante*.

"*Enter any premises.*" The power conferred is a power to enter or inspect without the express or implied agreement of the occupier. For implied permission, see *Robson* v. *Hallett*, [1967] 2 Q.B. 939. This paragraph does not authorise forcible entry; *cf.* sub-ss. (3) and (4), *post*.

"*Premises used only as a dwelling.*" The premises must in fact be used as a dwelling—*Oken* v. *Derraton*, [1947] 2 All E.R. 286; it is not sufficient that the premises are a yard attached to a dwelling—*McHole* v. *Davies* (1875), 1 Q.B. 59; or that the premises are occasionally used for keeping or taking meals—*MacMillan & Co., Ltd.* v. *Rees*, [1946] 1 All E.R. 675. The protection is available only if the premises are used exclusively as a dwelling. However the protection is not confined to a dwelling house, but may include other dwellings such as a caravan. *A fortiori* the protection is not confined to a private dwelling—*Tender* v. *Sponce*, [1947] 1 All E.R. 193.

"*Reasonable cause to suspect.*" Also "reasonable cause to believe." The authorised person must in fact suspect—*R.* v. *Banks*, [1916] 2 K.B. 621, and *R.* v. *Harrison*, [1938] 3 All E.R. 134; and the court must accept that there were in fact reasonable grounds for that belief—*Nakkuda Ali* v. *Jayaratne*, [1951] A.C. 66; *cf. Liversidge* v. *Anderson*, [1942] A.C. 206, and *Secretary of State for Employment* v. *Associated Society of Locomotive Engineers and Firemen* (*No. 2*), [1972] 2 Q.B. 455.

"*Any person.*" Person includes a limited company unless the contrary intention appears; Interpretation Act 1889, s. 2. In the present context the sense demands that person be confined to natural person and the expression should be so confined; see *Law Society* v. *United Service Bureau, Ltd.*, [1934] 1 K.B. 343.

"Carrying on a business." *Cf.* note to s. 25, *ante.* "Business means anything which is an occupation, as distinguished from a pleasure; anything which is an occupation or duty which requires attention is a business"—*Rolls* v. *Miller* (1884), 27 Ch.D. 71 at page 88, *per* Lindley, L.J. The involvement of transactions for payment or profit is not an essential part of a business—*Paddington Burial Board* v. *Inland Revenue Commissioners* (1884), 13 Q.B.D. 9. For discussion of the closely related words "trade and industry", see Trade Disputes Act 1906, s. 5 (3), and Citrine, *Trade Union Law*, 3rd Edition, at pages 608–613.

"Seize and detain." This paragraph probably authorises the officers to detain the goods only so long as is reasonably necessary; for the position at common law, see *Ghani* v. *Jones*, [1970] 1 Q.B. 693, and see s. 32, *post.*

"By testing or otherwise." For provisions relating to testing, see s. 31, *post.*

"Reason to believe may be required." See "reasonable cause to suspect" and note thereto above. It does not appear necessary that the goods or documents should actually be used.

"May . . . require." It appears as though a demand to an authorised person is a necessary precondition of the officer's own power to open or break open the container or machine—*sed quaere* what happens if such a person is not available.

Sub-s. (2): *"Shall inform."* This therefore imposes a mandatory obligation on the officer. It is not however clear whether a failure to comply with this obligation would render the seizure unlawful and tortious: it is submitted that it should; *cf. Christie* v. *Leachinsky*, [1947] A.C. 573.

"Name and address." This includes both the actual name and address of the person or company and a business name whether registered or not—see *Cameron* v. *Tyler*, [1899] 2 Q.B. 94, and *Edwards* v. *Pharmaceutical Society of Great Britain*, [1910] 2 K.B. 766.

"Occupier of the premises." This expression is ambiguous as an occupier for the purposes of the Occupiers Liability Act 1957 may not be an occupier for certain other purposes, such as title to sue for trespass to the land—see, *e.g.*, *Wheat* v. *E. Lacon & Co.*, [1956] A.C. 552.

Sub-s. (3): *"Justice of the peace."* A justice of the peace on the supplemental list may not grant a warrant under this section; see the Administration of Justice Act 1973, s. 5, Sch. 1, Part II. This disqualification does not however affect the validity of a warrant granted by such a justice.

"Sworn." In the case of persons allowed to affirm or declare instead of swearing, this includes affirm or declare; see Interpretation Act 1889, s. 3.

"Is satisfied"—The justice must be convinced on balance of probabilities. The validity of a warrant issued by the justice under sub-s. (3) can probably be impugned only on the ground that he acted *mala fide* or if the Court concludes that no reasonable justice could have been so satisfied if his mind had been properly directed—see *e.g.*, *Re City of Plymouth* (*City Centre*) *Declaratory Order, 1946, Robinson* v. *Minister of Town and Country Planning*, [1947] K.B. 702.

"Reasonable ground to believe." See note above.

"Is also satisfied." Thus the requirements of paragraphs (*a*) and (*b*) are cumulative, although the requirements of sub-paragraphs (i) and (ii) of each paragraph are alternative.

"May." The power is therefore discretionary.

"By warrant." Such a warrant does not appear to fall within the Magistrates' Courts Act 1952, s. 102 (3). It therefore appears as though the power of entry under the warrant cannot be granted on a Sunday; nor the warrant executed on a Sunday; see Sunday Observance Act 1677, s. 6.

"One month." I.e., a calendar month; Interpretation Act 1889, ss. 3 and 32.

"Authorise any such officer." The warrant cannot be delegated by the person to whom it is addressed; *Symonds* v. *Kurtz* (1889), 53 J.P. 727.

"By force." Only such force as is reasonably necessary in the circumstances. Excessive force would be an assault and, as such, actionable in tort or crime.

Sub-s. (4): *"As may appear to him necessary."* Although the decision is primarily one for the officer concerned, his decision must presumably be such as a reasonable officer might have reached.

"As he found them." This primarily poses a question of fact. If an officer failed to comply with this requirement and loss or damage resulted, he could be made liable for that loss in negligence and for breach of statutory duty.

Sub-s. (5): *"Barrister, advocate or solicitor."* This provision is designed to give effect to the common law rules of legal professional privilege. For a case concerning lawyers employed by a government department and commercial concerns, see *Alfred Crompton Amusement Machines, Ltd.* v. *Customs and Excise Commissioners,* [1971] 2 All E.R. 843; for a possible extension of the privilege to an advocate lacking formal legal qualifications—see *Grazebrook (M. and W.) Ltd.* v.. *Wallens,* [1973] 2 All E.R. 868; [1973] I.C.R. 256.

"*In that capacity.*" A lawyer, whether or not employed in a government department or commercial concern, is entitled to the protection afforded by sub-s. (5) only insofar as he acts in that capacity; see the *Alfred Crompton Amusements* case, cited above.

"*Such document.*" If the document contains both privileged and non-privileged material it appears from a strict reading of sub-s. (5) as though the whole of that document is protected from disclosure and may not be taken under the subsection—*sed quaere.*

30. Offences in connection with exercise of powers under s. 29

(1) Subject to subsection (6) of this section, any person who—

(*a*) wilfully obstructs any such officer or person as is mentioned in subsection (1) of section 29 of this Act acting in the exercise of any powers conferred on him by or under that section, or

(*b*) wilfully fails to comply with any requirement properly made to him by such an officer or person under that section, or

(*c*) without reasonable cause fails to give such an officer or person so acting any other assistance or information which he may reasonably require of him for the purpose of the performance of his functions under this Part of this Act,

shall be guilty of an offence.

(2) If any person, in giving any such information as is mentioned in subsection (1)(*c*) of this section, makes any statement which he knows to be false, he shall be guilty of an offence.

(3) If any person discloses to any other person—

(*a*) any information with respect to any manufacturing process or trade secret obtained by him in premises which he has entered by virtue of section 29 of this Act, or

(*b*) any information obtained by him under that section or by virtue of subsection (1) of this section,

he shall, unless the disclosure was made in the performance of his duty, be guilty of an offence.

(4) If any person who is neither a duly authorised officer of a weights and measures authority nor a person duly authorised in that behalf by the Secretary of State purports to act as such under section 29 of this Act or under this section, he shall be guilty of an offence.

(5) Any person guilty of an offence under subsection (1) of this section shall be liable on summary conviction to a fine not exceeding £50; and any person guilty of an offence under subsection (2), subsection (3) or subsection (4) of this section shall be liable—

(*a*) on summary conviction, to a fine not exceeding £400;

(*b*) on conviction on indictment, to a fine or to imprisonment for a term not exceeding two years or to both.

(6) Nothing in this section shall be construed as requiring a person to answer any question or give any information if to do so might incriminate that person or (where that person is married) the husband or wife of that person. [**130**]

COMMENCEMENT

See s. 140 (3), *post*, and the note to s. 29, *ante*.

GENERAL NOTE

"*Wilfully*." This expression in the words of Lord Russell of Killowen, C.J. in *R.* v. *Senior*, [1899] 1 Q.B. 283, at pages 290, 291, means "that the act is done deliberately and intentionally, not by accident or inadvertance, but so that the mind of the person who does the act goes with it"; see also *R.* v. *Walker* (1934), 24 Cr. App. Rep. 117; *Eaton* v. *Cobb*, [1950] 1 All E.R. 1016; *Arrowsmith* v. *Jenkins*, [1963] 2 Q.B. 561; *Rice* v. *Connolly*, [1966] 2 Q.B. 414; and *Ingleton* v. *Dibble*, [1972] 1 Q.B. 480. It is not however necessary that the defendant should have done the act knowing that it was wrongful.

"*Obstructs*." Obstruction need not necessarily involve physical violence, see especially *Borrow* v. *Howland* (1896), 74 L.T. 787; and *Hinchliffe* v. *Sheldon*, [1955] 3 All E.R. 406. It appears that obstruction means anything which makes it more difficult for a person to carry out his duties; see *Hinchliffe* v. *Sheldon*, supra. Standing by and doing nothing is not obstruction unless there is a legal duty to act; see *Swallow* v. *London County Council*, [1916] 1 K.B. 224; *cf.* also *Rice* v. *Connolly*, [1966] 2 Q.B. 414, and contrast *Baker* v. *Ellison*, [1914] 2 K.B. 762. See also *Ingleton* v. *Dibble*, [1972] 1 Q.B. 480.

"*Acting in the exercise of any powers*." Such officer or person must actually be so acting: it is not sufficient that he purports so to act—see *Davis* v. *Lisle*, [1936] 2 K.B. 434; but distinguish *Donnelly* v. *Jackman*, [1970] 1 All E.R. 987.

"*Without reasonable cause*." The wording of this provision suggests that the prosecution must prove absence of reasonable cause. Whether or not there was reasonable cause appears to be a question of fact depending upon all the circumstances.

"*Functions under this Part, etc*." See especially ss. 28 and 29, *ante*.

"*Guilty of an offence*." For time limit for prosecution, see s. 129, *post*.

"*Knows*". There is authority for saying that where a person refrains from making enquiries, the results of which he may not come to have, this constitutes knowledge of the facts in question; see *Knox* v. *Boyd*, 1941 S.C. (J.) 82 at page 86; and *Taylor's Central Garages (Exeter), Ltd.* v. *Roper* (1951), 115 J.P. 445, at pages 449, 450, *per* Devlin, J.; and see also, in particular, *Mallon* v. *Allon*, [1964] 1 Q.B. 385, at page 394. Mere neglect to find out what could have been ascertained by making reasonable enquiries is not tantamount to knowledge; see *Taylor's Central Garages (Exeter), Ltd.* v. *Roper*, *supra*; but cf. *London Computer, Ltd.* v. *Seymour*, [1944] 2 All E.R. 11; but further contrast *Mallon* v. *Allon*, *supra*.

"*False*." A statement may be false on account of what it omits even though it is literally true; see *R.* v. *Lord Kylsant*, [1932] 1 K.B. 442, and *R.* v. *Bishirgian*, [1936] 1 All E.R. 586; see also, *per* Lord Denning, L.J., in *Curtis* v. *Chemical Cleaning and Dyeing Co., Ltd.*, [1951] 1 K.B. 805, at pages 808, 809. However, unless a statement can be treated as a continuing statement, it will not become false because the circumstances change after it was made; *Sunair Holidays, Ltd.* v. *Dodd*, [1970] 2 All E.R. 410. It is immaterial whether or not advantage accrues from the statement; *Jones* v. *Meatyard*, [1939] 1 All E.R. 140, and *Stevens and Steeds, Ltd. and Evans* v. *King*, [1943] 1 All E.R. 314.

"*Weights and measures authority*." See s. 27 and note thereto, *ante*.

"*Secretary of State*". See the note to s. 1, *ante*.

"*Summary conviction: conviction on indictment: fine*." See s. 23 and note thereto, *ante*.

"*Might incriminate that person*." This provision seems, in essence, to enact the common law privilege against self-incrimination; for which, in particular, see *Blunt* v. *Park Lane Hotel, Ltd.*, [1942] 2 K.B. 253, *per* Goddard, L.J., at page 257. The provision removes any doubt as to whether the protection extends to incrimination of the person's spouse. Although the section does not in terms extend to documents, it seems probable that protection is similarly afforded to documents.

31. Notice of test

Where any goods seized or purchased by a person in pursuance of this Part of this Act are submitted to a test, then—

(*a*) if the goods were seized, he shall inform any such person as is mentioned in section 29(2) of this Act of the result of the test;

(*b*) if the goods were purchased and the test leads to the institution of proceedings for an offence under section 23 of this Act, he shall inform the person from whom the goods were purchased, or, in the case of goods sold through a vending machine, the person mentioned in relation to such goods in section 29(2) of this Act, of the result of the test;

and where, as a result of the test, proceedings for an offence under section 23 of this Act are instituted against any person, he shall allow that person to have the goods tested on his behalf if it is reasonably practicable to do so. [**131**]

COMMENCEMENT

See s. 140 (3), *post*, and the note to s. 29, *ante*.

DEFINITION

"goods": s. 137 (2).

GENERAL NOTE

"*Seized.*" *I.e.*, under s. 29, *ante*.

"*Purchased.*" *I.e.*, under s. 28, *ante*.

"*Submitted to a test.*" *I.e.*, after such purchase on seizure.

"*Shall inform.*" Thus, although there is a duty to inform the relevant person, the section imposes no sanction upon those in breach of this duty; nor are there any requirements as to the time or the manner of such information. It is submitted that the result of such tests should be indicated clearly before proceedings are instituted.

"*As is mentioned in section 29 (2).*" This is generally the person from whom the goods are seized. There is however special provision made in the case of vending machines.

"*If it is reasonably practicable to do so.*" The issue of practicability must be a question of fact to be answered in the light of all the circumstances of the case: this requirement probably governs the actual testing of the goods by the person; rather than the obligation to permit such testing.

32. Compensation for loss in respect of goods seized under s. 29

(1) Where in the exercise of his powers under section 29 of this Act a person seizes and detains any goods, and their owner suffers loss by reason of their being seized or by reason that the goods, during the detention, are lost or damaged or deteriorate, unless the owner is convicted of an offence under section 23 of this Act committed in relation to the goods, the appropriate authority shall be liable to compensate him for the loss so suffered.

(2) Any disputed question as to the right to or the amount of any compensation payable under this section shall be determined by arbitration and, in Scotland, by a single arbiter appointed, failing agreement between the parties, by the sheriff.

(3) In this section "the appropriate authority"—

(*a*) in relation to goods seized by an officer of a local weights and measures authority, means that authority, and

(*b*) in any other case, means the Secretary of State. [**132**]

COMMENCEMENT

See s. 140 (3), *post*, and the note to s. 29, *ante*.

DEFINITION

"goods": s. 137 (2).

GENERAL NOTE

"*Any goods.*" Under s. 29 the power of seizure extends to documents, presumably therefore the provisions of this section extend to such documents.

"*Their owner.*" There appears to be no liability to pay compensation if the loss is suffered by someone other than the owner. The provision is therefore much narrower than those provisions of the law of torts allowing recovery in the event of damage to chattels; see, *e.g.*, *The Winkfield*, [1902] P. 42. The word owner is not however defined: it may therefore be possible to construe it so as to include all those having a proprietary or possessory interest in the goods.

"*By reason of*," *etc.* Thus pure pecuniary loss appears to be potentially recoverable.

"*By reason that.*" It does not appear to be relevant to show that such loss, damage or deterioration resulted from negligence.

"*The owner is convicted of an offence.*" The right to compensation is not however lost if some other person is convicted of an offence in relation to the goods.

"*The appropriate authority.*" See generally s. 27 and the note thereto, *ante*.

"*Arbitration*". Subject to certain exceptions, the Arbitration Act 1950, Part I, applies to such arbitration; see also s. 31 of that Act.

33. Application of Part II to Northern Ireland

(1) It shall be the duty of the Ministry of Commerce for Northern Ireland to enforce in Northern Ireland the provisions of any order under section 22 of this Act.

(2) In the application of this Part of this Act to Northern Ireland—

(*a*) section 27 shall not apply;

(*b*) in sections 28 and 29, any reference to a local weights and measures authority shall be construed as a reference to the Ministry of Commerce for Northern Ireland, and the provisions of sections 30 to 32 shall be construed accordingly;

(*c*) in section 29(3), any reference to a justice of the peace shall be construed as a reference to a resident magistrate; and

(*d*) the provisions of the Arbitration Act (Northern Ireland) 1937, except the provisions set out in Schedule 3 thereto, shall apply to an arbitration under section 32 of this Act as if the arbitration were pursuant to an arbitration agreement (as defined in section 30(1) of that Act).

[133]

COMMENCEMENT

See s. 140 (3), *post*, and the note to s. 29, *ante*.

GENERAL NOTE

This section makes special provision for Northern Ireland.

PART III

ADDITIONAL FUNCTIONS OF DIRECTOR FOR PROTECTION OF CONSUMERS

34. Action by Director with respect to course of conduct detrimental to interests of consumers

(1) Where it appears to the Director that the person carrying on a business has in the course of that business persisted in a course of conduct which—

(*a*) is detrimental to the interests of consumers in the United Kingdom, whether those interests are economic interests or interests in respect of health, safety or other matters, and

(*b*) in accordance with the following provisions of this section is to be regarded as unfair to consumers,

the Director shall use his best endeavours, by communication with that person or otherwise, to obtain from him a satisfactory written assurance that he will refrain from continuing that course of conduct and from carrying on any similar course of conduct in the course of that business.

(2) For the purposes of subsection (1)(*b*) of this section a course of conduct

shall be regarded as unfair to consumers if it consists of contraventions of one or more enactments which impose duties, prohibitions or restrictions enforceable by criminal proceedings, whether any such duty, prohibition or restriction is imposed in relation to consumers as such or not and whether the person carrying on the business has or has not been convicted of any offence in respect of any such contravention.

(3) A course of conduct on the part of the person carrying on a business shall also be regarded for those purposes as unfair to consumers if it consists of things done, or omitted to be done, in the course of that business in breach of contract or in breach of a duty (other than a contractual duty) owed to any person by virtue of any enactment or rule of law and enforceable by civil proceedings, whether (in any such case) civil proceedings in respect of the breach of contract or breach of duty have been brought or not.

(4) For the purpose of determining whether it appears to him that a person has persisted in such a course of conduct as is mentioned in subsection (1) of this section, the Director shall have regard to either or both of the following, that is to say—

(*a*) complaints received by him, whether from consumers or from other persons;

(*b*) any other information collected by or furnished to him, whether by virtue of this Act or otherwise. [**134**]

COMMENCEMENT

See the note to s. 140 (3), *post*, and the note to s. 1, *ante*.

DEFINITIONS

"Director": s. 137 (2).

"business" and "consumer": s. 137 (2), and for supplementary definition, see s. 137 (6).

For further definitions, see s. 138.

GENERAL NOTE

Sub-s. (1): *"Where it appears to the Director."* Although the test is thus primarily made subjective, the decision must probably be based upon reasonable grounds; see *Padfield* v. *Minister of Agriculture*, [1968] A.C. 997 and *Secretary of State for Employment* v. *Associated Society of Locomotive Engineers and Firemen* (*No. 2*), [1972] 2 Q.B. 455. See also the note to s. 15, *ante*.

"Carrying on a business." See note to s. 29, *ante*.

"In the course of that business." See note to s. 25, *ante*. In that section the expression includes the additional word "ordinary". It therefore follows that this expression is broadly similar in meaning but probably somewhat wider.

"Persisted in." The decision in *Dale* v. *Smith*, [1967] 2 All E.R. 1133 concludes that this requires a degree of repetition exceeding one occasion.

"Course of conduct." The question whether a sequence of transactions amounts to a course of conduct must be one of fact and degree. The meaning is similar to the expression "course of dealing". In *Hollier* v. *Rambler Motors* (*A.M.C.*), *Ltd.*, [1972] 2 Q.B., at p. 76, Salmon, L.J., observed that 3 or 4 transactions over a period of 4 years did not constitute a course of dealing.

"Detrimental to the interests of consumers in the United Kingdom", *etc.* See the note to s. 2, *ante*.

"Shall use his best endeavours." This requires the Director to "do what can reasonably be done in the circumstances"; *Terrell* v. *Mabie Todd & Co.*, [1952] 2 T.L.R. 574. The duty thus imposed is a condition precedent to the Director's right to bring proceedings in the Restrictive Practices Court under s. 35, *post*.

"By communication with that person or otherwise." This appears to permit advertisements or other publicity directed to the world at large.

"Satisfactory written assurance." I.e., one which extends both to the course of conduct complained of and any similar course of conduct.

Sub-s. (2); *"Has or has not been convicted."* An assurance can accordingly be required on the basis of evidence which satisfies the Director that a criminal offence has been committed, even though such criminal offence could not be proved on balance of probabilities, let alone beyond reasonable doubt.

Sub-s. (3): "*Duty (other than contractual duty) owed to any person.*" This includes duties owed under the law of torts and such statutory duties as may confer an individual right of action in tort; but probably excludes other statutory duties on the ground that they are not owed to "any person". For the distinction see, *e.g.*, *Monk* v. *Warbey*, [1935] 1 K.B. 75.

Sub-s. (4): "*Shall have regard.*" The sender is obliged to take into account the matters specified in the section, but is not bound to abide by them; *Ishak* v. *Thowfeek*, [1968] 1 W.L.R. 1718.

"*Other information.*" This will probably be information collected pursuant to s. 2 of this Act—for which see note *ante*.

35. Proceedings before Restrictive Practices Court

If, in the circumstances specified in subsection (1) of section 34 of this Act,—

(*a*) the Director is unable to obtain from the person in question such an assurance as is mentioned in that subsection, or

(*b*) that person has given such an assurance and it appears to the Director that he has failed to observe it,

the Director may bring proceedings against him before the Restrictive Practices Court. **[135]**

COMMENCEMENT

See s. 140 (3), *post*, and the note to s. 1, *ante*.

DEFINITIONS

"Director": s. 137 (2).

GENERAL NOTE

"*If, in the circumstances*", *etc.* The power to bring proceedings under this section exists in two distinct circumstances: if no written assurance is forthcoming under s. 34; or if such an assurance is given and is then disregarded.

"*May bring proceedings.*" This clearly indicates that the Director has a discretion whether or not to bring such proceedings. There is no duty to do so.

"*Restrictive Practices Court.*" This is the Court established by s. 2 of the Restrictive Trade Practices Act 1956. This provision must, further, be read in the light of s. 41 of this Act which permits the Director, in an appropriate case, to bring proceedings before a county court (or its equivalent) instead of before the Restrictive Practices Court.

36. Evidence in proceedings under s. 35

(1) For the purposes of section 11 of the Civil Evidence Act 1968, section 10 of the Law Reform (Miscellaneous Provisions) (Scotland) Act 1968 or section 7 of the Civil Evidence Act (Northern Ireland) 1971 (each of which relates to convictions as evidence in civil proceedings), proceedings under section 35 of this Act shall (without prejudice to the generality of the relevant definition) be taken to be civil proceedings within the meaning of the Act in question.

(2) Where in any proceedings under section 35 of this Act the Director alleges such a breach of contract or breach of duty as is mentioned in section 34(3) of this Act, a judgment of any court given in civil proceedings, which includes a finding that the breach of contract or breach of duty in question was committed,—

(*a*) shall be admissible in evidence for the purpose of proving the breach of contract or breach of duty, and

(*b*) shall, unless the contrary is proved, be taken to be sufficient evidence that the breach of contract or breach of duty was committed.

(3) For the purposes of subsection (2) of this section no account shall be taken of a judgment given in any civil proceedings if it has subsequently been reversed on appeal, or has been varied on appeal so as to negative the finding referred to in that subsection.

(4) In subsection (1) of this section "the relevant definition" means section 18(1) of the Civil Evidence Act 1968, section 17(1) of the Law Reform (Miscellaneous Provisions) (Scotland) Act 1968 or section 14(1) of the Civil Evidence Act (Northern Ireland) 1971, as the case may be. [**136**]

COMMENCEMENT

See s. 140 (3), *post*, and the note to s. 1, *ante*.

DEFINITION

"Director": s. 137 (2).

GENERAL NOTE

"Section 11 of the Civil Evidence Act 1968" etc. This allows the fact that a person has been convicted of an offence by or before any court in the United Kingdom or by a court-martial to be admissible in evidence for the purpose of proving that the person concerned committed the offence in question.

"A judgment of any court given in civil proceedings." This allows a civil judgment to be admissible in evidence for the purpose of proving a relevant breach of contract or duty. The remaining provisions of sub-s. (2) are broadly similar to the provisions of s. 11 of the Civil Evidence Act 1968.

37. Order of, or undertaking given to, Court in proceedings under s. 35

(1) Where in any proceedings before the Restrictive Practices Court under section 35 of this Act—

(*a*) the Court finds that the person against whom the proceedings are brought (in this section referred to as "the respondent") has in the course of a business carried on by him persisted in such a course of conduct as is mentioned in section 34(1) of this Act, and

(*b*) the respondent does not give an undertaking to the Court under subsection (3) of this section which is accepted by the Court, and

(*c*) it appears to the Court that, unless an order is made against the respondent under this section, he is likely to continue that course of conduct or to carry on a similar course of conduct,

the Court may make an order against the respondent under this section.

(2) An order of the Court under this section shall (with such degree of particularity as appears to the Court to be sufficient for the purposes of the order) indicate the nature of the course of conduct to which the finding of the Court under subsection (1)(*a*) of this section relates, and shall direct the respondent—

(*a*) to refrain from continuing that course of conduct, and

(*b*) to refrain from carrying on any similar course of conduct in the course of his business.

(3) Where in any proceedings under section 35 of this Act the Court makes such a finding as is mentioned in subsection (1)(*a*) of this section, and the respondent offers to give to the Court an undertaking either—

(*a*) to refrain as mentioned in paragraphs (*a*) and (*b*) of subsection (2) of this section, or

(*b*) to take particular steps which, in the opinion of the Court, would suffice to prevent a continuance of the course of conduct to which the complaint relates and to prevent the carrying on by the respondent of any similar course of conduct in the course of his business,

the Court may, if it thinks fit, accept that undertaking instead of making an order under this section. [**137**]

COMMENCEMENT

See s. 140 (3), *post*, and the note to s. 1, *ante*.

DEFINITION

"business": s. 137 (2).

GENERAL NOTE

"*Where in any proceedings.*" The Court may make an order under this section only if three conditions are satisfied: the respondent has persisted in a course of conduct such as is mentioned in s. 34 (1); the respondent does not, or is unable to, give an undertaking acceptable to the Court; and it appears to the Court that the course of conduct (or a similar course of conduct) is likely to continue.

"*Undertaking to the Court.*" This section allows a respondent to give an undertaking to the Court. The provision is however subject to the requirement that the undertaking is acceptable to the Court. It may therefore become necessary for the Court to make an order either because no undertaking is forthcoming or because such undertaking as is offered is inadequate.

"*May make an order.*" This power is therefore discretionary and the Court is not obliged to make any order. For extensions of orders and appeals, see notes to ss. 40 and 42, *post*.

"*Shall . . . indicate.*" The Court is obliged to indicate the relevant course of conduct but has a discretion as to the degree of particularity used in indicating that course of conduct.

"*Shall direct the respondent.*" On making an order the Court is under a duty to direct the respondent to refrain from the conduct specified in this section.

"*May if it thinks fit.*" The Court therefore has a discretion whether to accept an undertaking instead of making an order. This discretion is, presumably, subject to the requirement that it is exercised reasonably.

38. Provisions as to persons consenting to or conniving at courses of conduct detrimental to interests of consumers

(1) The provisions of this section shall have effect where it appears to the Director—

(*a*) that a body corporate has in the course of a business carried on by that body persisted in such a course of conduct as is mentioned in section 34(1) of this Act, and

(*b*) that the course of conduct in question has been so persisted in with the consent or connivance of a person (in this and the next following section referred to as "the accessory") who at a material time fulfilled the relevant conditions in relation to that body.

(2) For the purposes of this section a person shall be taken to fulfil the relevant conditions in relation to a body corporate at any time if that person either—

(*a*) is at that time a director, manager, secretary or other similar officer of the body corporate or a person purporting to act in any such capacity, or

(*b*) whether being an individual or a body of persons, corporate or unincorporate, has at that time a controlling interest in that body corporate.

(3) If, in the circumstances specified in subsection (1) of this section,—

(*a*) the Director has used his best endeavours to obtain from the accessory such an assurance as is mentioned in the next following subsection and has been unable to obtain such an assurance from him, or

(*b*) the accessory has given such an assurance to the Director and it appears to the Director that he has failed to observe it,

the Director may bring proceedings against the accessory before the Restrictive Practices Court.

(4) The assurance referred to in subsection (3) of this section is a satisfactory written assurance given by the accessory that he will refrain—

(*a*) from continuing to consent to or connive at the course of conduct in question;

(*b*) from carrying on any similar course of conduct in the course of any business which may at any time be carried on by him; and

(*c*) from consenting to or conniving at the carrying on of any such course of conduct by any other body corporate in relation to which, at any time when that course of conduct is carried on, he fulfils the relevant conditions.

(5) Proceedings may be brought against the accessory under this section whether or not any proceedings are brought under section 35 of this Act against the body corporate referred to in subsection (1) of this section.

(6) Section 36 of this Act shall have effect in relation to proceedings under this section as it has effect in relation to proceedings under section 35 of this Act.

(7) For the purposes of this section a person (whether being an individual or a body of persons, corporate or unincorporate) has a controlling interest in a body corporate if (but only if) that person can, directly or indirectly, determine the manner in which one-half of the votes which could be cast at a general meeting of the body corporate are to be cast on matters, and in circumstances, not of such a description as to bring into play any special voting rights or restrictions on voting rights. [**138**]

COMMENCEMENT

See s. 140 (3), *post*, and the note to s. 1, *ante*.

DEFINITIONS

"the Director", "business': s. 137 (2); and see also s. 138.
"controlling interest": sub-s. (7) above.

GENERAL NOTE

Sub-s. (1): *"Where it appears to the Director"*. See the note to s. 34, *ante*.

"Body corporate." This expression is not defined in the Act. It clearly includes companies and other corporate bodies. The precise limit of this expression remains unclear because of the existence of certain quasi-corporate entities—see, *e.g.*, *Willis* v. *Association of Universities of the British Commonwealth*, [1965] 1 Q.B. 140.

"In the course of a business." See the notes to ss. 25 and 34, *ante*.

"Persisted in such a course of conduct." See the note to s. 34, *ante*.

"Consent." There is authority for saying that this presupposes knowledge; see *Re Caughey, Ex parte Ford* (1876), 1 Ch.D. 521, at page 528, and *Lamb* v. *Wright & Co.*, [1924] 1 K.B. 857. It is probable however that actual knowledge is unnecessary; see the discussion of the word "knows" at s. 30, *ante*, and the cases therein set out.

"Connivance." This, it has been said, implies knowledge and acquiescence, and as a legal doctrine has its source and its limits in the principle *volenti non fit injuria*, see *Boulting* v. *Boulting* (1864), 3 Sw. & Tr. 329, at page 335. Here also it appears that actual knowledge is unnecessary and suspicion is enough. However mere negligence or inattention is insufficient; see *Rogers* v. *Rogers* (1830), 3 Hag. Ecc. 57; see also *Douglas* v. *Douglas*, [1951] P. 85; *Godfrey* v. *Godfrey*, [1965] A.C. 444, and *Rumbelow* v. *Rumbelow and Hadden*, [1965] P. 207.

Sub-s. (2): *"Manager."* This must mean a person who has the management of the whole affairs of the company—see *Gibson* v. *Barton* (1875), L.R. 10 Q.B. 329 and also *Tesco Supermarkets, Ltd.* v. *Nattrass*, [1972] A.C. 153; [1971] 2 All E.R. 127, for the distinction between a manager in this sense and a manager of a shop.

"*Controlling interest.*" This is defined in sub-s. (7) above.

Sub-s. (3): "*Best endeavours.*" See note to s. 34, *ante.*

"*May bring proceedings.*" See note to s. 35, *ante.*

"*Restrictive Practices Court.*" See note to s. 35, *ante.*

Sub-s. (4): "*Satisfactory written assurance.*" See note to s. 34, *ante.*

"*Fulfills the relevant conditions.*" See note to s. 38, *ante.*

39. Order of, or undertaking given to, Court in proceedings under s. 38

(1) Where in any proceedings brought against the accessory before the Restrictive Practices Court under section 38 of this Act—

- (*a*) the Court finds that the conditions specified in paragraphs (*a*) and (*b*) of subsection (1) of that section are fulfilled in the case of the accessory, and
- (*b*) the accessory does not give an undertaking to the Court under subsection (3) of this section which is accepted by the Court, and
- (*c*) it appears to the Court that, unless an order is made against the accessory under this section, it is likely that he will not refrain from acting in one or more of the ways mentioned in paragraphs (*a*) to (*c*) of subsection (4) of that section,

the Court may make an order against the accessory under this section.

(2) An order of the Court under this section shall (with such degree of particularity as appears to the Court to be sufficient for the purposes of the order) indicate the nature of the course of conduct to which the finding of the Court under subsection (1)(*a*) of this section relates, and shall direct the accessory, in relation to the course of conduct so indicated, to refrain from acting in any of the ways mentioned in paragraphs (*a*) to (*c*) of subsection (4) of section 38 of this Act.

(3) Where in any proceedings under section 38 of this Act the Court makes such a finding as is mentioned in subsection (1)(*a*) of this section, and the accessory offers to give to the Court an undertaking either—

- (*a*) to refrain from acting in any of the ways mentioned in paragraphs (*a*) to (*c*) of subsection (4) of that section, or
- (*b*) to take particular steps which, in the opinion of the Court, would suffice to prevent him from acting in any of those ways,

the Court may, if it thinks fit, accept that undertaking instead of making an order under this section. **[139]**

COMMENCEMENT

See s. 140 (3), *post*, and the note to s. 1, *ante.*

GENERAL NOTE

"*Where in any proceedings.*" For the circumstances in which proceedings may be brought against an "accessory", see the note to s. 38, *ante.*

"*The accessory.*" For the meaning of "accessory" see s. 38 (1) (*b*), *ante.*

"*Restrictive Practices Court.*" See the note to s. 35, *ante.*

"*Undertaking to the Court.*" This section allows an accessory to give an undertaking to the Court. The provision is however subject to the requirement that the undertaking is acceptable to the Court. It may therefore become necessary for the Court to make an order either because no undertaking is forthcoming or because such undertaking as is offered is inadequate.

"*May make an order.*" This power is therefore discretionary and the Court is not obliged to make any order. For extensions of orders and appeals, see note to ss. 40 and 42, *post.*

"Shall . . . indicate." The Court is obliged to indicate the relevant course of conduct but has a discretion as to the degree of particularity used in indicating that course of conduct.

"Shall direct the accessory." On making an order the Court is under a duty to direct the accessory to refrain from acting in any of the ways specified at s. 38 (4) (*a*)–(*c*), *ante*.

"May, if it thinks fit." The Court therefore has a discretion whether to accept an undertaking instead of making an order. This discretion is, presumably, subject to the requirement that it is exercised reasonably.

40. Provisions as to interconnected bodies corporate

(1) This section applies to any order made under section 37 or section 39 of this Act.

(2) Where an order to which this section applies is made against a body corporate which is a member of a group of interconnected bodies corporate, the Restrictive Practices Court, on making the order, may direct that it shall be binding upon all members of the group as if each of them were the body corporate against which the order is made.

(3) Where an order to which this section applies has been made against a body corporate, and at a time when that order is in force—

(*a*) the body corporate becomes a member of a group of interconnected bodies corporate, or

(*b*) a group of interconnected bodies corporate of which it is a member is increased by the addition of one or more further members.

the Restrictive Practices Court, on the application of the Director, may direct that the order shall thereafter be binding upon each member of the group as if it were the body corporate against which the order was made.

(4) The power conferred by subsection (3) of this section shall be exercisable—

(*a*) whether, at the time when the original order was made, the body corporate against which it was made was a member of a group of interconnected bodies corporate or not, and

(*b*) if it was such a member, whether a direction under subsection (2) of this section was given or not. [**140**]

COMMENCEMENT

See s. 140 (3), *post*, and the note to s. 1, *ante*.

DEFINITIONS

"the Director": s. 137 (2).

"interconnected bodies corporate", "group of interconnected bodies corporate": s. 137 (5).

GENERAL NOTE

Sub-s. (2)*: "Body corporate."* See the note to s. 38, *ante*.

"Restrictive Practices Court." See the note to s. 35, *ante*.

"May direct." This power is therefore discretionary and the Court is not obliged to make any order under this section.

"As if each of them" etc. It appears from the wording as though the liability of bodies corporate subject to such an order is joint and several. Proceedings can probably therefore be brought either against each of them independently or against them all upon the basis of joint liability—for the position in contract see *Cabell* v. *Vaughan* (1669), 1 Wms. Saund. 291.

Sub-s. (3)*: "As if it were the body corporate."* See the previous note. It appears that, on the making of an extension order under sub-s. (3), the liability of all bodies corporate subject to the new order is joint and several. However the differences in wording between this, and the previous, provisions may make this conclusion controversial.

41. Concurrent jurisdiction of other courts in certain cases

(1) In any case where—

(*a*) the Director could bring proceedings against a person before the Restrictive Practices Court under section 35 or section 38 of this Act, and

(*b*) it appears to the Director that the conditions specified in the next following subsection are fulfilled,

the Director may, if he thinks fit, bring those proceedings in an appropriate alternative court instead of bringing them before the Restrictive Practices Court; and, in relation to any proceedings brought by virtue of this section, the appropriate alternative court in which they are brought shall have the like jurisdiction as the Restrictive Practices Court would have had if they had been brought in that Court.

(2) The conditions referred to in the preceding subsection are—

(*a*) that neither the person against whom the proceedings are to be brought nor the person against whom any associated proceedings have been or are intended to be brought is a body corporate having a share capital, paid up or credited as paid up, of an amount exceeding £10,000, and

(*b*) that neither those proceedings nor any associated proceedings involve or are likely to involve the determination of a question (whether of law or of fact) of such general application as to justify its being reserved for determination by the Restrictive Practices Court.

(3) For the purposes of this section, the following shall be appropriate alternative courts in relation to proceedings in respect of a course of conduct maintained in the course of a business, that is to say, the county court for any district (or, in Northern Ireland, any division) in which, or, in Scotland, any sheriff court within whose jurisdiction, that business is carried on.

(4) In relation to any proceedings brought in an appropriate alternative court by virtue of this section, or to any order made in any such proceedings, any reference in section 37, in section 39 or section 40 of this Act to the Restrictive Practices Court shall be construed as a reference to the appropriate alternative court in which the proceedings are brought.

(5) In this section " associated proceedings "—

(*a*) in relation to proceedings under section 35 of this Act, means proceedings under section 38 of this Act against a person as being a person consenting to or conniving at the course of conduct in question, and

(*b*) in relation to proceedings under section 38 of this Act, means proceedings under section 35 of this Act against a person as being the person by whom the course of conduct in question has been maintained. [**141**]

COMMENCEMENT

See s. 140 (3), *post*, and the note to s. 1, *ante*.

DEFINITIONS

"the Director": s. 137 (2).
"associated proceedings": sub-s. (5) above.

GENERAL NOTE

"Restrictive Practices Court." See note to s. 35, *ante*.

"It appears to the Director." Thus as long as the Director acts reasonably and directs himself to the relevant considerations, the Director and not the Courts must judge

whether or not those conditions are satisfied. For a similar provision, see *Secretary of State for Employment* v. *Associated Society of Locomotive Engineers and Firemen* (*No.* 2), [1972] 2 Q.B. 455.

"*May, if he thinks fit.*" Thus even if the Director considers that the above-mentioned conditions are satisfied, he has a discretion whether or not to proceed in an alternative Court. This discretion must presumably be exercised reasonably.

"*Body corporate.*" See the note to s. 38, *ante*.

"*Course of conduct.*" See note to s. 34, *ante*.

"*Course of a business.*" See note to s. 34, *ante*.

"*For any district.*" Thus where the business is carried on in more than one district, the Director may choose amongst the county courts for the districts in which that business is carried on.

"*Rules of court.*" Proceedings in the county court under this Part (ss. 34–43) of this Act are regulated by C.C.R. Ord. 46, r. 24 (added by S.I. 1974 No. 178).

42. Appeals from decisions or orders of courts under Part III

(1) Notwithstanding anything in any other enactment, an appeal, whether on a question of fact or on a question of law, shall lie from any decision or order of any court in proceedings under Part III of this Act.

(2) Any such appeal shall lie—

(*a*) in the case of proceedings in England and Wales, to the Court of Appeal;

(*b*) in the case of proceedings in Scotland, to the Court of Session;

(*c*) in the case of proceedings in Northern Ireland, to the Court of Appeal in Northern Ireland. [**142**]

COMMENCEMENT

See s. 140 (3), *post*, and the note to s. 1, *ante*.

GENERAL NOTE

"*Notwithstanding anything in any other enactment.*" See, in particular the Restrictive Trade Practices Act 1956, Schedule, para. 7, which provides that the decision of the Restrictive Practices Court on a question of fact is final and the County Courts Act 1959, s. 109, which provides for appeals on questions of fact in certain kinds of county court proceedings only.

"*Any Court.*" *I.e.*, the Restrictive Practices Court or, where it has jurisdiction by virtue of s. 41, *ante*, a county court.

"*Part III of this Act.*" *I.e.*, ss. 34–43 of this Act.

43. Legal aid in proceedings under Part III in Restrictive Practices Court

(1) The paragraph set out in the next following subsection shall be inserted—

(*a*) (*rep. by the Legal Aid Act* 1974, *s.* 42, *Sch.* 5, *Part I*);

(*b*) as paragraph 4, at the end of Part I of Schedule 1 to the Legal Aid (Scotland) Act 1967; and

(*c*) as paragraph 6, at the end of Part I of Schedule 1 to the Legal Aid and Advice Act (Northern Ireland) 1965.

(2) The paragraph referred to in subsection (1) of this section is as follows:—

"Proceedings in the Restrictive Practices Court under Part III of the Fair Trading Act 1973, and any proceedings in that Court in consequence of an order made, or undertaking given to the Court, under that Part of that Act". [**143**]

COMMENCEMENT

See s. 140 (3), *post*, and the note to s. 1, *ante*.

GENERAL NOTE

Sub-s. (1) (*a*) was replaced by the Legal Aid Act 1974, Sch. 1, Part I, para. 8, which makes legal aid under Part I of that Act available in proceedings in England and Wales of the kinds mentioned in sub-s. (2) above. Consequential amendments have been made to the Legal Aid (General) Regulations 1971, S.I. 1971 No. 62, by the Legal Aid (General) (Amendment) Regulations 1973, S.I. 1973 No. 2036.

"*Restrictive Practices Court.*" See the note to s. 35, *ante*.

PART IV

FUNCTIONS OF DIRECTOR AND COMMISSION IN RELATION TO MONOPOLY SITUATIONS AND UNCOMPETITIVE PRACTICES

Powers for Director to require information

44. General power for Director to require information

(1) Where it appears to the Director that there are grounds for believing—

(*a*) that a monopoly situation may exist in relation to the supply of goods or services of any description, or in relation to exports of goods of any description from the United Kingdom, and

(*b*) that in accordance with the following provisions of this Part of this Act he would not be precluded from making a monopoly reference to the Commission with respect to the existence or possible existence of that situation,

the Director, for the purpose of assisting him in determining whether to make a monopoly reference with respect to the existence or possible existence of that situation, may exercise the powers conferred by the next following subsection.

(2) In the circumstances and for the purpose mentioned in the preceding subsection the Director may require any person who supplies or produces goods of the description in question in the United Kingdom, or to whom any such goods are supplied in the United Kingdom, or (as the case may be) any person who supplies services of that description in the United Kingdom, or for whom any such services are so supplied, to furnish to the Director such information as the Director may consider necessary with regard to—

(*a*) the value, cost, price or quantity of goods of that description supplied or produced by that person, or of goods of that description supplied to him, or (as the case may be) the value, cost, price or extent of the services of that description supplied by that person or of the services of that description supplied for him, or

(*b*) the capacity of any undertaking carried on by that person to supply, produce or make use of goods of that description, or (as the case may be) to supply or make use of services of that description, or

(*c*) the number of persons employed by that person wholly or partly on work related to the supply, production or use of goods of that description, or (as the case may be) the supply or use of services of that description. **[144]**

COMMENCEMENT

See s. 140 (3), *post*, and the notes to s. 1, *ante*.

DEFINITIONS

"the Director": see s. 1 (1), *ante*, or s. 137 (2), *post*.
"monopoly reference" and "monopoly situation": s. 5 (3).
"goods", "price", "supply": s. 137 (2).
"supply of services": s. 137 (3).
"services": s. 137 (4).
"United Kingdom": see notes to s. 2, *ante*.

GENERAL NOTE

Ss. 44 to 46 contain provisions empowering the Director to seek information to assist him in deciding whether to make a monopoly reference under s. 50, *post*.

The Director's powers under s. 44 should be compared with the powers of the Commission to require information: see s. 85, *post*.

S. 44 gives the Director power to seek certain statistical information, mainly about turnover, capacity and employment when he has grounds for thinking that a monopoly may exist in relation to the supply of a description of goods, services or exports.

S. 44 does not prescribe the factors to be taken into account by the Director in deciding whether to make a reference, but merely confers on him powers of obtaining certain types of information helpful to him in making that decision.

Sub-s. (1) (*a*). See ss. 6, 7, 9, 10, *ante*.

Sub-s. (1) (*b*). The Director is precluded from making a monopoly reference in the cases mentioned in s. 50 (2), *post*.

45. Special power to require information with respect to complex monopoly situations

(1) Where it appears to the Director that there are grounds for believing—

(*a*) that a complex monopoly situation may exist in relation to the supply of goods or services of any description, or in relation to exports of goods of any description from the United Kingdom, and

(*b*) that in accordance with the following provisions of this Part of this Act he would not be precluded from making a monopoly reference to the Commission with respect to the existence or possible existence of that situation,

the Director may formulate proposals for requiring specified persons to furnish information to him in accordance with the proposals for the purpose of assisting him in determining whether to make a monopoly reference with respect to the existence or possible existence of that situation.

(2) The persons specified in any such proposals shall be persons appearing to the Director to be, or to be included among, those who, in relation to the production or supply of goods or to the supply of services of the description in question, or in relation to exports from the United Kingdom of goods of the description in question,—

(*a*) may be parties to any such agreement as is mentioned in paragraph (*d*) of section 6(1) or paragraph (*d*) of section 7(1) of this Act (or mentioned in either of those paragraphs as modified by section 9(2) of this Act) or may be parties to any such agreement as is mentioned in subsection (2) or subsection (3) of section 8 of this Act, or

(*b*) may be conducting their respective affairs as mentioned in section 6(2) or in section 7(2) of this Act.

(3) Any such proposals shall also specify the description of goods or services in question, and—

(*a*) in a case falling within paragraph (*a*) of subsection (2) of this section, shall indicate the particular respects in which it appears to the Director that any agreement in question may be such an agreement as is referred to in that paragraph, or

(*b*) in a case falling within paragraph (*b*) of that subsection, shall indicate the particular respects in which it appears to the Director that the persons specified in the proposals may be conducting their respective affairs in a manner referred to in that paragraph,

and shall state what information the Director proposes that the persons specified in the proposals should be required to furnish for the purpose of indicating whether, in those respects, they are parties to such an agreement, or are so conducting their respective affairs, and, if so, of indicating in what circumstances they are parties to such an agreement or are so conducting their affairs.

(4) Where the Director has formulated proposals under this section, he may submit those proposals to the Secretary of State for approval; and if the Secretary of State approves the proposals, with or without modifications, the Director may require any person specified in the proposals to furnish to the Director such information as the Director may specify in accordance with the proposals, or, if the proposals have been approved with modifications, in accordance with the proposals as so modified. **[145]**

COMMENCEMENT

See s. 140 (3), *post*, and note to s. 1, *ante*.

DEFINITIONS

"the Director": see s. 1 (1), *ante*, or s. 137 (2), *post*.
"monopoly reference": s. 5 (3).
"agreement", "goods", "produce" and "supply": s. 137 (2).
"supply of services": s. 137 (3).
"services": s. 137 (4).

GENERAL NOTE

S. 45 enables the Director to require the giving of information of a not purely quantitative nature (*cf.* s. 44) but which might be thought highly confidential and which is needed in order to establish a common feature in the behaviour of firms by way either of an agreement or parallel behaviour. This is a more far-reaching power than that under s. 44 in that it involves the investigation of a firm's behaviour and a firm's confidential dealings with other firms in order to establish whether or not a complex monopoly situation exists. This could involve the opening up of an individual's or a firm's records, documents and minutes of meetings. In view of the confidentiality of such information it can be required by the Director only after he has submitted proposals for his enquiries to the Secretary of State who must approve them. In approving the Director's enquiries the Secretary of State has power to require modification to prevent for example fishing enquiries of too general a nature. The enquiries will be made therefore when both the Director and the Secretary of State consider there is a likelihood of a complex monopoly situation and that discovery of confidential information is necessary.

Sub-s. (1): "*A complex monopoly situation may exist in relation to the supply of goods or services of any description.* See ss. 6, 7 and 11, *ante*.

"*A complex monopoly situation may exist . . . in relation to exports of goods of any description from the United Kingdom.*" See ss. 8 and 11, *ante*.

"*United Kingdom.*" See note to s. 2, *ante*.

"*Precluded from making a monopoly reference.*" The Director is precluded from making a monopoly reference in the cases mentioned in s. 50 (2), *post*.

"*Persons.*" See note "Person", s. 6, *ante*.

"*Monopoly reference.*" *I.e.*, a monopoly reference under s. 50, *post*. See generally as to monopoly references, ss. 47 *et seq.*, *post*.

Sub-s. (4): "*Require . . . to furnish . . . such information.*" See as to such requirements, s. 46, *post*.

46. Supplementary provisions as to requirements to furnish information

(1) Any power conferred on the Director by the preceding provisions of this Part of this Act to require a person to furnish information shall be exercisable by notice in writing served on that person.

(2) Any person who refuses or wilfully neglects to furnish to the Director information required by such a notice shall be guilty of an offence and shall be liable on summary conviction to a fine not exceeding £400.

(3) Any person who, in furnishing information required by such a notice, makes a statement which he knows to be false in a material particular, or recklessly makes a statement which is false in a material particular, shall be guilty of an offence and shall be liable—

(*a*) on summary conviction, to a fine not exceeding £400;
(*b*) on conviction on indictment, to imprisonment for a term not exceeding two years or to a fine or to both. [**146**]

COMMENCEMENT
See s. 140 (3), *post*, and the notes to s. 1, *aote*.

DEFINITION
"the Director": see s. 1 (1), *ante*, and s. 137 (2), *post*.

GENERAL NOTE
This section deals with enforecement of requests by the Director for information under ss. 44 and 45, *ante*.
The request by the Director under s. 46 (1) must be in writing but no particular form of request is prescribed.
S. 46 (2) covers failure otherwise than inadvertently to provide the required information. This is punishable summarily by way of fine only and is not an indictable offence.
S. 46 (3) covers the provision of false information deliberately or recklessly and this is punishable either summarily by way of a fine or on indictment by way of a fine or imprisonment or both.
Where the conviction under sub-s. (2) or (3) is summary any fine imposed cannot exceed £400.
As to offences under s. 46 of bodies corporate, see s. 132, *post*.
As to restrictions on disclosure of any information obtained by virtue of s. 85, see s. 133, *post*.
Sub-s. (1): *"Preceding provisions of this Part."* *I.e.*, ss. 44 and 45, *ante*.
"Writing." See the note to s. 1, *ante*.
Sub-s. (2): *"Any person."* As to offences by bodies corporate, see s. 132, *post*.
"Wilfully." See the note to s. 30, *ante*.
"Shall be guilty of an offence." As to time limit on prosecutions, see s. 129, *post*.
"Summary conviction." See note to s. 23, *ante*.
Sub-s. (3): *"Knows."* See the note to s. 25, *ante*.
"False." See the note to s. 30, *ante*.
"Material particular." A particular may be material in that it renders another statement more credible; see *R.* v. *Tyson* (1867), L.R. 1 C.C.R. 107.
"Recklessly." On the meaning of this expression see, in particular *Derry* v. *Peek* (1889), 14 App. Cas. 337; [1886–90] All E.R. Rep. 1; *Williams Brothers Direct Supply Stores, Ltd.* v. *Cloote* (1944), 60 T.L.R. 270; *R.* v. *Bates*, [1952] 2 All E.R. 842 (on appeal *sub nom. R.* v. *Russell*, [1953] 1 W.L.R. 77; 97 Sol. Jo. 12); *R.* v. *Mackinnon*, [1959] 1 Q.B. 150; [1958] 3 All E.R. 657; *R.* v. *Grunwald*, [1963] 1 Q.B. 935; [1960] 3 All E.R. 380; and *Shawinigan, Ltd.* v. *Vokins & Co., Ltd.*, [1961] 3 All E.R. 396.
"Conviction on indictment", *"fine"*. See notes to s. 23, *ante*.

Monopoly references

47. General provisions as to monopoly references

(1) A monopoly reference—

(*a*) shall specify the description of goods or services to which it relates;
(*b*) in the case of a reference relating to goods, shall state whether it relates to the supply of goods or to exports of goods from the United Kingdom or to both; and
(*c*) if, for the purposes of the reference, consideration is to be limited to a part of the United Kingdom, shall specify the part of the United Kingdom to which consideration is to be limited,

and (subject to the next following subsection) shall be framed in one or other of the ways specified in section 48 or section 49 of this Act.

(2) A monopoly reference (whether it falls within section 48 or within section 49 of this Act) may be so framed as to require the Commission to exclude from consideration, or to limit consideration to,—

(*a*) such agreements as are mentioned in paragraph (*d*) of section 6(1) or paragraph (*d*) of section 7(1) of this Act (or in either of those paragraphs as modified by section 9(2) of this Act) or as are mentioned in subsection (2) or subsection (3) of section 8 of this Act, or

(*b*) agreements or practices whereby persons conduct their affairs as mentioned in section 6(2) or section 7(2) of this Act,

or to exclude from consideration, or to limit consideration to, such one or more agreements or practices falling within paragraph (*a*) or paragraph (*b*) of this subsection as are specified in the reference. [**147**]

COMMENCEMENT

See s. 140 (3), *post*, and notes to s. 1, *ante*.

DEFINITIONS

"United Kingdom": see s. 2, *ante*.
"the Commission": see s. 4 (1), *ante*, or s. 137 (2), *post*.
"monopoly reference": s. 5 (3).
"agreement", "goods" and "supply": s. 137 (2).
"services": s. 137 (4).

GENERAL NOTE

Ss. 47, 48 and 49 describe the various ways in which a monopoly reference can be framed. A monopoly reference must always comply with the requirements of s. 47 (1) and it must then be framed either so as to be limited to an investigation of facts under s. 48 or so as not to be so limited under s. 49. In either case it may be framed in accordance with s. 47 (2).

S. 47 (2) allows further refinement of a monopoly reference, beyond the specifications of s. 47 (1), s. 48 or s. 49, in this way: as discussed in relation to ss. 6 to 8, *ante*, monopoly situations can be constituted by agreements or arrangements or parallel behaviour and such situations are complex monopoly situations within s. 11, *ante*. S. 47 (2) allows a reference to require the Commission either to exclude from its consideration or to limit its consideration to such specified agreements or arrangements or behaviour.

Further refinements of reference are possible under s. 9, *ante*, or s. 49 (3), *post*.

48. Monopoly reference limited to the facts

A monopoly reference may be so framed as to require the Commission only to investigate and report on the questions whether a monopoly situation exists in relation to the matters set out in the reference in accordance with section 47 of this Act and, if so,—

(*a*) by virtue of which provisions of sections 6 to 8 of this Act that monopoly situation is to be taken to exist;

(*b*) in favour of what person or persons that monopoly situation exists;

(*c*) whether any steps (by way of uncompetitive practices or otherwise) are being taken by that person or those persons for the purpose of exploiting or maintaining the monopoly situation and, if so, by what uncompetitive practices or in what other way; and

(*d*) whether any action or omission on the part of that person or those persons is attributable to the existence of the monopoly situation and, if so, what action or omission and in what way it is so attributable;

and a monopoly reference so framed is in this Act referred to as a "monopoly reference limited to the facts". [**148**]

COMMENCEMENT

See s. 140 (3), *post*, and notes to s. 1, *ante*.

DEFINITIONS

"the Commission": see s. 4 (1), *ante*, or s. 137 (2), *post*.
"Monopoly reference" and "monopoly situation", s. 5 (3).

GENERAL NOTE

In considering a reference under s. 48 the Commission is not concerned with any assessment of whether a monopoly situation operates or may be expected to operate against the public interest. The Commission's investigation is limited to the questions set out in s. 48, *i.e.*, broadly whether a monopoly situation exists, what sort of monopoly situation it is, in favour of whom it operates and whether that person is deliberately exploiting or maintaining the situation by uncompetitive practices or omissions. All and not merely some of the questions contained in the reference must be investigated by the Commission. A reference limited to the facts is in the nature of a probe only and cannot lead to an order under s. 56, *post* (*cf.* a reference not limited to the facts: see s. 49, *post*).

49. Monopoly reference not limited to the facts

(1) A monopoly reference may be so framed as to require the Commission to investigate and report on the question whether a monopoly situation exists in relation to the matters set out in the reference in accordance with section 47 of this Act and, if so, to investigate and report—

(*a*) on the questions mentioned in paragraphs (*a*) to (*d*) of section 48 of this Act, and

(*b*) on the question whether any facts found by the Commission in pursuance of their investigations under the preceding provisions of this subsection operate, or may be expected to operate, against the public interest.

(2) A monopoly reference may be so framed as to require the Commission to investigate and report on the questions whether a monopoly situation exists in relation to the matters set out in the reference in accordance with section 47 of this Act and, if so,—

(*a*) by virtue of which provisions of sections 6 to 8 of this Act that monopoly situation is to be taken to exist;

(*b*) in favour of what person or persons that monopoly situation exists; and

(*c*) whether any action or omission on the part of that person or those persons in respect of matters specified in the reference for the purposes of this paragraph operates, or may be expected to operate, against the public interest.

(3) For the purposes of subsection (2)(*c*) of this section any matter may be specified in a monopoly reference if it relates to any of the following, that is to say—

(*a*) prices charged, or proposed to be charged, for goods or services of the description specified in the reference;

(*b*) any recommendation or suggestion made as to such prices;

(*c*) any refusal to supply goods or services of the description specified in the reference;

(*d*) any preference given to any person (whether by way of discrimination in respect of prices or in respect of priority of supply or otherwise) in relation to the supply of goods or services of that description;

and any matter not falling within any of the preceding paragraphs may be specified for those purposes in a monopoly reference if, in the opinion of the person or persons making the reference, it is of a kind such that (if a monopoly situation is found to exist) that matter might reasonably be regarded as a step taken for the purpose of exploiting or maintaining that situation or as being attributable to the existence of that situation.

(4) A monopoly reference framed in either of the ways mentioned in subsections (1) and (2) of this section is in this Act referred to as a "monopoly reference not limited to the facts". [**149**]

COMMENCEMENT

See s. 140 (3), *post*, and notes to s. 1, *ante*.

DEFINITIONS

"the Commission": see s. 4 (1), *ante*, or s. 137 (2), *post*.
"monopoly reference" and "monopoly situation": s. 5 (3).
"goods", "price", "supply": s. 137 (2).
"supply of services": s. 137 (3).
"services": s. 137 (4).

GENERAL NOTE

Sub-s. (1): A reference framed under this subsection will require the Commission to consider the same questions as it would in a reference under s. 48, *ante*, and in addition to consider the question whether any facts found by the Commission in pursuance of their investigations under the other questions in the reference operate or may be expected to operate against the public interest.

Sub-s. (2): In a reference framed under this subsection the Commission's inquiry into the facts will be limited to whether a monopoly situation exists and in whose favour it operates. The Commission must then proceed straight to the issue contained in s. 49 (2) (*c*) involving again a consideration of the public interest. Its consideration of the public interest must be confined in a reference framed under s. 49 (2) to any or all of the matters provided for in s. 49 (3).

Sub-s. (3): This subsection contains a list of particular matters followed by a general provision allowing the person making the reference to specify any other matter if, in his opinion, it is of a kind such that (if a monopoly situation is found to exist) that matter might reasonably be regarded as a step taken for the purpose of exploiting or maintaining that situation or as being attributable to the existence of that situation.

The consequence of s. 49 (2) and s. 49 (3) which are new provisions in the legal regulation of monopolies is that a monopoly reference may be framed very specifically indeed and that once the Commission finds a monopoly situation exists in favour of someone it can turn immediately to the particular issue or issues specified in the reference.

50. Monopoly references by Director

(1) Where it appears to the Director that a monopoly situation exists or may exist in relation to—

(*a*) the supply of goods of any description, or
(*b*) the supply of services of any description, or
(*c*) exports of goods of any description from the United Kingdom, either generally or to any particular market,

the Director, subject to section 12 of this Act and to the following provisions of this section, may if he thinks fit make a monopoly reference to the Commission with respect to the existence or possible existence of such a monopoly situation.

(2) No monopoly reference shall be made by the Director with respect to the existence or possible existence of a monopoly situation in relation to the supply of goods or services of any description specified in Part I of Schedule 5 or in Part I of Schedule 7 to this Act.

(3) Notwithstanding anything in subsections (3) and (4) of section 10 of this Act—

(*a*) for the purposes of any monopoly reference made by the Director the supply of goods or services of any description specified in the first column of Part II of Schedule 5 or of Part II of Schedule 7 to this Act in any manner specified in relation to that description of goods or services in the second column of Part II of the relevant Schedule shall be taken to be a separate form of supply, and

(*b*) any monopoly reference made by the Director in relation to the supply of goods or services of any such description shall be limited so as to exclude that form of supply.

(4) For the purposes of any monopoly reference made by the Director in relation to goods of any description specified in the first column of Part III of Schedule 7 to this Act—

(*a*) the supply of goods of that description in Northern Ireland in any manner specified in relation to that description of goods in the second column of that Part of that Schedule shall be taken to be a separate form of supply, and, notwithstanding anything in section 10(3) and (4) of this Act, any monopoly reference so made in relation to the supply of goods of any such description in Northern Ireland shall be limited so as to exclude that form of supply, and

(*b*) for the purposes of any such monopoly reference the Director shall so exercise his powers under section 9 of this Act as to comply with the requirements of the preceding paragraph.

(5) The Secretary of State may by order made by statutory instrument vary any of the provisions of Schedule 7 to this Act, either by adding one or more further entries or by altering or deleting any entry for the time being contained in it; and any reference in this Act to that Schedule shall be construed as a reference to that Schedule as for the time being in force.

(6) On making a monopoly reference to the Commission, the Director shall send a copy of it to the Secretary of State; and if, before the end of the period of fourteen days from the day on which the reference is first published in the Gazette in accordance with section 53 of this Act, the Secretary of State directs the Commission not to proceed with the reference,—

(*a*) the Commission shall not proceed with that reference, but

(*b*) nothing in the preceding paragraph shall prevent the Commission from proceeding with any subsequent monopoly reference, notwithstanding that it relates wholly or partly to the same matters.

[150]

COMMENCEMENT

See s. 140 (1), *post*, and notes to s. 1, *ante*.

DEFINITIONS

"United Kingdom": see notes to s. 2, *ante*.
"the Director": see s. 1 (1), *ante*, or s. 137 (2), *post*.
"the Commission": see s. 4 (1), *ante*, or s. 137 (2), *post*.
"monopoly reference" and "monopoly situation": s. 5 (3).
"goods" and "supply": s. 137 (2).
"supply of services": s. 137 (3).
"services": s. 137 (4).

GENERAL NOTE

Sub-s. (1): *"A monopoly situation exists or may exist in relation to . . . the supply of goods of any description."* See s. 6, *ante*.

"A monopoly situation exists or may exist in relation to . . . the supply of services of any description." See s. 7, *ante*.

"A monopoly situation exists or may exist in relation to . . . exports of goods of any description from the United Kingdom, either generally or to any particular market." See s. 8, *ante*. The phrase "either generally or to any particular market" is otiose as it is comprehended by the definition in s. 8.

Sub-ss. (2), (3), (4): See notes to s. 10, *ante*.

Sub-s. (5): *Orders*. At the time of going to press no orders had been made under this section.

For general provision as to orders, see s. 134, *post*.

Sub-s. (6). This subsection contains a veto power for the Secretary of State. No reason need be given by the Secretary of State when exercising this power though under s. 53 (2), *post*, he must publish his direction to the Commission not to proceed with the reference in the London, Edinburgh and Belfast Gazettes or in such one as is appropriate to the reference.

It was indicated in Committee in the House of Commons that it was the then Government's intention that the power under sub-s. (6) above should be used infrequently and that reasons would be given for refusing a reference. It was further indicated that ministerial decisions on this matter would be reviewable by Parliamentary Question.

51. Monopoly references by Ministers

(1) Subject to the following provisions of this section, the Secretary of State, or the Secretary of State and any other Minister acting jointly, where it appears to him or them that a monopoly situation exists or may exist in relation to—

(*a*) the supply of goods of any description, or

(*b*) the supply of services of any description, or

(*c*) export of goods of any description from the United Kingdom, either generally or to any particular market,

may, if the Secretary of State (or, in the case of joint action by the Secretary of State and another Minister, each of them) thinks fit, make a monopoly reference to the Commission with respect to the existence or possible existence of such a monopoly situation.

(2) Where it appears to the Secretary of State that a monopoly situation exists or may exist as mentioned in the preceding subsection, and that the goods or services in question are of a description specified in Part I of, or in the first column of Part II of, Schedule 5 or Schedule 7 to this Act, the Secretary of State shall not make a monopoly reference with respect to the existence or possible existence of that situation except jointly with such one or more of the Ministers mentioned in the next following subsection as appear to him to have functions directly relating—

(*a*) to the supply of goods or services of that description in the area (whether consisting of the whole or part of the United Kingdom) in relation to which the question arises, or

(*b*) to exports of goods of that description from the United Kingdom,

as the case may be.

(3) The Ministers referred to in subsection (2) of this section are the Secretary of State for Scotland, the Secretary of State for Wales, the Secretary of State for Northern Ireland, the Secretary of State for the Environment, the Minister of Agriculture, Fisheries and Food, the Minister of Agriculture for Northern Ireland, the Minister of Commerce for Northern Ireland . . .

(4) Where it appears to the Secretary of State that a monopoly situation exists or may exist as mentioned in subsection (1) of this section in relation to the supply in Northern Ireland of goods of a description specified in the first column of Part III of Schedule 7 to this Act, the Secretary of State shall not make a monopoly reference with respect to the existence or possible existence of that situation except jointly with the Minister of Agriculture for Northern Ireland. [**151**]

COMMENCEMENT

See s. 140 (3), *post*, and notes to s. 1, *ante*.

AMENDMENT

The words omitted from sub-s. (3) at the place indicated by dots were repealed by the Ministry of Posts and Telecommunications (Dissolution) Order 1974, S.I. 1974 No. 691, art. 4 (1), Schedule.

DEFINITIONS

"the Commission": see s. 4 (1), *ante*, or s. 137 (2), *post*.
"monopoly reference" and "monopoly situation": s. 5 (3).
"goods", "Minister" and "supply": s. 137 (2).
"supply of services": s. 137 (3).
"services": s. 137 (4).

GENERAL NOTE

The powers of the Secretary of State acting alone, to make a monopoly reference, are identical with those of the Director except that the former is subject to no veto (*cf.* s. 50 (6), *ante*).

When acting together with another Minister or Ministers from the list in s. 51 (3), chosen by him on the grounds specified in s. 51 (2) (*a*) or 51 (2) (*b*) the Secretary of State has substantially wider powers than the Director since the exemptions in Part I of, or in the first column of Part II of, Schedule 5 or in Schedule 7 are not then operative: s. 51 (2) (*cf.* s. 50 (2)).

52. Variation of monopoly reference

(1) Subject to the following provisions of this section, the Director may at any time vary a monopoly reference made by him, and the Secretary of State (or, in the case of a monopoly reference made by the Secretary of State jointly with one or more other Ministers, the Secretary of State and that Minister or those Ministers acting jointly) may vary a monopoly reference made by him or them.

(2) A monopoly reference not limited to the facts shall not be varied so as to become a monopoly reference limited to the facts; but (subject to the following provisions of this section) a monopoly reference limited to the facts may be varied so as to become a monopoly reference not limited to the facts, whether the Commission have already reported on the reference as originally made or not.

(3) A monopoly reference made by the Director shall not be varied so as to become a reference which he is precluded from making by any provisions of section 50 of this Act.

(4) On varying a monopoly reference made by him, the Director shall send a copy of the variation to the Secretary of State; and if, before the end of the period of fourteen days from the day on which the variation is first published in the Gazette in accordance with the next following section, the Secretary of State directs the Commission not to give effect to the variation,—

(*a*) the Commission shall proceed with the reference as if that variation had not been made, but

(*b*) nothing in the preceding paragraph shall prevent the Commission from proceeding with any subsequent monopoly reference, or from giving effect to any subsequent variation, notwithstanding that it relates wholly or partly to the matters to which that variation related.

(5) In this section and in sections 53 to 55 of this Act "Ministers" includes the Minister of Agriculture for Northern Ireland and the Minister of Commerce for Northern Ireland. [**152**]

COMMENCEMENT

See s. 140 (3), *post*, and notes to s. 1, *ante*.

DEFINITIONS

"the Director": see s. 1 (1), *ante*, or s. 137 (2), *post*.
"the Commission": see s. 4 (1), *ante*, or s. 137 (2), *post*.
"monopoly reference": s. 5 (3).
"monopoly reference limited to the facts": s. 48.
"monopoly reference not limited to the facts": s. 49 (4).
"Minister": see s. 137 (2), *post*, and note also s. 52 (5).

GENERAL NOTE

A monopoly reference may be varied at any time by the person or persons who made it whether or not the Commission has already reported on the original reference.

By s. 52 (4) consideration by the Commission of a variation by the Director but not of one made by any other referring person can be subjected to disallowance by the Secretary of State just as, under s. 50 (6) consideration of an original reference by the Director can be disallowed (see s. 50, *ante*). A direction not to give effect to the Director's variation allows the Commission to proceed subsequently in accordance with s. 52 (4) (*a*) and (*b*).

Limits on variation of the contents of a reference:—

(i) By any person making a reference.

Under s. 52 (2) a variation cannot be made so as to take away considerations of the public interest once a reference not limited to the facts has been made. However a reference limited to the facts can be varied to one not so limited, having the effect of adding to the reference questions involving consideration of the public interest (see ss. 48, 49, *ante*).

(ii) By the Director.

S. 52 (3): In addition, the Director's power to vary, like his power to make the original reference, is subject to s. 50 (2), *ante*.

53. Publication of monopoly references and variations, and of directions relating to them

(1) On making a monopoly reference, or a variation of a monopoly reference, the Director or, as the case may be, the Secretary of State (or, in the case of a monopoly reference or variation made by the Secretary of State acting jointly with one or more other Ministers, the Secretary of State and that Minister or those Ministers acting jointly) shall arrange for the reference or variation to be published in full in the Gazette, and shall arrange for the reference or variation to be published in such other manner as he or they may think most suitable for bringing it to the attention of persons who, in his or their opinion, would be affected by it.

(2) Where the Secretary of State gives a direction under section 50(6) of this Act with respect to a monopoly reference, or gives a direction under section 52(4) of this Act with respect to a variation of a monopoly reference, the Secretary of State shall arrange for the direction to be published in the Gazette and otherwise in the same manner as the monopoly reference or variation was published in accordance with the preceding subsection.

(3) In this section "the Gazette" means the London, Edinburgh and Belfast Gazettes, except that, in relation to a monopoly reference under which consideration is limited to a particular part of the United Kingdom in accordance with section 9 of this Act (including a reference under which consideration is required to be so limited by section 50(4)(*b*) of this Act), it means such one or more of those Gazettes as are appropriate to that part of the United Kingdom.

(4) In sections 50 and 52 of this Act any reference to publication in the Gazette is a reference to publication in the London Gazette, the Edinburgh Gazette or the Belfast Gazette, whichever first occurs. [**153**]

COMMENCEMENT

See s. 140 (3), *post*, and the notes to s. 1, *ante*.

DEFINITIONS

"Secretary of State": see note to s. 1, *ante*.
"the Director": see s. 1 (1), *ante*, or s. 137 (2), *post*.
"monopoly reference": s. 5 (3).
"Minister": see s. 52 (5), *ante*, and s. 137 (2), *post*.
"the Gazette": note s. 53 (3).

GENERAL NOTE

There is provision here for publication in the Gazette at least and, in the discretion of the publisher, elsewhere, of all monopoly references, variations of such references and directions by the Secretary of State under s. 50 (6), *ante*, or s. 52 (4), *ante*.

54. Report of Commission on monopoly reference

(1) A report of the Commission on a monopoly reference—

(*a*) if the reference was made by the Director, shall be made to the Secretary of State, and

(*b*) in any other case, shall be made to the Minister or Ministers by whom the reference was made.

(2) In making their report on a monopoly reference, the Commission shall include in it definite conclusions on the questions comprised in the reference, together with—

(*a*) such an account of their reasons for those conclusions, and

(*b*) such a survey of the general position with respect to the subject-matter of the reference, and of the developments which have led to that position,

as in their opinion are expedient for facilitating a proper understanding of those questions and of their conclusions.

(3) Where, on a monopoly reference not limited to the facts, the Commission find that a monopoly situation exists and that facts found by the Commission in pursuance of their investigations under subsection (1) or subsection (2) of section 49 of this Act operate, or may be expected to operate, against the public interest, the report shall specify those facts, and the conclusions to be included in the report, in so far as they relate to the operation of those facts, shall specify the particular effects, adverse to the public interest, which in their opinion those facts have or may be expected to have; and the Commission—

(*a*) shall, as part of their investigations, consider what action (if any) should be taken for the purpose of remedying or preventing those adverse effects, and

(*b*) may, if they think fit, include in their report recommendations as to such action.

(4) In paragraph (*a*) of subsection (3) of this section the reference to action to be taken for the purpose mentioned in that paragraph is a reference to action to be taken for that purpose either—

(*a*) by one or more Ministers (including Ministers or departments of the Government of Northern Ireland) or other public authorities, or

(*b*) by the person or (as the case may be) one or more of the persons in whose favour, in accordance with the findings of the Commission, the monopoly situation in question exists.

(5) Where, on a monopoly reference not limited to the facts, the Commission find—

(*a*) that a monopoly situation exists, and

(*b*) that the person (or, if more than one, any of the persons) in whose favour it exists is a party to an agreement to which Part I of the Act of 1956 applies,

the Commission, in making their report on that reference, shall exclude from their consideration the question whether the provisions of that agreement, in so far as they are provisions by virtue of which it is an agreement to which Part I of that Act applies, operate, or may be expected to operate, against the public interest; and subsection (3) of this section, in so far as it refers to facts found by the Commission in pursuance of their investigations, shall have effect subject to the provisions of this subsection. [**154**]

COMMENCEMENT

See s. 140 (3), *post*, and notes to s. 1, *ante*.

DEFINITIONS

"monopoly reference": see ss. 47, 48 and 49, *ante*.
"operate . . . against the public interest": s. 84.
"Secretary of State": see note to s. 1, *ante*.
"the Director": see s. 1 (1), *ante*, or s. 137 (2), *post*.
"the Commission": see s. 4 (1), *ante*, or s. 137 (2), *post*.
"monopoly reference" and "monopoly situation": s. 5 (3).
"monopoly reference not limited to the facts": s. 49 (4).
"Minister": see s. 52 (5), *ante*, and s. 137 (2), *post*.
"Act of 1956": see note to s. 10, *ante*.

GENERAL NOTE

S. 54 covers the report by the Commission on a monopoly reference. The Commission's report is always made to a Minister and not to the Director though, under s. 86, *post*, the Commission must transmit to the Director a copy of a report on every monopoly reference except one that the Director is precluded from making by s. 50 (2), *ante*.

S. 88, *post*, gives the Director certain powers to act on a report so transmitted.

55. Time-limit for report on monopoly reference

(1) A monopoly reference shall specify a period within which the Commission are to report on the reference; and, if a report of the Commission on the reference—

(*a*) is not made before the end of the period so specified, or
(*b*) if one or more extended periods are allowed under the next following subsection, is not made before the end of that extended period or of the last of those extended periods, as the case may be,

the reference shall cease to have effect and no action, or (if action has already been taken) no further action, shall be taken in relation to that reference under this Act.

(2) Directions may be given—

(*a*) in the case of a monopoly reference made by the Director or by the Secretary of State otherwise than jointly with one or more Ministers, by the Secretary of State, or
(*b*) in the case of a monopoly reference made by the Secretary of State jointly with one or more other Ministers, by the Secretary of State and that Minister or those Ministers acting jointly,

allowing to the Commission such extended period for the purpose of reporting on the reference as may be specified in the directions, or, if the period has already been extended once or more than once by directions under this subsection, allowing to the Commission such further extended period for that purpose as may be so specified. [**155**]

COMMENCEMENT

See s. 140 (3), *post*, and notes to s. 1, *ante*.

DEFINITIONS

"the Director": see s. 1 (1), *ante*, or s. 137 (2), *post*.
"the Commission": see s. 4 (1), *ante*, or s. 137 (2), *post*.
"monopoly reference": s. 5 (3).
"Minister": see s. 52 (5), *ante*, and s. 137 (2), *post*.
"Secretary of State": see note to s. 2, *ante*.

GENERAL NOTE

There has hitherto in U.K. monopoly legislation been no provision for time limits for reports on monopoly references. The provision is mandatory and there will be a time limit for report in every reference made to the Commission. The limit will be set by the party, whether the Director or a Minister, making the reference. No maximum time is specified in contrast to the provision on merger references in ss. 60 and 70, *post*. Furthermore, under s. 55 (2) (*a*) the Secretary of State may direct on a reference by himself or the Director that the time specified in the reference be extended and under s. 55 (2) (*b*) the Secretary of State and a Minister or Ministers acting jointly may direct extension in a reference made by them. There may be any number of extensions under s. 55 (2).

56. Order of appropriate Minister on report on monopoly reference

(1) The provisions of this section shall have effect where a report of the Commission on a monopoly reference not limited to the facts has been laid before Parliament in accordance with the provisions of Part VII of this Act, and the conclusions of the Commission set out in the report, as so laid,—

(*a*) include conclusions to the effect that a monopoly situation exists and that facts found by the Commission in pursuance of their investigations under section 49 of this Act operate, or may be expected to operate, against the public interest, and

(*b*) specify particular effects, adverse to the public interest, which in their opinion those facts have or may be expected to have.

(2) In the circumstances mentioned in the preceding subsection the appropriate Minister may (subject to subsection (6) of this section) by order made by statutory instrument exercise such one or more of the powers specified in Parts I and II of Schedule 8 to this Act as he considers it requisite to exercise for the purpose of remedying or preventing the adverse effects specified in the report as mentioned in the preceding subsection; and those powers may be so exercised to such extent and in such manner as the appropriate Minister considers requisite for that purpose.

(3) In determining whether, or to what extent or in what manner, to exercise any of those powers, the appropriate Minister shall take into account any recommendations included in the report of the Commission in pursuance of section 54(3)(*b*) of this Act and any advice given by the Director under section 88 of this Act.

(4) Subject to the next following subsection, in this section "the appropriate Minister" means the Secretary of State.

(5) Where, in any such report as is mentioned in subsection (1) of this section, the person or one of the persons specified as being the person or persons in whose favour the monopoly situation in question exists is a body corporate fulfilling the following conditions, that is to say—

(*a*) that the affairs of the body corporate are managed by its members, and

(*b*) that by virtue of an enactment those members are appointed by a Minister, then for the purpose of making any order under this section in relation to that body corporate (but not for the purpose of making any such order in relation to any other person) "the appropriate Minister" in this section means the Minister by whom members of that body corporate are appointed.

(6) In relation to any such body corporate as is mentioned in subsection (5) of this section, the powers exercisable by virtue of subsection (2) of this section shall not include the powers specified in Part II of Schedule 8 to this Act. [**156**]

COMMENCEMENT

See s. 140 (3), *post*, and notes to s. 1, *ante*.

DEFINITIONS

"the Director": see s. 1 (1), *ante*, or s. 137 (2), *post*.
"the Commission": see s. 4 (1), *ante*, or s. 137 (2), *post*.
"monopoly reference" and "monopoly situation": s. 5 (3).
"monopoly reference not limited to the facts": s. 49 (4).
"enactment" and "Minister": s. 137 (2).
"appropriate" Minister: s. 56 (4).

GENERAL NOTE

S. 56 (1) lays down the conditions all of which must obtain before an appropriate Minister may make an order under this section. The Commission must have found that a monopoly situation exists and that it operates or may be expected to operate against the public interest and the Commission must have gone on to specify particular effects adverse to the public interest. A report which does not specify particular adverse effects cannot be the foundation of a valid order under s. 56.

Undsr s. 56 (5) and (6) where, in a report by the Commission the person or one of the persons specified as being the person or one of the persons in whose favour the monopoly situation in question exists is the board of a nationalised industry then, for the purpose of making an order against the Board the appropriate Minister is the Minister who appoints the members of that Board. The Minister cannot, in making an order against such a Board, use any of the powers listed in Part II of Sch. 8 to this Act. Against any other person the appropriate Minister is the Secretary of State and all of the powers contained in Parts I and II of Sch. 8 can be used.

S. 56 is permissive only. The Minister does not have to act on the Commission's analysis nor, though he must take them into account, on its recommendations. There is no time limit for ministerial action under s. 56. The Minister must before making an order take into account any advice given by the Director under s. 88, *post*. In practice wide and deep consultations will be entered into with persons involved in the considerations of public interest to which the report of the Commission gives rise.

As to what powers a Minister may use, assuming it has been decided that an order should be made, there is a complete discretion, subject only to the limitation described above in s. 56 (6), to use to any extent any of the powers listed in Sch. 8.

ORDERS UNDER THIS SECTION

At the time of going to press no order had been made under this section, but by virtue of s. 139 (2) and Sch. 11, para. 1, *post*, the Monopolies and Restrictive Practices (Dental Goods) Order 1951, S.I. 1951 No. 1200, the Monopolies and Restrictive Practices (Imported Hardwood and Softwood Timber) Order 1960, S.I. 1960 No. 1211, the Restrictions on Agreement's (Estate Agents) Order 1970, S.I. 1970 No. 1696, and the Regulation of Prices (Tranquillising Drugs) (No. 3) Order 1973, S.I. 1973 No. 1993, have effect as if made under this section.

For general provisions as to orders, see s. 134, *post*.

PART V

MERGERS

Newspaper merger references

57. Meaning of "newspaper", "transfer of newspaper or of newspaper assets" and related expressions

(1) In this Part of this Act—

(*a*) "newspaper" means a daily, Sunday or local (other than daily or

Sunday) newspaper circulating wholly or mainly in the United Kingdom or in a part of the United Kingdom;

(*b*) "newspaper proprietor" includes (in addition to an actual proprietor of a newspaper) any person having a controlling interest in a body corporate which is a newspaper proprietor, and any body corporate in which a newspaper proprietor has a controlling interest;

and any reference to the newspapers of a newspaper proprietor includes all newspapers in relation to which he is a newspaper proprietor and, in the case of a body corporate, all newspapers in relation to which a person having a controlling interest in that body corporate is a newspaper proprietor.

(2) In this Part of this Act "transfer of a newspaper or of newspaper assets" means any of the following transactions, that is to say—

(*a*) any transaction (whether involving a transfer or not) by virtue of which a person would become, or would acquire the right to become, a newspaper proprietor in relation to a newspaper;

(*b*) any transfer of assets necessary to the continuation of a newspaper as a separate newspaper (including goodwill or the right to use the name of the newspaper);

(*c*) any transfer of plant or premises used in the publication of a newspaper, other than a transfer made without a view to a change in the ownership or control of the newspaper or to its ceasing publication;

and " the newspaper concerned in the transfer ", in relation to any transaction falling within paragraph (*a*), paragraph (*b*) or paragraph (*c*) of this subsection, means the newspaper in relation to which (as mentioned in that paragraph) the transaction is or is to be effected.

(3) In this Part of this Act "average circulation per day of publication", in relation to a newspaper, means its average circulation for the appropriate period, ascertained by dividing the number of copies to which its circulation amounts for that period by the number of days on which the newspaper was published during that period (circulation being calculated on the basis of actual sales in the United Kingdom of the newspaper as published on those days); and for the purposes of this subsection " the appropriate period "—

(*a*) in a case in which an application is made for consent under the next following section, means the period of six months ending six weeks before the date of the application, or

(*b*) in a case in which a transfer or purported transfer is made without any such application for consent, means the period of six months ending six weeks before the date of the transfer or purported transfer.

(4) For the purposes of this section a person has a controlling interest in a body corporate if (but only if) he can, directly or indirectly, determine the manner in which one-quarter of the votes which could be cast at a general meeting of the body corporate are to be cast on matters, and in circumstances, not of such a description as to bring into play any special voting rights or restrictions on voting rights. [**157**]

COMMENCEMENT

See s. 140 (3), *post*, and the note to s. 1, *ante*.

GENERAL NOTE

"*United Kingdom.*" See notes to s. 2, *ante*.

"*This Part of this Act.*" *I.e.*, Part V (ss. 57–77) of this Act.

"*Wholly or mainly.*" See on this phrase *Re Hatschek's Patents, Ex parte Zerenner*,

[1909] 2 Ch. 68; *Miller* v. *Ottilie* (*Owners*), [1944] 1 All E.R. 277; *Berthelemy* v. *Neale*, [1952] 1 All E.R. 437, C.A., and *Franklin* v. *Gramophone Co., Ltd.*, [1948] 1 All E.R. 353, C.A. at p. 358, *per* Somervell, L.J.

"*Months.*" *I.e.*, calendar months; see the Interpretation Act 1889, s. 3.

"*Newspaper.*" National publications which are not published daily and which are not Sunday newspapers are not within the definition. Thus national weekly journals are not covered. Local publications are within the definition even if they are not published daily and are not Sunday newspapers. Local weekly journals therefore are covered provided they can be said to be newspapers.

There is no definition of "local" except that there is an implication that a publication cannot be local if it circulates in the whole of the United Kingdom.

Whether local or national, for a newspaper to qualify within the statutory definition most or all of its circulation must be in the United Kingdom or part of it.

"*Newspaper proprietor.*" This includes:

(i) an actual proprietor of a newspaper, *i.e.*, the person who owns the assets and goodwill of which a newspaper is comprised. Most actual proprietors are companies;

(ii) any person having a controlling interest in terms of ownership or control of shares in a company which is a newspaper proprietor is in turn a newspaper proprietor under s. 57 (1) (*b*).

"Controlling interest" is defined in s. 57 (4) and includes indirect control of voting rights of shareholders as well as direct ownership of voting shares;

(iii) further, a company in which a person who is a newspaper proprietor under (i) or (ii) has a controlling interest as defined in s. 57 (4) will itself be a newspaper proprietor by virtue of being so controlled;

(iv) s. 77 provides that for the purpose of determining under s. 57 (1) whether a person is a newspaper proprietor and, if so, which newspapers are that proprietor's newspapers, associated persons and any companies which they or any of them control are to be treated as one person.

"Associated persons" are defined in s. 57 (4) and the consequence of s. 57 (1) in the light of s. 77 and s. 57 (4) is that a man may be a newspaper proprietor by virtue of his wife's or his partners' or his relatives' shareholdings or control.

"Control" in this context is defined in s. 77 (5) by reference to s. 57 (5) and "relatives" by s. 77 (6).

58. Prohibition of certain newspaper mergers

(1) Subject to the following provisions of this section, a transfer of a newspaper or of newspaper assets to a newspaper proprietor whose newspapers have an average circulation per day of publication amounting, together with that of the newspaper concerned in the transfer, to 500,000 or more copies shall be unlawful and void, unless the transfer is made with written consent given (conditionally or unconditionally) by the Secretary of State.

(2) Except as provided by subsections (3) and (4) of this section and by section 60(3) of this Act, the consent of the Secretary of State under the preceding subsection shall not be given in respect of a transfer until after the Secretary of State has received a report on the matter from the Commission.

(3) Where the Secretary of State is satisfied that the newspaper concerned in the transfer is not economic as a going concern and as a separate newspaper, then—

(*a*) if he is also satisfied that, if the newspaper is to continue as a separate newspaper, the case is one of urgency, he may give his consent to the transfer without requiring a report from the Commission under this section;

(*b*) if he is satisfied that the newspaper is not intended to continue as a separate newspaper, he shall give his consent to the transfer, and shall give it unconditionally, without requiring such a report.

(4) If the Secretary of State is satisfied that the newspaper concerned in

the transfer has an average circulation per day of publication of not more than 25,000 copies, he may give his consent to the transfer without requiring a report from the Commission under this section.

(5) The Secretary of State may by order made by statutory instrument provide, subject to any transitional provisions contained in the order, that for any number specified in subsection (1) or subsection (4) of this section (whether as originally enacted or as previously varied by an order under this subsection) there shall be substituted such other number as is specified in the order.

(6) In this section "satisfied" means satisfied by such evidence as the Secretary of State may require. [**158**]

COMMENCEMENT

See s. 140 (3), *post*, and the note to s. 1, *ante*.

DEFINITIONS

"The Commission": s. 4 (1), *ante*, or s. 137 (2), *post*.
"newspaper", "newspaper proprietor": s. 57 (1), *ante*.
"transfer of a newspaper or newspaper assets" and "the newspaper concerned in the transfer": s. 57 (2), *ante*.
"average circulation per day of publication": s. 57 (3), *ante*.
"satisfied": s. 58 (6) above.

GENERAL NOTE

"*Secretary of State.*" See note to s. 1, *ante*.
"*Statutory instrument.*" See note to s. 3, *ante*.
"*Shall be unlawful . . . unless . . . made with written consent, etc.*" For provisions as to enforcement, see s. 62, *post*, and as to laying a copy of the consent before Parliament, see s. 87 (1), *post*.
"*Writing.*" See note to s. 1, *ante*.
"*Report . . . from the Commission.*" *I.e.*, a report on a reference made under s. 59, *post*.

Exceptions to the rule that newspaper mergers cannot take place without first being considered by the Commission are contained in s. 58 (3) and (4). Mergers falling within s. 58 (3) (*a*) and s. 58 (4) may be referred to the Commission. Mergers within s. 58 (3) (*b*) cannot be referred to the Commission and the Secretary of State must give his unconditional consent without such a reference.

59. Newspaper merger reference

(1) Where an application is made to the Secretary of State for his consent to a transfer of a newspaper or of newspaper assets, the Secretary of State, subject to the next following subsection, shall, within one month after receiving the application, refer the matter to the Commission for investigation and report.

(2) The Secretary of State shall not make a reference to the Commission under the preceding subsection in a case where—

(*a*) by virtue of subsection (3) of section 58 of this Act he is required to give his consent unconditionally without requiring a report from the Commission under this section, or

(*b*) by virtue of subsection (3) or subsection (4) of that section he has power to give his consent without requiring such a report from the Commission, and determines to exercise that power,

or where the application is expressed to depend on the operation of subsection (3) or subsection (4) of that section.

(3) On a reference made to them under this section (in this Act referred to as a "newspaper merger reference") the Commission shall report to the Secretary of State whether the transfer in question may be expected to operate

against the public interest, taking into account all matters which appear in the circumstances to be relevant and, in particular, the need for accurate presentation of news and free expression of opinion. [**159**]

COMMENCEMENT

See s. 140 (3), *post*, and the note to s. 1, *ante*.

DEFINITIONS

"The Commission": s. 4 (1), *ante*, or s. 137 (2), *post*.
"transfer of a newspaper or newspaper assets": s. 57 (2), *ante*.

GENERAL NOTE

"*Application is made . . . for his consent.*" Such consent is required by s. 58, *ante*.
"*Secretary of State.*" See note to s. 1, *ante*.
"*Refer the matter to the Commission etc.*" See further as to references to the Commission, Part VII (ss. 81–83) and Part VIII (ss. 84–93) of this Act, etc.
"*Report to the Secretary of State.*" Further provisions as to such reports are contained in s. 60, *post* (time-limit); s. 61, *post* (contents of report); s. 82, *post* (general provisions) and s. 83, *post* (laying before Parliament and publication); and see also s. 87 (1), *post* (laying of consent before Parliament).

60. Time-limit for report on newspaper merger reference

(1) A report of the Commission on a newspaper merger reference shall be made before the end of the period of three months beginning with the date of the reference or of such further period (if any) as the Secretary of State may allow for the purpose in accordance with the next following subsection.

(2) The Secretary of State shall not allow any further period for a report on such a reference except on representations made by the Commission and on being satisfied that there are special reasons why the report cannot be made within the original period of three months; and the Secretary of State shall allow only one such further period on any one reference, and no such further period shall be longer than three months.

(3) If on such a reference the Commission have not made their report before the end of the period specified in subsection (1) or of any further period allowed under subsection (2) of this section, the Secretary of State may, without waiting for the report, give his consent to the transfer to which the reference relates. [**160**]

COMMENCEMENT

See s. 140 (3), *post*, and the note to s. 1, *ante*.

DEFINITIONS

"Commission": s. 4 (1), *ante*, or s. 137 (2), *post*.
"newspaper merger reference": s. 59 (3), *ante*.
"Secretary of State": see note to s. 1, *ante*.

GENERAL NOTE

"*Three months beginning, etc.*": see note to s. 20, *ante*.
"*Report . . . on a newspaper merger reference.*" As to such references and reports thereon, see s. 59, *ante*, and the other relevant provisions of this Act mentioned in the notes thereto.

61. Report on newspaper merger reference

(1) In making their report on a newspaper merger reference, the Commission shall include in it definite conclusions on the questions comprised in the reference, together with—

(*a*) such an account of their reasons for those conclusions, and

(*b*) such a survey of the general position with respect to the transfer of a newspaper or of newspaper assets to which the reference relates, and of the developments which have led to that position,

as in their opinion are expedient for facilitating a proper understanding of those questions and of their conclusions.

(2) Where on such a reference the Commission find that the transfer of a newspaper or of newspaper assets in question might operate against the public interest, the Commission shall consider whether any (and, if so, what) conditions might be attached to any consent to the transfer in order to prevent the transfer from so operating, and may, if they think fit, include in their report recommendations as to such conditions. [**161**]

COMMENCEMENT

See s. 140 (3), *post*, and the note to s. 1, *ante*.

DEFINITIONS

"The Commission": s. 4 (1), *ante*, or s. 137 (2), *post*.
"transfer of a newspaper or newspaper assets": s. 57 (2), *ante*.
"newspaper merger reference": s. 59 (3), *ante*.

GENERAL NOTE

Report on a newspaper merger reference." As to such references and reports thereon, see s. 59, *ante*, and the other relevant provisions of this Act mentioned in the notes thereto.

"*Operate against the public interest.*" On the factors to be taken into account, see s. 84, *post*.

62. Enforcement provisions relating to newspaper mergers

(1) Any person who is knowingly concerned in, or privy to, a purported transfer of a newspaper or of newspaper assets which is unlawful by virtue of section 58 of this Act shall be guilty of an offence.

(2) Where under that section the consent of the Secretary of State is given to a transfer of a newspaper or of newspaper assets, but is given subject to one or more conditions, any person who is knowingly concerned in, or privy to, a breach of that condition, or of any of those conditions, as the case may be, shall be guilty of an offence.

(3) A person guilty of an offence under this section shall be liable, on conviction on indictment, to imprisonment for a term not exceeding two years or to a fine or to both.

(4) No proceedings for an offence under this section shall be instituted—

(*a*) in England or Wales, except by, or with the consent of, the Director of Public Prosecutions, or

(*b*) in Northern Ireland, except by, or with the consent of, the Director of Public Prosecutions for Northern Ireland. [**162**]

COMMENCEMENT

See s. 140 (3), *post*, and the note to s. 1, *ante*.

GENERAL NOTE

"*Any person.*" As to offences by bodies corporate, see s. 132, *post*.
"*Knowingly.*" See the note "Did not know, etc." to s. 25, *ante*.
"*Transfer of a newspaper or of newspaper assets.*" See s. 57 (2), *ante*.
"*Secretary of State.*" See the note to s. 1, *ante*.
"*Shall be guilty of an offence.*" As to time limit on prosecutions, see s. 129 (1), *post*.

"Conviction on indictment; fine." See the notes to s. 23, *ante*.

"Director of Public Prosecutions." Provision for the appointment of the Director of Public Prosecutions and of assistant directors is made by the Prosecution of Offences Act 1908, s. 1 (8 Halsbury's Statutes (3rd Edn.) 238). By s. 1 (5) thereof an assistant director may do any act or thing which the Director is required or authorised to do. See also as to evidence of his consent the Criminal Justice Act 1925, s. 34 (21 Halsbury's Statutes (3rd Edn.) 83).

Other merger references

63. Mergers references to which ss. 64 to 75 apply

(1) Sections 64 to 75 of this Act shall have effect in relation to merger references other than newspaper merger references; and accordingly in those sections "merger reference" shall be construed—

(*a*) as not including a reference made under section 59 of this Act, but

(*b*) as including any merger reference relating to a transfer of a newspaper or of newspaper assets, if the reference is made under section 64 or section 75 of this Act in a case falling within section 59(2) of this Act.

(2) In the following provisions of this Part of this Act "enterprise" means the activities, or part of the activities, of a business. [**163**]

COMMENCEMENT

See s. 140 (3), *post*, and the note to s. 1, *ante*.

DEFINITIONS

"Following provisions of this Act": i.e., ss. 64–77, *post*.
"transfer of a newspaper or of newspaper assets": s. 57 (2), *ante*.
"newspaper merger reference": s. 59 (3), *ante*.
"business": s. 137 (2), *post*.

GENERAL NOTE

This section and ss. 64–75, *post*, replace with modifications the provisions in the Monopolies and Mergers Act 1965, ss. 6, 7 (37 Halsbury's Statutes (3rd Edn.) 186, 189) relating to the reference of mergers other than newspaper mergers, to the Monopolies Commission (renamed the Monopolies and Mergers Commission by s. 4, *ante*) and their duty to report upon them.

64. Merger situation qualifying for investigation

(1) A merger reference may be made to the Commission by the Secretary of State where it appears to him that it is or may be the fact that two or more enterprises (in this section referred to as "the relevant enterprises"), of which one at least was carried on in the United Kingdom or by or under the control of a body corporate incorporated in the United Kingdom, have, at a time or in circumstances falling within subsection (4) of this section, ceased to be distinct enterprises, and that either—

(*a*) as a result, the condition specified in subsection (2) or in subsection (3) of this section prevails, or does so to a greater extent, with respect to the supply of goods or services of any description, or

(*b*) the value of the assets taken over exceeds £5 million.

(2) The condition referred to in subsection (1)(*a*) of this section, in relation to the supply of goods of any description, is that at least one-quarter of all the goods of that description which are supplied in the United Kingdom, or in a substantial part of the United Kingdom, either—

(*a*) are supplied by one and the same person or are supplied to one and the same person, or (*b*) are supplied by the persons by whom the relevant enterprises (so far as they continue to be carried on) are carried on, or are supplied to those persons.

(3) The condition referred to in subsection (1)(*a*) of this section, in relation to the supply of services of any description, is that the supply of services of that description in the United Kingdom, or in a substantial part of the United Kingdom, is, to the extent of at least one-quarter, either—

(*a*) supply by one and the same person, or supply for one and the same person, or

(*b*) supply by the persons by whom the relevant enterprises (so far as they continue to be carried on) are carried on, or supply for those persons.

(4) For the purposes of subsection (1) of this section enterprises shall be taken to have ceased to be distinct enterprises at a time or in circumstances falling within this subsection if either—

(*a*) they did so not earlier than six months before the date on which the merger reference relating to them is to be made, or

(*b*) they did so under or in consequence of arrangements or transactions which were entered into without prior notice being given to the Secretary of State or to the Director of material facts about the proposed arrangements or transactions and in circumstances in which those facts had not been made public, and notice of those facts was not given to the Secretary of State or to the Director or made public more than six months before the date mentioned in the preceding paragraph.

(5) In determining whether to make a merger reference to the Commission the Secretary of State shall have regard, with a view to the prevention or removal of uncertainty, to the need for making a determination as soon as is reasonably practicable.

(6) On making a merger reference, the Secretary of State shall arrange for it to be published in such manner as he thinks most suitable for bringing it to the attention of persons who in his opinion would be affected by it.

(7) The Secretary of State may by order made by statutory instrument provide, subject to any transitional provisions contained in the order, that for the sum specified in subsection (1)(*b*) of this section (whether as originally enacted or as previously varied by an order under this subsection) there shall be substituted such other sum (not being less than £5 million) as is specified in the order.

(8) The fact that two or more enterprises have ceased to be distinct enterprises in the circumstances described in subsection (1) of this section (including in those circumstances the result specified in paragraph (*a*), or fulfilment of the condition specified in paragraph (*b*), of that subsection) shall, for the purposes of this Act, be regarded as creating a merger situation qualifying for investigation; and in this Act "merger situation qualifying for investigation" and any reference to the creation of such a situation shall be construed accordingly.

(9) In this section "made public" means so publicised as to be generally known or readily ascertainable. [**164**]

COMMENCEMENT

See s. 140 (3), *post*, and the note to s. 1, *ante*.

DEFINITIONS

"The Director": s. 1 (1), *ante*, or s. 137 (2), *post*.

"The Commission": s. 4 (1), *ante*, or s. 137 (2), *post*.
"merger reference": ss. 5 (3) and 63 (1), *ante*.
"enterprise": s. 63 (2), *ante*.
"goods" and "supply": s. 137 (2), *post*.
"supply of services": s. 137 (3), *post*.
"services": s. 137 (4), *post*.
"the relevant enterprises": s. 64 (1), above.
"made public": s. 64 (9), above.

GENERAL NOTE

The aim of merger control legislation in the first place is negative in that the primary effect of control is to prevent two or more businesses from ceasing to be distinct enterprises. This is spelled out in the definition of "merger situation qualifying for investigation" in s. 64 (8). Under s. 64 (1) it must appear to the Secretary of State and, it is submitted, must reasonably appear—

(i) that such a disappearance of distinctness has occurred or may have occurred;
(ii) in addition, the Secretary of State must be reasonably satisfied that either of the conditions described in s. 64 (1) *(a)* or 64 (1) *(b)* obtains.

S. 64 (1) *(a)* lays down that one of the things of which the Secretary of State must be satisfied is that as a result of the ceasing of the relevant enterprises to be distinct the condition specified in s. 64 (2) or in s. 64 (3) prevails. He may also make a reference if he is satisfied that either of those conditions already obtains before the merger but is increased as a result of the merger. If the enterprises are concerned with the supply of goods, s. 64 (2) is relevant, if with services s. 64 (3) applies

S. 64 (1) *(a)* is a general provision that a monopoly situation in regard to the supply of goods or services of a particular description is produced or prevails to a greater extent as a result of the relevant merger or mergers.

As to the criteria to be adopted in arriving at a description of the goods whether by the Secretary of State in deciding whether to make a reference or by the Commission in considering one, s. 68 (4), *post*, gives an unfettered discretion, while s. 68 (1) and (2), *post*, give the Secretary of State or the Commission a discretion as to how to treat different forms of supply of a particular description of goods and s. 68 (3) does the same as regards the criterion of value to be adopted in assessing whether one-quarter of the supply is affected.

Under s. 64 (1) *(a)* the monopoly situation in question for the purposes of a merger reference may be either in the whole or in a substantial part of the U.K. and the criterion of monopoly within the area is one-quarter of the supply of the particular description of goods or services.

Furthermore a merger may be referable either where it directly produces or strengthens a monopoly situation for the companies controlling the merging enterprises (s. 64 (2) *(b)* and (3) *(b)*, *post*) or alternatively where it produces or strengthens a monopoly in the supply or purchase by persons not involved in the merger of the particular goods or services (s. 64 (2) *(a)* and (3) *(a)*, *post*). The latter result could occur where, for example, a merger resulted in an enterprise going out of business altogether, allowing a monopoly to another supplier or buyer in the industry not involved in the merger.

S. 64 (1) *(b)*. The assets "taken over" are the assets of the enterprise resulting from the ceasing to be distinct of the merging enterprises leaving out of account the assets of any enterprise remaining under the same ownership or control. If none do so remain, the assets of the enterprise with assets of the highest value must be left out of account (see s. 77 (2) *(a)*, *post*).

These assets "taken over" must exceed £5 million in value. This figure may be amended by the Secretary of State by Statutory Instrument (see s. 64 (7)). Valuation of assets must be in accordance with s. 67, *post*.

Mergers leading to the taking over of assets of value less than £5 million are not subject to statutory control unless they are caught by s. 64 (1) *(a)*—*e.g.*, in the case of the takeover of an enterprise producing more than one-quarter of the supply of a particular description of goods or services which has a low capitalisation of assets.

PARTICULAR EXPRESSIONS

Sub-s. (1): "*Merger reference.*" Further provisions relating to merger references are contained in s. 69, *post* (different kinds of reference); s. 70, *post* (time-limit for report); s. 71, *post* (variation of certain references); s. 72, *post* (report on reference); s. 73, *post* (order of Secretary of State on report); s. 74, *post* (interim orders); and s. 75, *post* (reference in anticipation of a merger); and provisions relating to references to the

Monopolies and Mergers Commission generally are contained in Part VII (ss. 81–83) and Part VIII (ss. 84–93) of this Act, *post.*

"Secretary of State." See the note to s. 1, *ante.*

"United Kingdom." See the note to s. 2, *ante.*

"Body corporate." See generally 7 Halsbury's Laws (4th edn.), paras. 82, *et seq.*

"Have . . . ceased to be distinct enterprises." In this connection, see, in addition to sub-s. (4) above, s. 65, *post,* as to when enterprises are to be regarded as ceasing to be distinct enterprises, and s. 66, *post,* as to the time when enterprises cease to be distinct.

"Value of assets taken over." As to the valuation of assets taken over, see s. 67, *post.*

Sub-s. (2): *"Supply of goods."* As to the construction of the expression in sub-s. (2) above, see s. 68 (1), (2), *post.*

"Any description." As to when goods or services can be treated for the purposes of this section as goods or services of a separate description, see s. 68 (4), *post.*

"One-quarter." As to whether this proportion is fulfilled, see s. 68 (3), *post.*

Sub-s. (3): *"Supply of services."* As to the construction of this expression in sub-s. (3) above, see s. 68 (1), (2), *post.*

"Any description." See s. 68 (4), *post,* and note above.

"One-quarter." See s. 68 (3), *post.*

Sub-s. (4): *"Months." I.e.,* calendar months; see the Interpretation Act 1889, s. 3, 32 Halsbury's Statutes (3rd Edn.) 436.

Sub-s. (7): *"Statutory instrument."* See the note to s. 3, *ante.*

65. Enterprises ceasing to be distinct enterprises

(1) For the purposes of this Part of this Act any two enterprises shall be regarded as ceasing to be distinct enterprises if either—

(*a*) they are brought under common ownership or common control (whether or not the business to which either of them formerly belonged continues to be carried on under the same or different ownership or control), or

(*b*) either of the enterprises ceases to be carried on at all and does so in consequence of any arrangements or transaction entered into to prevent competition between the enterprises.

(2) For the purposes of the preceding subsection enterprises shall (without prejudice to the generality of the words "common control" in that subsection) be regarded as being under common control if they are—

(*a*) enterprises of interconnected bodies corporate, or

(*b*) enterprises carried on by two or more bodies corporate of which one and the same person or group of persons has control, or

(*c*) an enterprise carried on by a body corporate and an enterprise carried on by a person or group of persons having control of that body corporate.

(3) A person or group of persons able, directly or indirectly, to control or materially to influence the policy of a body corporate, or the policy of any person in carrying on an enterprise, but without having a controlling interest in that body corporate or in that enterprise, may for the purposes of subsections (1) and (2) of this section be treated as having control of it.

(4) For the purposes of subsection (1)(*a*) of this section, in so far as it relates to bringing two or more enterprises under common control, a person or group of persons may be treated as bringing an enterprise under his or their control if—

(*a*) being already able to control or materially to influence the policy of the person carrying on the enterprise, that person or group of persons acquires a controlling interest in the enterprise or, in the case of an enterprise carried on by a body corporate, acquires a controlling interest in that body corporate, or (*b*) being already able materially to influence the policy of the person carrying on the enterprise, that person or group of persons becomes able to control that policy. [**165**]

COMMENCEMENT

See s. 140 (3), *post*, and the note to s. 1, *ante*.

DEFINITIONS

"enterprise": s. 63 (2), *ante*.
"group": s. 137 (2), *post*.
"interconnected bodies corporate": s. 137 (5), *post*.
"enterprises . . . brought under common ownership or common control": note the provisions in s. 77, *post*, concerning associated persons.

GENERAL NOTE

S. 65 (1) utilises the concept of "common control" of enterprises and the rest of s. 65 explains this concept.

S. 65 (2) states that, for the purposes of deciding whether there is common control of enterprises, the following types of linkage of enterprises will qualify:

(i) "enterprises of interconnected bodies corporate." This must be read in the light of s. 137 (5), *post*, and includes companies where one is a shareholder in the other and companies in which the shares are held by other holding company.

(ii) "enterprises carried on by two or more bodies corporate of which one and the same person or group of persons has control" (s. 65 (2) (*b*)).

"*Control*"; (I). This concept, in the case of an enterprise carried on by one or more bodies corporate is elaborated in s. 65 (3) to include three types of relationship between the "controller" and the company controlled:

(*a*) "material influence over policy";
(*b*) "control of policy";
(*c*) "controlling interest".

This last is not defined but presumably signifies the capacity to exercise the same power over an enterprise that a holding company can exercise over its "subsidiary" (cf. s. 154 of the Companies Act 1948).

(II). In addition the possibility of a variety of types of control of enterprises through unincorporated persons, *e.g.*, the members of a partnership, is recognised in s. 65 (5). Suppose a person, P, is able to control or materially influence the policy of the person, Q, carrying on the enterprise. P, under s. 65 (4) (*a*) will come to be in control of the enterprise if Q acquires a controlling interest in the enterprise or a controlling share interest in any company which carries on the enterprise. Suppose a person, Q, carries on an enterprise and suppose P is able materially to influence Q's policy. P is not then in control of the enterprise but becomes so under s. 65 (4) (*b*) where P becomes able to control Q's policy. Accordingly, in the above examples where P already controls one enterprise, that enterprise and the one coming into P's control will be under P's common control for the purposes of s. 65 (1) (*a*).

"*Controlling interest in a body corporate carrying on the enterprise.*" See the reference to s. 154 of the Companies Act 1948 above.

"*Controlling interest in the enterprise.*" "Enterprise" is defined in s. 63 (2) as "the activities or any part of the activities of a trade or business" and under s. 65 (1) (*a*) "any two enterprises shall be regarded as ceasing to be distinct enterprises if . . . they are brought under common ownership or common control". Where an enterprise is carried on by a person which is not a corporate body, control or ownership of that enterprise can consist in ownership of the capital assets used in the business activities of the enterprise. Accordingly transfer of such capital assets may lead to a transfer of control of the enterprise constituted by those activities and may therefore lead to a situation of control of that enterprise in common with another.

"*Person or group of persons.*" One enterprise may be controlled by person, P, another by his wife, Q. Under s. 77 (4) (*a*) P and Q are associated persons and under s. 77 (1) (*b*) associated persons shall for the purposes of s. 65 be treated as one person and therefore the two enterprises controlled by P and Q are in common control. Suppose an enterprise is controlled by X & Co. Ltd. in which P has a controlling interest and that another enterprise is controlled by Y & Co. Ltd. in which P's wife, Q, has a controlling interest. Again, by virtue of s. 77 (4) and (1) (*b*) those enterprises will be taken to be under common control for the purposes of s. 65. Where consideration of what is a controlling interest in a company is necessary under s. 77 in relation to s. 65 then under s. 77 (5) (*b*) it is defined by s. 65 (3) and (4).

Other relationships between persons which constitute them associated persons and therefore bring enterprises controlled by them or by companies in which they have a controlling interest are contained in s. 77 (4) and "relative" is defined in s. 77 (6).

Under s. 77 (2) (*b*) application of s. 77 (1) so as to constitute two or more persons one person for the purposes of s. 65 shall not be such as to exclude from s. 65 any case which otherwise would fall within s. 65. Accordingly where person, P, carries on two enterprises and passes control of one of them to his wife, Q, who controls several other enterprises, s. 77 (1) will not prevent the transferred enterprise from being taken to be controlled by Q in common with her other enterprises even though by virtue of s. 77 the transferred enterprise is still under P's control also.

66. Time when enterprises cease to be distinct

(1) Where under or in consequence of the same arrangements or transaction, or under or in consequence of successive arrangements or transactions between the same parties or interests, successive events to which this subsection applies occur within a period of two years, then for the purposes of a merger reference those events may, if the Secretary of State thinks fit, be treated as having occurred simultaneously on the date on which the latest of them occurred.

(2) The preceding subsection applies to any event whereby, under or in consequence of the arrangements or the transaction or transactions in question, any enterprises cease as between themselves to be distinct enterprises.

(3) For the purposes of subsection (1) of this section any arrangements or transactions may be treated by the Secretary of State as arrangements or transactions between the same interests if it appears to him to be appropriate that they should be so treated, having regard to the persons who are substantially concerned in them.

(4) Subject to the preceding provisions of this section, the time at which any two enterprises cease to be distinct enterprises, where they do so under or in consequence of any arrangements or transaction not having immediate effect, or having immediate effect in part only, shall be taken to be the time when the parties to the arrangements or transaction become bound to such extent as will result, on effect being given to their obligations, in the enterprises ceasing to be distinct enterprises.

(5) In accordance with subsection (4) of this section (but without prejudice to the generality of that subsection) for the purpose of determining the time at which any two enterprises cease to be distinct enterprises no account shall be taken of any option or other conditional right until the option is exercised or the condition is satisfied. [**166**]

COMMENCEMENT

See s. 140 (3), *post*, and the note to s. 1, *ante*.

DEFINITIONS

"merger reference": ss. 5 (3) and 63 (1), *ante*
"enterprise": s. 63 (2), *ante*.

GENERAL NOTE

Under s. 64 (1) and s. 64 (4) the capacity of the Secretary of State to make a valid merger reference depends on when the enterprises in question ceased to be distinct. Section 66 defines the latest time when that event can be said in law to have taken place. The key provision is s. 66 (4) which concentrates attention on the arrangements or transactions leading to a merger. Section 66 (1) allows the time on which a series of such arrangements transactions takes place to be the time when the last in the series happens, provided the series is between the "same parties or interests".

"Interests" is not defined but they are the "same" under s. 66 (3) where it appears to him appropriate to do so "having regard to the persons who are substantially concerned in them". Thus where negotiations take place between different subsidiaries of the same two holding companies, the latter will be the interests involved throughout and therefore the whole negotiation if they take place within two years will be taken to end on the last episode although different subsidiaries may have figured in them from time to time. S. 66 (5) directs that a merger dependent on the exercise of an option will not for the purposes of a reference under s. 64 be taken to have happened until the option is exercised.

Reference in anticipation of a merger. This may be made under s. 75, *post,* and in relation to such a reference this section and ss. 67, 69 and 71–74 apply as modified by s. 75 (4), *post.*

67. Valuation of assets taken over

(1) The provisions of this section shall have effect for the purposes of section 64(1)(*b*) of this Act.

(2) Subject to subsection (4) of this section, the value of the assets taken over—

(*a*) shall be determined by taking the total value of the assets employed in, or appropriated to, the enterprises which cease to be distinct enterprises, except any enterprise which remains under the same ownership and control, or if none of the enterprises remains under the same ownership and control, then that one of the enterprises having the assets with the highest value, and

(*b*) shall be so determined by reference to the values at which, on the enterprises ceasing to be distinct enterprises or (if they have not then done so) on the making of the merger reference to the Commission, the assets stand in the books of the relevant business, less any relevant provisions for depreciation, renewals or diminution in value.

(3) For the purposes of subsection (2) of this section any assets of a body corporate which, on a change in the control of the body corporate or of any enterprise of it, are dealt with in the same way as assets appropriated to any such enterprise shall be treated as appropriated to that enterprise.

(4) Where in accordance with subsection (1) of section 66 of this Act events to which that subsection applies are treated as having occurred simultaneously, subsection (2) of this section shall apply with such adjustments as appear to the Secretary of State or to the Commission to be appropriate. [**167**]

COMMENCEMENT

See s. 140 (3), *post,* and the note to s. 1, *ante.*

DEFINITIONS

"the Commission": s. 4 (1), *ante,* or s. 137 (2), *post.*
"merger reference": ss. 5 (3) and 63 (1), *ante.*
"enterprise": s. 63 (2), *ante.*
"business": s. 137 (2), *post.*

GENERAL NOTE

See the note to s. 64 (1) (*b*), *ante,* and the note under "Reference in anticipation of a merger" to s. 66, *ante.*

"*Secretary of State.*" See the note to s. 1, *ante.*

68. Supplementary provisions as to merger situations qualifying for investigation

(1) In relation to goods or services of any description which are the subject of different forms of supply—

(*a*) references in subsection (2) of section 64 of this Act to the supply of goods, or

(*b*) references in subsection (3) of that section to the supply of services,

shall be construed in whichever of the following ways appears to the Secretary of State or the Commission, as the case may be, to be appropriate in all the circumstances, that is to say, as references to any of those forms of supply taken separately, to all those forms of supply taken together, or to any of those forms of supply taken in groups.

(2) For the purposes of the preceding subsection the Secretary of State or the Commission may treat goods or services as being the subject of different forms of supply whenever the transactions in question differ as to their nature, their parties, their terms or their surrounding circumstances, and the difference is one which, in the opinion of the Secretary of State or of the Commission, as the case may be, ought for the purposes of that subsection to be treated as a material difference.

(3) For the purpose of determining whether the proportion of one-quarter mentioned in subsection (2) or subsection (3) of section 64 of this Act is fulfilled with respect to goods or services of any description, the Secretary of State or the Commission, as the case may be, shall apply such criterion (whether it be value or cost or price or quantity or capacity or number of workers employed or some other criterion, of whatever nature) or such combination of criteria as may appear to the Secretary of State or the Commission to be most suitable in all the circumstances.

(4) The criteria for determining when goods or services can be treated, for the purposes of section 64 of this Act, as goods or services of a separate description shall be such as in any particular case the Secretary of State thinks most suitable in the circumstances of that case. [**168**]

COMMENCEMENT

See s. 140 (3), *post*, and the note to s. 1, *ante*.

DEFINITIONS

"the Commission": s. 4 (1), *ante*, or s. 137 (2), *post*.
"goods", "price", "supply": s. 137 (1), *post*.
"supply of services": s. 137 (3), *post*.
"services": s. 137 (4), *post*.

GENERAL NOTE

See the note to s. 64 (1) (*a*), *ante*.

"*Secretary of State.*" See the note to s. 1, *ante*.

69. Different kinds of merger references

(1) Subject to the following provisions of this Part of this Act, on a merger reference the Commission shall investigate and report on the questions—

(*a*) whether a merger situation qualifying for investigation has been created, and

(*b*) if so, whether the creation of that situation operates, or may be expected to operate, against the public interest.

(2) A merger reference may be so framed as to require the Commission, in relation to the question whether a merger situation qualifying for investigation has been created, to exclude from consideration paragraph (*a*) of subsection (1) of section 64 of this Act, or to exclude from consideration paragraph (*b*) of that subsection, or to exclude one of those paragraphs if the Commission find the other satisfied.

(3) In relation to the question whether any such result as is mentioned in section 64(1)(*a*) of this Act has arisen, a merger reference may be so framed as to require the Commission to confine their investigation to the supply of goods or services in a specified part of the United Kingdom.

(4) A merger reference may require the Commission, if they find that a merger situation qualifying for investigation has been created, to limit their consideration thereafter to such elements in, or possible consequences of, the creation of that situation as may be specified in the reference, and to consider whether, in respect only of those elements or possible consequences, the situation operates, or may be expected to operate, against the public interest. [**169**]

COMMENCEMENT

See s. 140 (3), *post*, and the note to s. 1, *ante*.

DEFINITIONS

"this Part of this Act": *i.e.*, Part V (ss. 57–77) of this Act.
"the Commission": s. 4 (1), *ante*, or s. 137 (2), *post*.
"goods" and "supply": s. 137 (2), *post*.
"supply of services": s. 137 (3), *post*.
"services": s. 137 (4), *post*.
"merger situation qualifying for investigation" and as to the creation of such a situation: s. 64 (8), *ante*.

GENERAL NOTE

See the note under "Reference in anticipation of a merger" to s. 66, *ante*.

"*Merger reference.*" *I.e.*, a merger reference made under s. 64, *ante*. For further provisions relating to such references, cf. the note "Merger reference" to that section. See also ss. 5 (3) and 63 (1), *ante*.

"*Operates . . . against the public interest.*" For the factors to be taken into account, see s. 84, *post*.

"*United Kingdom.*" See the note to s. 2, *ante*.

70. Time-limit for report on merger reference

(1) Every merger reference shall specify a period (not being longer than six months beginning with the date of the reference) within which a report on the reference is to be made; and a report of the Commission on a merger reference shall not have effect, and no action shall be taken in relation to it under this Act, unless the report is made before the end of that period or of such further period (if any) as may be allowed by the Secretary of State in accordance with the next following subsection.

(2) The Secretary of State shall not allow any further period for a report on a merger reference except on representations made by the Commission and on being satisfied that there are special reasons why the report cannot be made within the period specified in the reference; and the Secretary of State shall allow only one such further period on any one reference, and no such further period shall be longer than three months. [**170**]

COMMENCEMENT

See s. 140 (3), *post*, and the note to s. 1, *ante*.

DEFINITIONS

"the Commission": s. 4 (1), *ante*, or s. 137 (2), *post*.
"merger reference": ss. 5 (3) and 63 (1), *ante*.

GENERAL NOTE

"*Six months beginning with.*" See the note "Three months beginning, etc." to s. 20, *ante*.

"*Report on the reference.*" See further as to such reports, s. 72, *post*.

"*No action shall be taken.*" *I.e.*, in particular no action under s. 73, *post*. See also s. 89, *post*.

"*Secretary of State.*" See the note to s. 1, *ante*.

71. Variation of certain merger references

(1) Subject to the following provisions of this section, the Secretary of State may at any time vary a merger reference made under section 69(4) of this Act.

(2) A merger reference made under section 69(4) of this Act shall not be so varied that it ceases to be a reference limited in accordance with that subsection.

(3) Without prejudice to the powers of the Secretary of State under section 70 of this Act, a merger reference shall not be varied so as to specify a period within which a report on the reference is to be made which is different from the period specified in the reference in accordance with that section. [**171**]

COMMENCEMENT

See s. 140 (3), *post*, and the note to s. 1, *ante*.

DEFINITION

"Merger reference": ss. 5 (3) and 63 (1), *ante*.

GENERAL NOTE

See the note "Reference in anticipation of a merger" to s. 66, *ante*.

"*Secretary of State.*" See the note to s. 1, *ante*.

72. Report of Commission on merger reference

(1) In making their report on a merger reference, the Commission shall include in it definite conclusions on the questions comprised in the reference, together with—

(*a*) such an account of their reasons for those conclusions, and

(*b*) such a survey of the general position with respect to the subject-matter of the reference, and of the developments which have led to that position,

as in their opinion are expedient for facilitating a proper understanding of those questions and of their conclusions.

(2) Where on a merger reference the Commission find that a merger situation qualifying for investigation has been created and that the creation of that situation operates or may be expected to operate against the public interest (or, in a case falling within subsection (4) of section 69 of this Act, find that one or more elements in or consequences of that situation which were specified in the reference in accordance with that subsection so operate or may be expected so to operate) the Commission shall specify in their report the particular effects, adverse to the public interest, which in their opinion the creation of that situation (or, as the case may be, those elements in or consequences of it) have or may be expected to have; and the Commission—

(*a*) shall, as part of their investigations, consider what action (if any) should be taken for the purpose of remedying or preventing those adverse effects, and

(*b*) may, if they think fit, include in their report recommendations as to such action.

(3) In paragraph (*a*) of subsection (2) of this section the reference to action

to be taken for the purpose mentioned in that paragraph is a reference to action to be taken for that purpose either—

(*a*) by one or more Ministers (including Ministers or departments of the Government of Northern Ireland) or other public authorities, or

(*b*) by one or more persons specified in the report as being persons carrying on, owning or controlling any of the enterprises which, in accordance with the conclusions of the Commission, have ceased to be distinct enterprises. [**172**]

COMMENCEMENT

See s. 140 (3), *post*, and the note to s. 1, *ante*.

DEFINITIONS

"public interest": s. 84, *post*.
"the Commission": s. 4 (1), *ante*, or s. 137 (2), *post*.
"merger reference": ss. 5 (3) and 63 (1), *ante*.
"enterprise": s. 63 (2), *ante*.
"merger situation qualifying for investigation": s. 64 (8), *ante*.
"Minister": s. 137 (2), *post*.

GENERAL NOTE

Further provisions on a report on a merger reference made under s. 64 are contained in s. 70, *ante* (time-limit); s. 73, *post* (order of Secretary of State on report); s. 82, *post* (general provisions); s. 83, *post* (laying before Parliament and publication); s. 86, *post* (Director General of Fair Trading to receive copy); s. 87 (2), (3), *post* (laying before Parliament of Northern Ireland); s. 88, *post* (action by Director General of Fair Trading in consequence of report) and s. 89, *post* (interim order after report).

See also the note "Reference in anticipation of a merger" to s. 66, *ante*.

73. Order of Secretary of State on report on merger reference

(1) The provisions of this section shall have effect where a report of the Commission on a merger reference has been laid before Parliament in accordance with the provisions of Part VII of this Act, and the conclusions of the Commission set out in the report, as so laid,—

(*a*) include conclusions to the effect that a merger situation qualifying for investigation has been created and that its creation, or particular elements in or consequences of it specified in the report, operate or may be expected to operate against the public interest, and

(*b*) specify particular effects, adverse to the public interest, which in the opinion of the Commission the creation of that situation, or (as the case may be) those elements in or consequences of it, have or may be expected to have.

(2) In the circumstances mentioned in the preceding subsection the Secretary of State may by order made by statutory instrument exercise such one or more of the powers specified in Parts I and II of Schedule 8 to this Act as he may consider it requisite to exercise for the purpose of remedying or preventing the adverse effects specified in the report as mentioned in the preceding subsection; and those powers may be so exercised to such extent and in such manner as the Secretary of State considers requisite for that purpose.

(3) In determining whether, or to what extent or in what manner, to exercise any of those powers, the Secretary of State shall take into account any recommendations included in the report of the Commission in pursuance of section 72(2)(*b*) of this Act and any advice given by the Director under section 88 of this Act. [**173**]

COMMENCEMENT

See s. 140 (3), *post*, and the note to s. 1, *ante*.

DEFINITIONS

"the Director": s. 1 (1), *ante*, or s. 137 (2), *post*.
"the Commission": s. 4 (1), *ante*, or s. 137 (2), *post*.
"merger reference": ss. 5 (3) and 63 (1), *ante*.
"merger situation qualifying for investigation": s. 64 (8), *ante*.
"public interest": s. 84, *post*.

GENERAL NOTE

On the question of orders of the Secretary of State see also ss. 74 and 89, *post* (interim orders); s. 90, *post* (general provisions); s. 91, *post* (procedure); s. 92, *post* (investigation of company or association with reference to order). As to enforcement, see s. 93, *post*, and see also s. 88, *post*, on possible action by the Director General of Fair Trading.

As to patents, see s. 126, *post*.

See also the note "Reference in anticipation of a merger" to s. 66, *ante*.

"*Report . . . on a merger reference.*" See s. 72, *ante*, and the other relevant provisions of this Act noted thereto.

"*Laid before Parliament . . . in accordance with . . . Part VII.* See s. 83, *post*.

74. Interim order in respect of merger reference

(1) Where a merger reference has been made to the Commission, and does not impose on the Commission a limitation under section 69(4) of this Act, then, with a view to preventing action to which this subsection applies, the Secretary of State, subject to subsection (3) of this section, may by order made by statutory instrument—

(*a*) prohibit or restrict the doing of things which in his opinion would constitute action to which this subsection applies, or
(*b*) impose on any person concerned obligations as to the carrying on of any activities or the safeguarding of any assets, or
(*c*) provide for the carrying on of any activities or the safeguarding of any assets either by the appointment of a person to conduct or supervise the conduct of any activities (on such terms and with such powers as may be specified or described in the order) or in any other manner, or
(*d*) exercise any of the powers which, by virtue of paragraph 12 of Schedule 8 to this Act, are exercisable by an order under section 73 of this Act.

(2) In relation to a merger reference the preceding subsection applies to any action which might prejudice the reference or impede the taking of any action under this Act which may be warranted by the Commission's report on the reference.

(3) No order shall be made under this section in respect of a merger reference after whichever of the following events first occurs, that is to say—

(*a*) the time (including any further period) allowed to the Commission for making a report on the reference expires without their having made such a report;
(*b*) the period of forty days beginning with the day on which a report of the Commission on the reference is laid before Parliament expires.

(4) An order under this section made in respect of a merger reference (if it has not previously ceased to have effect) shall cease to have effect on the occurrence of whichever of those events first occurs, but without prejudice to anything previously done under the order.

(5) Subsection (4) of this section shall have effect without prejudice—

(*a*) to the operation, in relation to any such order, of section 134(1) of this Act, or (*b*) to the operation of any order made under section 73 of this Act which exercises the same or similar powers to those exercised by the order under this section. [**174**]

COMMENCEMENT

See s. 140 (3), *post*, and the note to s. 1, *ante*.

DEFINITIONS

"the Commission": s. 4 (1), *ante*, or s. 137 (2), *post*.
"merger reference": ss. 5 (3) and 63 (1), *ante*.

GENERAL NOTE

See further s. 90, *post* (general provisions); s. 91, *post* (procedure); s. 92, *post* (investigation of company or association with reference to order); and s. 93, *post* (enforcement). See also s. 89, *post* (interim order after report under s. 72, *ante*).

See also note "Reference in anticipation of merger" to s. 66, *ante*.

"*Secretary of State.*" See the note to s. 1, *ante*.

"*Statutory instrument.*" See the note to s. 3, *ante*.

75. Reference in anticipation of merger

(1) A merger reference may be made to the Commission by the Secretary of State where it appears to him that it is or may be the fact that arrangements are in progress or in contemplation which, if carried into effect, will result in the creation of a merger situation qualifying for investigation.

(2) Subject to the following provisions of this section, on a merger reference under this section the Commission shall proceed in relation to the prospective and (if events so require) the actual results of the arrangements proposed or made as, in accordance with the preceding provisions of this Part of this Act, they could proceed if the arrangements in question had actually been made, and the results in question had followed immediately before the date of the reference under this section.

(3) A merger reference under this section may require the Commission, if they find that a merger situation qualifying for investigation has been created, or will be created if the arrangements in question are carried into effect, to limit their consideration thereafter to such elements in, or possible consequences of, the creation of that situation as may be specified in the reference, and to consider whether, in respect only of those elements or possible consequences, the situation might be expected to operate against the public interest.

(4) In relation to a merger reference under this section, sections 66, 67, 69, 71, 72, 73 and 74 of this Act shall apply subject to the following modifications, that is to say—

(*a*) section 66 shall apply with the necessary adaptations in relation to enterprises which will or may cease to be distinct enterprises under or in consequence of arrangements not yet carried into effect or not yet fully carried into effect;

(*b*) in section 67(4) the reference to subsection (1) of section 66 shall be construed as a reference to that subsection as modified in accordance with the preceding paragraph;

(*c*) in section 69, subsection (1) shall be construed as modified by subsection (2) of this section; in subsections (2) and (3) any reference to the question whether a merger situation qualifying for investigation has been created, or whether a result mentioned in section 64(1)(*a*) of this Act has arisen, shall be construed as including a reference to the question whether such a situation will be created or such a result will arise if the arrangements in question are carried into effect; and subsection (4) of that section shall not apply;

(*d*) in section 71, in section 72(2) and in section 74(1), the references to section 69(4) of this Act shall be construed as references to subsection (3) of this section; and

(*e*) in section 73(1), the reference to conclusions to the effect that a merger situation qualifying for investigation has been created shall be construed as including a reference to conclusions to the effect that such a situation will be created if the arrangements in question are carried into effect.

(5) If, in the course of their investigations on a merger reference under this section, it appears to the Commission that the proposal to make arrangements such as are mentioned in the reference has been abandoned, the Commission—

(*a*) shall, if the Secretary of State consents, lay the reference aside, but

(*b*) shall in that case furnish to the Secretary of State such information as he may require as to the results until then of the investigations.

[175]

COMMENCEMENT

See s. 140 (3), *post*, and the note to s. 1, *ante*.

DEFINITIONS

"merger situation qualifying for investigation": s. 64 (8), *ante*.
"preceding provisions of this Part": *I.e.*, ss. 64–74, in particular.
"public interest": s. 84, *post*.
"cease to be distinct enterprises": s. 65, *ante*.
"the Commission": s. 4 (1), *ante*, or s. 137 (2), *post*.
"merger references": ss. 5 (3) and 63 (1), *ante*.
"enterprise": s. 63 (2), *ante*.

GENERAL NOTE

"*Secretary of State.*" See the note to s. 1, *ante*.

Supplementary

76. Functions of Director in relation to merger situations

It shall be the duty of the Director—

(*a*) to take all such steps as are reasonably practicable for keeping himself informed about actual or prospective arrangements or transactions which may constitute or result in the creation of merger situations qualifying for investigation, and

(*b*) to make recommendations to the Secretary of State as to any action under this Part of this Act which in the opinion of the Director it would be expedient for the Secretary of State to take in relation to any such arrangements or transactions. **[176]**

COMMENCEMENT

See s. 140 (3), *post*, and the note to s. 1, *ante*.

DEFINITIONS

"Director": s. 1 (1), *ante*, or s. 137 (2), *post*.
"merger situation qualifying for investigation": s. 64 (8), *ante*.

GENERAL NOTE

S. 76 should be compared with s. 88, *post*, concerning action by the Director in consequence of a report on a merger reference.

77. Associated persons

(1) For the following purposes, that is to say—

(*a*) for the purpose of determining under section 57(1) of this Act whether a person is a newspaper proprietor and, if so, which newspapers are his newspapers;

(*b*) for the purpose of determining under section 65 of this Act whether any two enterprises have been brought under common ownership or common control; and

(*c*) for the purpose of determining what activities are carried on by way of business by any one person, in so far as that question arises in the application, by virtue of an order under section 73 of this Act, of paragraph 14 of Schedule 8 to this Act,

associated persons, and any bodies corporate which they or any of them control, shall (subject to the next following subsection) be treated as one person.

(2) The preceding subsection shall not have effect—

(*a*) for the purpose mentioned in paragraph (*a*) of that subsection so as to exclude from section 58 of this Act any case which would otherwise fall within that section, or

(*b*) for the purpose mentioned in paragraph (*b*) of the preceding subsection so as to exclude from section 65 of this Act any case which would otherwise fall within that section.

(3) A merger reference other than a newspaper merger reference (whether apart from this section the reference could be made or not) may be so framed as to exclude from consideration, either altogether or for any specified purpose or to any specified extent, any matter which, apart from this section, would not have been taken into account on that reference.

(4) For the purposes of this section the following persons shall be regarded as associated with one another, that is to say—

(*a*) any individual and that individual's husband or wife and any relative, or husband or wife of a relative, of that individual or of that individual's husband or wife;

(*b*) any person in his capacity as trustee of a settlement and the settlor or grantor and any person associated with the settlor or grantor;

(*c*) persons carrying on business in partnership and the husband or wife and relatives of any of them;

(*d*) any two or more persons acting together to secure or exercise control of a body corporate or other association or to secure control of any enterprise or assets.

(5) The reference in subsection (1) of this section to bodies corporate which associated persons control shall be construed as follows, that is to say—

(*a*) in its application for the purpose mentioned in paragraph (*a*) of that subsection, "control" in that reference means having a controlling interest within the meaning of section 57(4) of this Act, and

(*b*) in its application for any other purpose mentioned in subsection (1) of this section, "control" in that reference shall be construed in accordance with section 65(3) and (4) of this Act.

(6) In this section "relative" means a brother, sister, uncle, aunt, nephew, niece, lineal ancestor or descendant (the stepchild or illegitimate child of any person, or anyone adopted by a person, whether legally or otherwise, as his

child, being taken into account as a relative or to trace a relationship in the same way as that person's child); and references to a wife or husband shall include a former wife or husband and a reputed wife or husband. [**177**]

COMMENCEMENT

See s. 140 (3), *post*, and the note to s. 1, *ante*.

DEFINITIONS

"merger reference": s. 5 (3).

"newspaper" and "newspaper proprietor" and as to the newspapers of a newspaper proprietor: s. 57 (1), *ante*.

"newspaper merger reference": s. 59 (3), *ante*.

"enterprise": s. 63 (2), *ante*.

"business': s. 137 (2), *post*.

"bodies corporate which associated persons control": s. 77 (5), above.

"relative": s. 77 (6), above.

GENERAL NOTE

See the General Note to s. 65, *ante*.

"*Settlement*": "*settlor*." See 34 Halsbury's Laws (3rd Edn.) 428.

"*Partnerships*." For the criteria to be applied in determining whether a partnership exists, see the Partnership Act 1890, s. 2.

"*Reputed wife or husband*." This is a person who has the reputation of being a spouse *Ledwith* v. *Roberts*, [1937] 1 K.B. 232; [1936] 3 All E.R. 570, C.A., at p. 259 and 581 respectively, *per* Greene, L.J. The expression therefore does not cover a person living with someone of the opposite sex as if married to that person but known not to be so married.

PART VI

REFERENCES TO COMMISSION OTHER THAN MONOPOLY AND MERGER REFERENCES

78. General references

(1) The Secretary of State, or the Secretary of State and any other Minister acting jointly, may at any time require the Commission to submit to him or them a report on the general effect on the public interest—

(*a*) of practices of a specified class which, in his or their opinion, are commonly adopted as a result of, or for the purpose of preserving, monopoly situations, or

(*b*) of any specified practices which appear to him or them to be uncompetitive practices.

(2) The Secretary of State, or the Secretary of State and any other Minister acting jointly, may also at any time require the Commission to submit to him or them a report on the desirability of action of any specified description for the purpose of remedying or preventing effects, adverse to the public interest, which result or might result from monopoly situations or from any such practices as are mentioned in the preceding subsection.

(3) The matters to be taken into consideration by the Commission on any reference under this section shall not include any provisions of any agreement in so far as they are provisions by virtue of which it is an agreement to which Part I of the Act of 1956 applies. [**178**]

COMMENCEMENT

See s. 140 (3), *post*, and the note to s. 1, *ante*.

DEFINITIONS

"the Commission": s. 4 (1), *ante*, or s. 137 (2), *post*.
"monopoly situation": s. 5 (3).
"Minister", "uncompetitive practices": s. 137 (2), *post*.
"Act of 1956": see note to s. 10, *ante*.

GENERAL NOTE

s.78, which replaces the Monopolies and Mergers Act 1965, s. 5, enables Ministers but not the Director to seek from the Commission reports upon the general effect on the public interest of particular things commonly done in connection with monopoly situations or of particular uncompetitive practices or upon proposed remedies for dealing with the adverse effects of monopoly situations or of uncompetitive practices.

Reports of the Commission under s. 78 do not provide a basis for the exercise of any order making power comparable to those conferred by ss. 56 and 73, *ante*.

As to the public interest, see s. 84, *post*.

As under s. 10, *ante*, agreements subject to registration under the Restrictive Trade Practices Act 1956 are excluded from reference to the Commission.

79. References as to restrictive labour practices

(1) The Secretary of State, or the Secretary of State and any other Minister acting jointly, may at any time refer to the Commission the questions—

(*a*) whether a practice of a description specified in the reference exists and, if so, whether it is a restrictive labour practice, and

(*b*) if it exists and is a restrictive labour practice, whether it operates or may be expected to operate against the public interest and, if so, what particular effects, adverse to the public interest, it has or may be expected to have.

(2) A reference under this section may refer those questions to the Commission either—

(*a*) in relation to commercial activities in the United Kingdom generally, or

(*b*) in relation to such commercial activities in the United Kingdom as consist of the supply of goods of a description specified in the reference, or of the supply of services of a description so specified, or of the export from the United Kingdom of goods of a description so specified.

(3) The Commission shall examine any questions referred to them under this section and shall report to the Minister or Ministers who referred them to the Commission.

(4) For the purposes of their functions under subsection (3) of this section the Commission shall disregard anything which appears to them to have been done, or omitted to be done, in contemplation or furtherance of an industrial dispute within the meaning of the Industrial Relations Act 1971.

(5) In this section "restrictive labour practice" means any practice whereby restrictions or other requirements, not being restrictions or requirements relating exclusively to rates of remuneration, operate in relation to the employment of workers in any commercial activities in the United Kingdom or in relation to work done by any such workers, and are restrictions or requirements which—

(*a*) could be discontinued without thereby contravening the provisions of an enactment or of any instrument having effect by virtue of an enactment, and

(*b*) are not necessary for, or are more stringent than is necessary for, the efficient conduct of those activities. [**179**]

COMMENCEMENT

See s. 140 (3), *post*, and the note to s. 1, *ante*.

DEFINITIONS

"public interest": s. 84, *post*.
"the Commission": s. 4 (1), *ante*, and s. 137 (2), *post*.
"commercial activities in the United Kingdom", "enactment", "goods", "Minister", "practice", "supply" and "worker": s. 137 (2), *post*; and as to "worker" see also s. 137 (7), *post*.
"supply of services": s. 137 (3), *post*.
"services": s. 137 (4), *post*.
"restrictive labour practice": note s. 79 (5) above.

GENERAL NOTE

The purpose of s. 79 is to enable the Commission to investigate the existence and extent of restrictive labour practices and to make public the facts about these practices and their effects. The exclusion of rates of remuneration under s. 79 (5) and of anything done in furtherance or contemplation of an industrial dispute is intended to make it clear that the Commission is to be concerned exclusively with practices which are generally restrictive and against the public interest in a general way.

80. Variation of reference under Part VI

A reference made under this Part of this Act may at any time be varied by the Minister or Ministers by whom the reference was made. [**180**]

COMMENCEMENT

See s. 140 (3), *post*, and the note to s. 1, *ante*.

GENERAL NOTE

There is no time limit or variation under this section.
"*Reference under this Part.*" *I.e.*, a reference to the Commission under s. 78 or 79.

PART VII

PROVISIONS RELATING TO REFERENCES TO ADVISORY COMMITTEE OR TO COMMISSION

81. Procedure in carrying out investigations

(1) The Advisory Committee, in carrying out an investigation on a reference to which section 17 of this Act applies, and the Commission, in carrying out an investigation on a reference made to them under this Act (whether it is a monopolyreference or a merger reference or a reference under Part VI of this Act),—

(*a*) shall take into consideration any representations made to them by persons appearing to them to have a substantial interest in the subject-matter of the reference, or by bodies appearing to them to represent substantial numbers of persons who have such an interest, and

(*b*) unless in all the circumstances they consider it not reasonably necessary or not reasonably practicable to do so, shall permit any such person or body to be heard orally by the Advisory Committee or the Commission, as the case may be, or by a member of the Committee or of the Commission nominated by them for that purpose.

(2) Subject to subsection (1) of this section, the Advisory Committee or the Commission may determine their own procedure for carrying out any investigation on a reference under this Act, and in particular may determine—

(*a*) the extent, if any, to which persons interested or claiming to be interested in the subject-matter of the reference are allowed to be present or to be heard, either by themselves or by their representatives, or to cross-examine witnesses or otherwise take part in the investigation, and

(*b*) the extent, if any, to which the sittings of the Advisory Committee or of the Commission are to be held in public.

(3) In determining their procedure under subsection (2) of this section, and in the case of the Commission, in exercising any powers conferred on them by section 85 of this Act, the Advisory Committee or the Commission, as the case may be, shall act in accordance with any general directions which may from time to time be given to them by the Secretary of State.

(4) The Secretary of State shall lay before each House of Parliament a copy of any directions given by him under subsection (3) of this section. [**181**]

COMMENCEMENT

See s. 140 (3), *post*, and the note to s. 1, *ante*.

DEFINITIONS

"the Advisory Committee": s. 3 (1), *ante*, and s. 137 (2), *post*.
"the Commission": s. 4 (1), *ante*, and s. 137 (2), *post*.
"monopoly reference"; "merger reference": s. 5 (3).

GENERAL NOTE

"*Monopoly reference.*" As to such references, see ss. 47 *et seq.*, *ante*.

"*Merger reference.*" As to such references, see ss. 57 *et seq.* and 63 *et seq.*, *ante*.

"*Reference under Part VI of this Act.*" As to such references, see ss. 58 and 80, *ante*.

"*They consider it.*" Thus the Advisory Committee and the Commission are entitled to judge whether or not it is reasonably necessary or practicable to allow any such person to give oral evidence. Although the provision is thus rendered subjective, it seems probable that the Advisory Committee and the Commission must act reasonably.

"*Reasonably necessary.*" This expression was considered in *Re Chemists' Federation Agreement* (*No.* 2), [1958] 3 All E.R. 448. It seems as though this requirement will be satisfied if a reasonable and prudent man would be prepared to dispense with the oral evidence concerned.

"*Reasonably practicable.*" This expression was considered in *Marshall* v. *Gotham Co., Ltd.*, [1954] A.C. 360, H.L. It appears as though this requirement will be satisfied where the time, trouble and expense involved in obtaining the oral evidence would be disproportionate to the risks involved in dispensing with such evidence.

"*Or by a member of the Committee.*" This expressly empowers the Committee or the Commission to delegate the task of hearing the evidence to one of its members. The statute thus expressly excludes the application of the maxim "*delegatus non potest delegare*".

"*May determine their own procedure.*" Although the Committee and the Commission are thus given a discretion it is submitted that the procedure adopted must comply with the basic requirements of fairness and probably with the rules of natural justice as well.

"*Shall act in accordance with.*" This imposes a duty on the Commission and the Committee to comply with the directions. It is probable that any failure to comply with such directions could be used as a basis for quashing a report produced by one of those bodies.

"*Secretary of State.*" See the note to s. 1, *ante*.

"*Shall lay before each House of Parliament.*" This provision imposes a duty on the Secretary of State, it is however not clear whether the directions, and thus a report of the Commission or the Committee, could be impugned on the ground that the directions had not been laid before the Houses of Parliament—see generally *British Railways Board* v. *Pickin*, [1974] A.C. 765, H.L.

82. General provisions as to reports

(1) In making any report under this Act the Advisory Committee or the Commission shall have regard to the need for excluding, so far as that is practicable,—

(*a*) any matter which relates to the private affairs of an individual, where the publication of that matter would or might, in their opinion, seriously and prejudicially affect the interests of that individual, and

(*b*) any matter which relates specifically to the affairs of a particular body of persons, whether corporate or uncorporate, where publication of that matter would or might, in the opinion of the Advisory Committee or of the Commission, as the case may be, seriously and prejudicially affect the interests of that body, unless in their opinion the inclusion of that matter relating specifically to that body is necessary for the purposes of the report.

(2) For the purposes of the law relating to defamation, absolute privilege shall attach to any report of the Advisory Committee or of the Commission under this Act.

(3) Subject to the next following subsection, if—

(*a*) on a reference to the Advisory Committee under this Act, or

(*b*) on a reference to the Commission, other than a monopoly reference limited to the facts,

a member of the Advisory Committee or of the Commission, as the case may be, dissents from any conclusions contained in the report on the reference as being conclusions of the Committee or of the Commission, the report shall, if that member so desires, include a statement of his dissent and of his reasons for dissenting.

(4) In relation to a report made by a group of members of the Commission in pursuance of paragraph 10 or paragraph 11 of Schedule 3 to this Act, subsection (3) of this section shall have effect subject to paragraph 14(1) of that Schedule. [**182**]

COMMENCEMENT

See s. 140 (3), *post*, and the note to s. 1, *ante*.

DEFINITIONS

"The Advisory Committee"; "the Commission": s. 137 (2).
"monopoly reference limited to the facts": s. 48.

GENERAL NOTE

"*Any report under this Act.*" For such reports see s. 40, *ante* (report on consumer trade practice); s. 21, *ante* (report on consumer trade practice and on recommendations); s. 54, *ante* (report on monopoly reference); s. 61, *ante* (report on newspaper merger reference); s. 72, *ante* (report on merger reference); s. 78, *ante* (general reference); and s. 79, *ante* (reference of restrictive labour practices).

"*Shall have regard.*" This section imposes a duty on the Advisory Committee. This duty can, probably, be enforced by any person adversely affected by means of an injunction or, probably, an action for damages.

"*So far as that is practicable.*" The issue of practicability must be a question of fact to be answered in the light of all the circumstances of the particular case.

"*In their opinion.*" This wording probably has the same meaning as the somewhat fuller wording included at paragraph (*b*) of this subsection, as follows—the opinion of the Advisory Committee or of the Commission, as the case may be.

"*Unless in their opinion*", *etc.* Although the wording of this provision is not entirely clear, it seems likely that this restriction governs both paragraph (*a*) and paragraph (*b*).

"*Reference to the Advisory Committee.*" Such a reference may be made under either s. 14 or 17, *ante*.

"*Reference to the Commission.*" Such references may be made under ss. 47, 57, 63, 78 and 79, *ante*.

"*Other than a monopoly reference limited to the facts.*" See the definition in s. 48, *ante*.

"*In relation to a report*", *etc.* Where the functions of the Commission are performed by a group of members, rather than by the Commission as a whole, no member of the Commission who is not a member of the group is entitled to have a statement of his dissent from a conclusion of the group included in a report made by them.

83. Laying before Parliament and publication of reports

(1) The Minister or Ministers to whom any report of the Advisory Committee on a reference to which section 17 of this Act applies, or any report of the Commission under this Act, is made shall lay a copy of the report before each House of Parliament, and shall arrange for the report to be published in such manner as appears to the Minister or Ministers to be appropriate.

(2) If such a report is presented by command of Her Majesty to either House of Parliament otherwise than at or during the time of a sitting of that House, the presentation of the report shall for the purposes of this section be treated as the laying of a copy of it before that House by the Minister or Ministers to whom the report was made.

(3) If it appears to the Minister or Ministers to whom any report of the Advisory Committee or of the Commission under this Act is made that the publication of any matter in the report would be against the public interest, the Minister or Ministers shall exclude that matter from the copies of the report as laid before Parliament and from the report as published under this section.

(4) Any reference in this Act to a report of the Advisory Committee or of the Commission as laid before Parliament shall be construed as a reference to the report in the form in which copies of it are laid (or by virtue of subsection (2) of this section are treated as having been laid) before each House of Parliament under this section. [**183**]

COMMENCEMENT

See s. 140 (3), *post*, and the note to s. 1, *ante*.

DEFINITIONS

"Advisory Committee'; "the Commission"; "Minister": s. 137 (2), *post*.

GENERAL NOTE

"Reference to which Section 17 of this Act applies." This provision does not apply to a report made by the Advisory Committee on a reference under s. 14, *ante*.

"Any report of the Commission." For the references upon which Reports might be made see the note to s. 82, *ante*.

"Lay a copy of the report." For meaning, see the Laying of Documents before Parliament (Interpretation) Act, 1948, s. 1 (1), and for supplementary provisions see also s. 87, *post*.

"Such manner as appears to the Minister or Ministers." The Minister is thus entrusted with a discretion as to the manner of publication but this discretion must probably be exercised reasonably—see *Padfield* v. *Minister of Agriculture*, [1968] A.C. 997, and *Secretary of State for Employment* v. *Associated Society of Locomotive Engineers and Firemen* (*No.* 2), [1972] 2 Q.B. 455.

"If it appears to the Minister." Thus the test is again made subjective and is probably again subject to the obligation to act reasonably—see the previous note.

"The public interest." This expression was best defined in *Duncan* v. *Cammell Laird & Co.*, [1942] A.C. 624 at p. 642. The expression includes those circumstances in which publication would be injurious to national defence or to good diplomatic relations or where secrecy is essential for the proper functioning of the public service.

PART VIII

ADDITIONAL PROVISIONS RELATING TO REFERENCES TO COMMISSION

84. Public interest

(1) In determining for any purposes to which this section applies whether any particular matter operates, or may be expected to operate, against the public interest, the Commission shall take into account all matters which appear to them in the particular circumstances to be relevant and, among other things, shall have regard to the desirability—

(*a*) of maintaining and promoting effective competition between persons supplying goods and services in the United Kingdom;

(*b*) of promoting the interests of consumers, purchasers and other users of goods and services in the United Kingdom in respect of the prices charged for them and in respect of their quality and the variety of goods and services supplied;

(*c*) of promoting, through competition, the reduction of costs and the development and use of new techniques and new products, and of facilitating the entry of new competitors into existing markets;

(*d*) of maintaining and promoting the balanced distribution of industry and employment in the United Kingdom; and

(*e*) of maintaining and promoting competitive activity in markets outside the United Kingdom on the part of producers of goods, and of suppliers of goods and services, in the United Kingdom.

(2) This section applies to the purposes of any functions of the Commission under this Act other than functions to which section 59(3) of this Act applies. **[184]**

COMMENCEMENT

See s. 140 (3), *post*, and the note to s. 1, *ante*.

DEFINITIONS

"the Commission": s. 4 (1), *ante*, or s. 137 (2), *post*.
"consumer", "goods", "price" and "supply": s. 137 (2), *post*.
"consumer": see also s. 137 (6), *post*.
"supply of services": s. 137 (3), *post*.
"services": s. 137 (4), *post*.

GENERAL NOTE

Under s. 84 (2) the public interest guidelines in s. 84 (1) apply for the purposes of all functions of the Commission under this Act except the consideration of newspaper mergers, for which a different set of criteria is provided in s. 59 (3), *ante*.

In all other functions of the Commission, it is enjoined by s. 84 (1) merely to take the desirability of the various factors listed into account. The list in s. 84 (1) (*a*) to (*e*) is therefore not exhaustive and furthermore the alleged monopolist or those contemplating a merger are not compelled to prove that they will bring about a positive benefit before the Commission's approval can be secured (cf. s. 21 of the Restrictive Trade Practices Act 1956). Accordingly the fact that the desirability of maintaining competition and the interests of consumers are now expressly included is not so very significant.

85. Attendance of witnesses and production of documents

(1) For the purposes of any investigation on a reference made to them under this Act the Commission may, by notice in writing signed on their behalf by any of their members or by their secretary,—

(*a*) require any person to attend at a time and place specified in the notice, and to give evidence to the Commission or a member of the Commission nominated by them for the purpose, or

(*b*) require any person to produce, at a time and place specified in the notice, to the Commission or to any person nominated by the Commission for the purpose, any documents which are specified or described in the notice and which are documents in his custody or under his control and relating to any matter relevant to the investigation, or

(*c*) require any person carrying on any business to furnish to the Commission such estimates, returns or other information as may be specified or described in the notice, and specify the time, the manner and the form in which any such estimates, returns or information are to be furnished.

(2) For the purposes of any such investigation the Commission, or a member of the Commission nominated by them for that purpose, may take evidence on oath, and for that purpose may administer oaths.

(3) No person shall be compelled for the purpose of any such investigation to give any evidence or produce any document which he could not be compelled to give or produce in civil proceedings before the court or, in complying with any requirement for the furnishing of information, to give any information which he could not be compelled to give in evidence in such proceedings.

(4) No person shall be required, in obedience to a notice under subsection (1) of this section, to go more than ten miles from his place of residence unless the necessary expenses of his attendance are paid or tendered to him.

(5) Any person who refuses or, without reasonable excuse, fails to do anything duly required of him by a notice under subsection (1) of this section shall be guilty of an offence and liable on summary conviction to a fine not exceeding £400.

(6) Any person who—

(*a*) wilfully alters, suppresses or destroys any document which he has been required by any such notice to produce, or

(*b*) in furnishing any estimate, return or other information required of him under any such notice, makes any statement which he knows to be false in a material particular or recklessly makes any statement which is false in a material particular,

shall be guilty of an offence and liable on summary conviction to a fine not exceeding £400 or, on conviction on indictment, to imprisonment for a term not exceeding two years or to a fine or to both.

(7) If a person makes default in complying with a notice under subsection (1) of this section, the court may, on the application of the Secretary of State, make such order as the court thinks fit for requiring the default to be made good; and any such order may provide that all the costs or expenses of and incidental to the application shall be borne by the person in default or by any officers of a company or other association who are responsible for its default.

(8) In this section "the court"—

(*a*) in relation to England and Wales, means the High Court;

(*b*) in relation to Scotland means the Court of Session; and

(*c*) in relation to Northern Ireland, means the High Court or a judge of the High Court. [**185**]

COMMENCEMENT

See s. 140 (3), *post*, and the note to s. 1, *ante*.

DEFINITIONS

"The Commission": s. 4 (1), *ante*, or s. 137 (2), *post*.
"business": s. 137 (2), *post*.
"court": note s. 85 (8), above.

GENERAL NOTE

The Commission by notice in writing can compel persons and firms to provide information for the purposes of an investigation. Its powers of compulsion are those available in the High Court. The Commission and any of its members have power to take evidence on oath.

Information which can be demanded by the Commission may be in documentary form. If so it can insist on the production of the documents. It can also insist on the attendance of witnesses and on the giving of evidence by witnesses called. The Commission's notice may also require the production of estimates. Precise information on certain aspects of a business may not always be available and records may not be available either so that an estimate has to be made. S. 85 (1) (*c*) empowers the Commission to seek an estimate from a party being investigated so that the Commission is not forced to make its own estimate though it can still do that.

Enforcement. S. 85 (5) covers refusal or failure to provide the required information. This is punishable summarily by way of fine only and is not an indictable offence.

S. 85 (6) covers the provision of false information deliberately or recklessly and this is punishable summarily by way of a fine or on indictment by way of a fine or imprisonment or both.

Where the conviction under s. 85 (5) or (6) is summary the fine imposed cannot exceed £400.

In relation to s. 85 (6) see also s. 132, *post*.

In addition, under s. 85 (7) the Secretary of State can apply in one of the courts listed in s. 85 (8) for an order for requiring any default in providing information requested by the Commission to be made good. Refusal to comply with such an order could be a contempt of the court making it.

The Commission's powers under s. 85 (1) (*a*) and (*b*) are available against "any person" and under s. 85 (1) (*c*) against "any person carrying on any business". By s. 81 (3) (and see also 81 (4)) the Commission in exercising their powers under s. 85 must act in accordance with any directions given by the Secretary of State.

As to restrictions on disclosure of any information obtained by virtue of s. 85, see s. 133, *post*.

As to the procedure of the Commission in carrying out investigations, see s. 81, *ante*.

"Reference . . . under this Act." See ss. 47 *et seq.*, 57 *et seq.*, 63 *et seq.*, 78 and 79, *ante*.

"Writing." See the note to s. 1, *ante*.

"Oath." In the case of a person allowed in law to affirm or declare, this includes affirmation and declaration; see the Interpretation Act 1889, s. 3.

"Ten miles." Any distance is, unless the contrary indication appears, to be measured in a straight line on a horizontal plane; see the Interpretation Act 1889, s. 34.

"Shall be guilty of an offence." As to time limit on prosecutions, see s. 129, *post*.

"Summary conviction." See note to s. 23, *ante*.

"Any person." As to offences by bodies corporate under s. 85 (6), see s. 132, *post*.

"Wilfully"; "false." See notes to s. 30, *ante*.

"Knows." See note "Did not know, etc." to s. 25, *ante*.

"Material particular"; "recklessly." See notes to s. 46, *ante*.

"Summary conviction"; "conviction on indictment"; fine." See the notes to s. 23, *ante*.

"Secretary of State." See the note to s. 1, *ante*.

86. Director to receive copies of reports

(1) Subject to the next following subsection, a copy of every report of the Commission on a monopoly reference, or on a merger reference other than a newspaper merger reference, shall be transmitted by the Commission to the Director; and the Minister or Ministers to whom any such report is made shall take account of any advice given to him or them by the Director with respect to a report of which a copy is transmitted to the Director under this section.

(2) The preceding subsection shall not apply to a report made on a monopoly reference, where the reference was made by a Minister or Ministers and (by virtue of any of the provisions of section 50 of this Act) could not have been made by the Director.

(3) In this section "Minister" includes the Minister of Agriculture for Northern Ireland and the Minister of Commerce for Northern Ireland. [**186**]

COMMENCEMENT

See s. 140 (3), *post*, and the note to s. 1, *ante*.

DEFINITIONS

"Report . . . on a monopoly reference, or, on a merger reference, etc": see in particular ss. 54 and 72, *ante*.

"The Director": s. 1 (1), *ante*, or s. 137 (2), *post*.

"The Commission": s. 4 (1), *ante*, or s. 137 (2), *post*.
"monopoly reference" and "merger reference": s. 5 (3), *ante*.
"newspaper merger reference": s. 59 (3), *ante*.
"minister": s. 137 (2), *post*, and note s. 86 (3) above.

GENERAL NOTE

See the General Note to s. 54, *ante*.

87. Supplementary provisions as to laying reports before Parliament

(1) Where under section 83 of this Act the Secretary of State lays before Parliament a copy of a report of the Commission on a newspaper merger reference, then—

(*a*) if before laying it the Secretary of State has consented to the transfer of a newspaper or of newspaper assets to which the report relates, he shall annex a copy of that consent to the copy of the report laid before Parliament, or

(*b*) if he subsequently consents to that transfer, he shall thereupon lay before Parliament a copy of that consent.

(2) Where the persons to whom a report of the Commission is made under this Act include the Minister of Agriculture for Northern Ireland, that Minister shall lay a copy of the report before the Senate and House of Commons of Northern Ireland, and shall arrange for it to be published in Northern Ireland in such manner as appears to him to be appropriate.

(3) If a report to which subsection (2) of this section applies is presented by command of the Governor of Northern Ireland to the Senate or House of Commons of Northern Ireland otherwise than at or during the time of a sitting of the Senate or of that House, as the case may be, the presentation of the report shall for the purposes of that subsection be treated as the laying of a copy of it before the Senate or that House as required by that subsection. [**187**]

COMMENCEMENT

See s. 140 (3), *post*, and the note to s. 1, *ante*.

DEFINITIONS

"The Commission": s. 4 (1), *ante*, or s. 137 (2), *post*.
"transfer of a newspaper or of newspaper assets": s. 57 (2), *ante*.
"newspaper merger reference": s. 59 (3), *ante*.

GENERAL NOTE

Sub-s. (1): *"Secretary of State."* See note to s. 1, *ante*.
"Lays before Parliament." See the note to s. 83, *ante*.
"Report of the Commission." See in particular ss. 54, 61 and 72, *ante*.
"Consented to the transfer of a newspaper, etc." Such consent is required by s.58, *ante*.
Sub-s. (2): *Lay before the Senate; presented . . . to the Senate*. These are to be construed as references to laying or presenting before or to the Northern Ireland Assembly; see the Northern Ireland Constitution Act 1973, s. 40 (1), Sch. 5, para. 3 (2). But, by the Northern Ireland Act 1974, s. 1 (2), that Assembly is prorogued pending dissolution, and by *ibid.*, s. 1 (3), Sch. 1, para. 3 (4), so much of any enactment as makes the taking of any step conditional on the laying of any document before the Assembly is not to apply during the interim period defined by s. 1 (4) of that Act.

88. Action by Director in consequence of report of Commission on monopoly or merger reference

(1) Where a report of the Commission on a monopoly reference, or on a merger reference other than a newspaper merger reference, as laid before Parliament,—

(*a*) in the case of a monopoly reference, sets out such conclusions as are mentioned in section 56(1) of this Act, or (*b*) in the case of a merger reference, sets out such conclusions as are mentioned in section 73(1) or in section 75(4)(*e*) of this Act,

and a copy of the report is transmitted to the Director under section 86 of this Act, it shall be the duty of the Director, if requested by the appropriate Minister or Ministers to do so, to consult the relevant parties with a view to obtaining from them undertakings to take action indicated in the request made to the Director as being action requisite, in the opinion of the appropriate Minister or Ministers, for the purpose of remedying or preventing the adverse effects specified in the report.

(2) The Director shall report to the appropriate Minister or Ministers the outcome of his consultations under the preceding subsection; and if any undertaking is given by any of the relevant parties to take action indicated in the request made to the Director as mentioned in that subsection (in this section referred to as an "appropriate undertaking") the Minister to whom the undertaking is given shall furnish particulars of it to the Director.

(3) Where in his consultations under subsection (1) of this section the Director seeks to obtain an appropriate undertaking from any of the relevant parties, and either—

(*a*) he is satisfied that no such undertaking is likely to be given by that party within a reasonable time, or

(*b*) having allowed such time as in his opinion is reasonable for the purpose, he is satisfied that no such undertaking has been given by that party,

the Director shall give such advice to the appropriate Minister or Ministers as he may think proper in the circumstances (including, if the Director thinks fit, advice with respect to the exercise by the appropriate Minister or Ministers of his or their powers under section 56 or section 73 of this Act, as the case may be).

(4) Where the Director has made a report under subsection (2) of this section, and particulars of an undertaking given by any of the relevant parties have been furnished to the Director in accordance with that subsection, it shall be the duty of the Director—

(*a*) to keep under review the carrying out of that undertaking, and from time to time to consider whether, by reason of any change of circumstances, it needs to be varied or to be superseded by a new undertaking, and

(*b*) if it appears to him that it has not been or is not being fulfilled, or needs to be varied or superseded, to give such advice to the appropriate Minister or Ministers as he may think proper in the circumstances.

(5) Where, in consequence of a report of which a copy is transmitted to the Director under section 86 of this Act, an order is made under section 56 or section 73 of this Act in relation to any of the matters to which the report relates, it shall be the duty of the Director to keep under review the action (if any) taken in compliance with that order, and from time to time to consider whether, by reason of any change of circumstances, the order should be varied or should be superseded by a new order, and—

(*a*) if it appears to him that the order has in any respect not been complied with, to consider whether any action (by way of proceedings in accordance with section 93 of this Act or otherwise) should be taken for the purpose of securing compliance with the order, and (where in his opinion it is appropriate to do so) to take such action himself or give advice to any Minister or other person by whom such action might be taken, or

(*b*) if it appears to him that the order needs to be varied, or to be superseded by a new order, to give such advice to the appropriate Minister or Ministers as he may think proper in the circumstances.

(6) In this section "the relevant parties"—

(*a*) in relation to a report of the Commission on a monopoly reference, means the person or persons specified in the report as being the person or persons in whose favour the monopoly situation in question exists;

(*b*) in relation to a report of the Commission on a merger reference under section 75 of this Act, which includes a finding that a merger situation qualifying for investigation will be created if the arrangements in question are carried into effect, means any person indicated in the report as being a person by whom in accordance with the arrangements any assets are to be taken over;

(*c*) in relation to a report of the Commission on a merger reference, other than a newspaper merger reference, or a reference falling within paragraph (*b*) of this subsection, means the persons specified in the report as being persons carrying on, owning or controlling any of the enterprises which, in accordance with the conclusions of the Commission, have ceased to be distinct enterprises;

and, in relation to a report of the Commission, "the appropriate Minister or Ministers" means the Minister or Ministers to whom the report is made, "undertaking" means an undertaking given to that Minister or to one of those Ministers, as the case may be, and, in subsections (3) and (5) of this section, the references to section 73 of this Act shall be construed as including references to that section as applied by section 75(4) of this Act. **[188]**

COMMENCEMENT

See s. 140 (3), *post*, and the note to s. 1, *ante*.

DEFINITIONS

"the Director": s. 1 (1), *ante*, and s. 137 (2), *post*.
"the Commission": s. 4 (1), *ante*, or s. 137 (2), *post*
"monopoly reference", "merger reference" and "monopoly situation": s. 5 (3), *ante*.
"newspaper merger reference": s. 59 (3), *ante*.
"merger situation qualifying for investigation": s. 64 (8), *ante*.
"Minister": s. 137 (2), *post*.
Note as to "appropriate undertaking" s. 88 (2) above and as to "the relevant parties", "the appropriate Minister or Ministers" and "undertaking" s. 88 (6) above.

GENERAL NOTE

S. 88 makes provision for undertakings to be given to the Director following a report of the Commission which contains conclusions as to the existence of a monopoly situation and its adverse effects in specified ways on the public interest.

The Director can only seek undertakings when requested to do so by the Minister to whom the report is made. No time limit is placed on the Director's endeavours and if, having sought and failed to get a promise of proper undertakings within a reasonable time he must advise the Minister accordingly. His advice may include the exercise by the Minister of powers to make orders under s. 56 or s. 73 of this Act.

If the Minister is, after the report and after a request for undertakings has been made by the Director, given undertakings, he must disclose them to the Director. To that extent the Minister's discretion is subject to the Director's scrutiny.

The Director is given powers to supervise the carrying out of undertakings given and accepted and also action needed to comply with a ministerial order under s. 56 or s. 73. If he, in either case, notes slack or non-compliance he must advise the Minister. Failure to carry out undertakings will probably result in the Director recommending an order. He can also agree to vary the undertaking when that is needed for perfectly bona fide reasons.

PARTICULAR EXPRESSIONS

Report . . . on a monopoly reference or on a merger reference, etc." See ss. 54 and 72, *ante*.

"*Laid before Parliament.*" I.e., under s. 83, *ante*.

"*Consult.*" See the note "After consulting" to s. 20, *ante*.

"*Ceased to be distinct enterprises.*" See s. 65, *ante*.

FURTHER PROVISIONS

See ss. 44–46, *ante*, concerning the powers of the Director General to require information concerning monopoly situations and s. 76, *ante*, concerning the functions of the Director in relation to merger situations.

See also Sch. 11, paras. 9, 10, *post*, in respect of reports made under the Monopolies and Restrictive Practices (Inquiry and Control) Act 1948 or the Monopolies and Mergers Act 1965.

89. Interim order after report of Commission under s. 54 or s. 72

(1) The provisions of this section shall have effect where—

(*a*) in the circumstances specified in subsection (1) of section 56 of this Act the Secretary of State makes, or has under consideration the making of, an order under that section exercising any of the powers specified in Part II of Schedule 8 to this Act, or

(*b*) in the circumstances specified in subsection (1) of section 73 of this Act the Secretary of State makes, or has under consideration the making of, an order under that section exercising any of those powers;

and in those provisions "the principal order" means the order which the Secretary of State makes, or has it under consideration to make, as mentioned in paragraph (*a*) or paragraph (*b*) of this subsection.

(2) With a view to achieving the purpose for which any of the powers specified in Part II of that Schedule are, or are proposed to be, exercised by the principal order, the Secretary of State may by order made by statutory instrument exercise any of the powers mentioned in the next following subsection.

(3) An order under this section may—

(*a*) prohibit or restrict the doing of things which, in the opinion of the Secretary of State, might impede the operation of the principal order or, where it has not yet been made, might be an impediment to making it;

(*b*) impose on any person concerned obligations as to the carrying on of any activities or the safeguarding of any assets;

(*c*) provide for the carrying on of any activities or the safeguarding of any assets either by the appointment of a person to conduct or supervise the conduct of any activities (on such terms and with such powers as may be specified or described in the order under this section) or in any other manner. [**189**]

COMMENCEMENT

See s. 140 (3), *post*, and the note to s. 1, *ante*.

GENERAL NOTE

The Secretary of State is given the powers listed in s. 89 (3) where he makes or is considering making an order under s. 56 or s. 73, *ante*. The powers are ancillary and intended to prevent actions or inaction which renders the principal order difficult or impossible to execute.

"*Secretary of State.*" See the note to s. 1, *ante*.

"*Statutory instrument.*" See the note to s. 3, *ante*.

90. General provisions as to orders under ss. 56, 73, 74 and 89

(1) This section applies to any order under section 56, section 73, section 74 or section 89 of this Act.

(2) Any such order declaring anything to be unlawful may declare it to be unlawful either for all persons or for such persons as may be specified or described in the order.

(3) Nothing in any such order shall have effect so as to apply to any person in relation to his conduct outside the United Kingdom unless that person is—

(*a*) a citizen of the United Kingdom and Colonies, or
(*b*) a body corporate incorporated under the law of the United Kingdom or of a part of the United Kingdom, or
(*c*) a person carrying on business in the United Kingdom, either alone or in partnership with one or more other persons,

but, in the case of a person falling within paragraph (*a*), paragraph (*b*) or paragraph (*c*) of this subsection, any such order may extend to acts or omissions outside the United Kingdom.

(4) An order to which this section applies may extend so as to prohibit the carrying out of agreements already in existence on the date on which the order is made.

(5) Nothing in any order to which this section applies shall have effect so as to restrict the doing of anything for the purpose of restraining an infringement of a United Kingdom patent or so as to restrict any person as to the conditions which he attaches to a licence to do anything the doing of which would, but for the licence, be an infringement of a United Kingdom patent.

(6) Nothing in any such order shall affect the conduct of a board established under a scheme made under the Agricultural Marketing Act 1958 or under the Agricultural Marketing Act (Northern Ireland) 1964.

(7) An order to which this section applies may authorise the Minister making the order to give directions to a person specified in the directions, or to the holder for the time being of an office so specified in any company or association,—

(*a*) to take such steps within his competence as may be specified or described in the directions for the purpose of carrying out, or securing compliance with, the order, or
(*b*) to do or refrain from doing anything so specified or described which he might be required by the order to do or refrain from doing,

and may authorise that Minister to vary or revoke any directions so given. [**190**]

COMMENCEMENT

See s. 140 (3), *post*, and the note to s. 1, *ante*.

DEFINITIONS

"Agreement", "business" and "Minister": s. 137 (2), *post*.

GENERAL NOTE

S. 90 (3) allows an extraterritorial effect to orders under the Act provided one of the conditions in (*a*), (*b*) or (*c*) is fulfilled.

S. 90 (4) provides that orders under the Act can affect agreements in existence before the order was made. An order cannot be invalidated for being retroactive therefore.

S. 90 (5) permits holders of U.K. patents or licensors of patented processes to protect their patents or licences despite possible infringement of an order under this Act.

PARTICULAR EXPRESSIONS

"*United Kingdom.*" See note to s. 2, *ante*.

"*Citizen of the United Kingdom and Colonies.*" Citizenship of the United Kingdom and Colonies is mainly governed by the British Nationality Act 1948, ss. 4 *et seq.* (1 Halsbury's Statutes (3rd Edn.) 866 *et seq.*).

"*Body corporate.*" See the note to s. 38, *ante*.

"Carrying on business." These words connote something of a permanent character not merely an isolated transaction, and a business is carried on only where there is some degree of management or control; see *Brown* v. *London and North Western Rail. Co.* (1863), 32 L.J.Q.B. 318; [1861–73] All E.R. Rep. 487; *Graham* v. *Lewis* (1888), 22 Q.B.D. 1, C.A.; and *Cain* v. *Butler*, [1916] 1 K.B. 759, at 766; but contrast *Cornelius* v. *Philips*, [1918] A.C. 199; [1916–17] 1 All E.R. Rep. 685.

"Restraining an infringement of a . . . patent." As to proceedings for infringement of a patent see the Patents Act 1949, ss. 59 *et seq.* (24 Halsbury's Statutes 615 *et seq.*) and note special provisions as to patents in s. 126, *post.*

"Directions." As to the enforcement of directions given under s. 90 (7), see s. 93 (3)–(5), *post.*

Agricultural Marketing Act 1958. See 1 Halsbury's Statutes 460.

Agriculture Marketing Act (*Northern Ireland*) 1964. 1964 c. 13 (N.I.).

91. Procedure relating to orders to which s. 90 applies

(1) No order to which section 90 of this Act applies and which exercises any of the powers specified in Part II of Schedule 8 to this Act, and no order varying or revoking any such order, shall be made unless a draft of the order has been laid before Parliament and approved by a resolution of each House of Parliament; and the provisions of Schedule 9 to this Act shall have effect with respect to the procedure to be followed before laying before Parliament a draft of any such order.

(2) Before making any order under section 56 or section 73 of this Act other than any such order as is mentioned in the preceding subsection, the Minister proposing to make the order shall publish, in such manner as appears to him to be appropriate, a notice—

(*a*) stating his intention to make the order;

(*b*) indicating the nature of the provisions to be embodied in the order; and

(*c*) stating that any person whose interests are likely to be affected by the order, and who is desirous of making representations in respect of it, should do so in writing (stating his interest and the grounds on which he wishes to make the representations) before a date specified in the notice (that date being not earlier than the end of the period of thirty days beginning with the day on which publication of the notice is completed);

and the Minister shall not make the order before the date specified in the notice in accordance with paragraph (*c*) of this subsection and shall consider any representations duly made to him in accordance with the notice before that date.

[191]

COMMENCEMENT

See s. 140 (3), *post*, and the note to s. 1, *ante*.

DEFINITION

"Minister": s. 137 (2), *post.*

GENERAL NOTE

The powers specified in Part II of Schedule 8 are powers of divestment and are exercisable by a Minister making an order under s. 56 in all cases except in respect of nationalised industries which fall within s. 56 (6) when only the powers specified in Part I of Schedule 8 are exercisable. In an order under s. 56 powers in Part I of Sch. 8 are always exercisable and in an order under s. 73 powers in Parts I and II are all exercisable without exception.

An order exercising Part II powers is covered by s. 91 (1) and the procedure therein together with Schedule 9 must be followed in relation to such an order.

An order exercising Part I powers is within s. 91 (2) which prescribes the procedure appropriate to such an order.

"Laid before Parliament." See the Laying of Documents before Parliament (Interpretation) Act 1948, s. 1 (1).

"Thirty days beginning with." See the note "Three months beginning, etc." to s. 20, *ante*.

92. Investigation of company or association with reference to order to which s. 90 applies

(1) For the purpose of determining whether to make an order to which section 90 of this Act applies whereby any powers are to be exercised in relation to a company or association, or for the purpose of obtaining information on which to exercise by or under any such order any powers in relation to a company or association, the Secretary of State may appoint an inspector to investigate and report to him on any such matters falling within the next following subsection as are specified or described in the appointment.

(2) The matters which may be so specified or described are any matters which, in the case of a company registered under the Companies Act 1948,—

(*a*) could in accordance with sections 165 and 166 of that Act be investigated by an inspector appointed under section 165 of that Act, or

(*b*) could in accordance with section 172 of that Act, or in accordance with any provisions as applied by subsection (5) of that section, be investigated by an inspector appointed under that section.

(3) For purposes connected with any investigation made by an inspector appointed under this section—

(*a*) section 167 (or that section as applied by section 172(5)) of the Companies Act 1948 shall have effect as it has effect for the purposes of any investigation under section 165 or section 172 of that Act, and

(*b*) the provisions of that Act referred to in this and the last preceding subsection shall be taken to extend throughout the United Kingdom. [**192**]

COMMENCEMENT

See s. 140 (3), *post*, and the note to s. 1, *ante*.

GENERAL NOTE

This section allows the Secretary of State in considering whether to make an order under this Act against a company to appoint an inspector to investigate the affairs of the company. The powers of such an inspector may go as far as but no further than powers of inspection under the provisions of the Companies Act 1948 mentioned in sub-s. (2) above.

"Secretary of State." See the note to s. 1, *ante*.

"United Kingdom." See the note to s. 2, *ante*.

"Companies Act 1948." See 5 Halsbury's Statutes (3rd Edn.) 110, and for ss. 165–167 and 172 of that Act, see *ibid*., pp. 243, 244, 248.

93. Enforcement of orders to which s. 90 applies

(1) No criminal proceedings shall, by virtue of the making of an order to which section 90 of this Act applies, lie against any person on the grounds that he has committed, or aided, abetted, counselled or procured the commission of, or conspired or attempted to commit, or incited others to commit, any contravention of the order.

(2) Nothing in the preceding subsection shall limit any right of any person to bring civil proceedings in respect of any contravention or apprehended contravention of any such order, and (without prejudice to the generality of the

preceding words) compliance with any such order shall be enforceable by civil proceedings by the Crown for an injunction or interdict or for any other appropriate relief.

(3) If any person makes default in complying with any directions given under section 90(7) of this Act, the court may, on the application of the Secretary of State, make an order requiring him to make good the default within a time specified in the order, or, if the directions related to anything to be done in the management or administration of a company or association, requiring the company or association or any officer of it to do so.

(4) Any order of the court under subsection (3) of this section may provide that all the costs or expenses of or incidental to the application for the order shall be borne by any person in default or by any officers of a company or association who are responsible for its default.

(5) In this section "the court"—

(*a*) in relation to England and Wales, means the High Court;
(*b*) in relation to Scotland means the Court of Session; and
(*c*) in relation to Northern Ireland, means the High Court or a judge of the High Court. [**193**]

COMMENCEMENT

See s. 140 (3), *post*, and the note to s. 1, *ante*.

GENERAL NOTE

Sub-s. (1). There were two grounds for not making a breach of an order under ss. 56, 73, 74 or 89 a criminal offence. First, it was considered that summary proceedings would be unlikely to be appropriate because magistrates' courts are not suitable for lengthy or complicated cases, while if proceedings were by indictment, the issues would be so complicated as to be difficult to put to a jury.

Secondly, once an order had been made about a category of goods or services, it would be difficult, in any subsequent investigation into the industry or firms connected with it to get further information from persons concerned if they should claim privilege on the ground that what they said might tend to show they had committed an offence.

Sub-ss. (3) *and* (4). See s. 90 (7), *ante*.

Sub-s. (2). Proceedings in civil conspiracy against those who contravene an order under the Act are not excluded by the Act.

"Secretary of State." See the note to s. 1, *ante*.

PART IX

AMENDMENTS OF RESTRICTIVE TRADE PRACTICES ACTS

94. Transfer of functions of Registrar to Director

(1) Subject to the transitional provisions having effect by virtue of section 139 of this Act, the functions of the Registrar of Restrictive Trading Agreements are hereby transferred to the Director, and the office of Registrar of Restrictive Trading Agreements is hereby abolished.

(2) In accordance with the preceding subsection, but without prejudice to any amendment made by any other provisions of this Act, in the Act of 1956, the Act of 1964 and the Act of 1968, for the words "the Registrar" or the words "the Registrar of Restrictive Trading Agreements", in each place where they occur, there shall be substituted the words "the Director". [**194**]

COMMENCEMENT

See s. 140 (3), *post*, and the note to s. 1, *ante*.

TRANSITIONAL PROVISIONS HAVING EFFECT BY VIRTUE OF S. 137

The relevant provisions are those contained in Sch. 11, para. 11, *post*. See also para. 15 of that Schedule.

DEFINITIONS

"Registrar of Restrictive Trading Agreements": this officer was appointed under, and his main functions were set out in, the Restrictive Trade Practices Act 1956, s. 1, which is largely repealed by s. 139 (1) and Sch. 13, *post*.

"The Director": *I.e.*, the Director General of Fair Trading; see s. 1 (1), *ante*, or s. 137 (2), *post*.

"Act of 1956": the Restrictive Trade Practices Act 1956; see s. 137 (1), *post*.

"Act of 1964": the Resale Prices Act 1964; see s. 137 (1), *post*.

"Act of 1968": the Restrictive Trade Practices Act 1968; see s. 137 (1), *post*.

GENERAL NOTE

This section abolishes the office of Registrar of Restrictive Trading Agreements and transfers the functions of that office to the Director General of Fair Trading who thus has functions in relation both to references to the Monopolies and Mergers Commission and to agreements registrable as restrictive trade agreements under Part I of the Restrictive Trade Practices Act 1956. The division of control over monopolies and restrictive trade agreements between the Commission and the Restrictive Practices Court continues (see s. 10 (2), *ante*) but the Director will be able to adjust the timing of his references to the Commission under s. 50, *ante*, so as to coincide with his consideration of registrable agreements under the Act of 1956. When investigating a possible monopoly or merger situation under ss. 44, 45 and 76, *ante*, the Director may discover in addition registrable agreements and may persuade the parties to abandon them without registration being necessary. Furthermore if the Director's investigations under the Fair Trading Act 1973 gives him reasonable cause to believe that a person is a party to a registrable agreement then he has powers to obtain information under the Act of 1956, powers enforceable under the provisions of ss. 15, 16 and 17 of that Act.

95. Agreements as to prices to be recommended or suggested for resale of goods

Section 6(1) of the Act of 1956 (which provides for agreements under which restrictions are accepted on certain matters to be subject to Part I of the Act) and section 5(1) of the Act of 1968 (which makes similar provision in relation to information agreements) shall each be amended by inserting the following paragraph after paragraph (*a*):—

"(*aa*) the prices to be recommended or suggested as the prices to be charged or quoted in respect of the resale of goods supplied". **[195]**

COMMENCEMENT

See s. 140 (3), *post*, and the note to s. 1, *ante*.

DEFINITIONS

"goods", "price", supply": see the Restrictive Trade Practices Act 1956, s. 36 (1), the definitions in which apply also to the Act of 1968 by virtue of s. 14 (2) of the Restrictive Trade Practices Act 1968.

"information agreement": see s. 5 (1) of the Act of 1968.

"Act of 1956": the Restrictive Trade Practices Act 1956; see s. 137 (1), *post*. For Part I and s. 6 (1) of that Act see 37 Halsbury's Statutes (3rd Edn.) 78, 82. Section 6 (1) of the Act of 1956 is also amended by s. 139 (1) and Sch. 12, *post*, as to which see the General Note to s. 94, *ante*.

"Act of 1968": the Restrictive Trade Practices Act 1968; see s. 137 (1), *post*. For s. 5 (1) of that Act see 37 Halsbury's Statutes (3rd Edn.) 320.

GENERAL NOTE

This section brings within the ambit of the Restrictive Trade Practices Act 1956, Part I, agreements relating to the recommendation of resale prices of goods and enables information agreements relating to the recommendation of resale prices to be brought within the ambit of Part I of the Act of 1956 by order of the Secretary of State under s. 5 of the Act of 1968.

96. Subscriptions to trade associations

In section 6 of the Act of 1956 (agreements to which Part I applies), after subsection (5) (which relates to obligations to make payments calculated by reference to certain variable factors) there shall be inserted the following proviso:—

"Provided that this subsection does not apply to any obligation on the part of any person to make payments to a trade association of which he is a member, if the payments are to consist only of bona fide subscriptions for membership of the association". **[196]**

COMMENCEMENT

See s. 140 (3), *post*, and the note to s. 1, *ante*.

DEFINITIONS

"Trade Association": see the Restrictive Trade Practices Act 1956, s. 6 (8), 37 Halsbury's Statutes (3rd Edn.) 83, as amended by s. 97, *post*.

"Act of 1956": the Restrictive Trade Practices Act 1956; see s. 137 (1), *post*. For Part I and s. 6 (5) of that Act, see 37 Halsbury's Statutes (3rd Edn.) 78, 83.

GENERAL NOTE

This section amends s. 6 (5) of the Act of 1956 so that rules and recommendations relating to bona fide subscriptions to trade associations are no longer registrable.

97. "Trade association" not to include certain approved societies

In section 6(8) of the Act of 1956 (which contains a definition of "trade association"), after the words "or of persons represented by its members" there shall be inserted the words "and which is not a society for the time being approved under section 6A of this Act". **[197]**

COMMENCEMENT

See s. 140 (3), *post*, and the note to s. 1, *ante*.

DEFINITIONS

"Act of 1956": the Restrictive Trade Practices Act 1956; see s. 137 (1), *post*. For s. 6 (8) of that Act see 37 Halsbury's Statutes (3rd Edn.) 83 and for s. 6A, see s. 98, *post*.

GENERAL NOTE

See the General Note to s. 98, *post*.

98. Wholesale co-operative societies

After section 6 of the Act of 1956 there shall be inserted the following section:—

"**6A.**—(1) The Secretary of State may approve under this section any industrial and provident society which in his opinion fulfils the following conditions, that is to say—

(*a*) that it carries on business in the production or supply of goods or in the supply of services or in the application to goods of any process of manufacture;

(*b*) that its shares are wholly or mainly held by industrial and provident societies; and

(*c*) that those societies are retail societies or societies whose shares are wholly or mainly held by retail societies.

(2) An approval given in respect of a society under this section shall (if it has not been previously withdrawn) expire at the end of the period of two years beginning with the date on which it was given or, if that

period is extended (once or more than once) under the next following subsection, at the end of that period as so extended, or further extended, as the case may be.

(3) The Secretary of State may extend or, if it has already been extended under this subsection, may further extend the period of two years referred to in subsection (2) of this section by such period, not exceeding two years, as he may specify.

(4) The Secretary of State may at any time withdraw an approval given in respect of a society under this section if it appears to him—

(*a*) that the society has made an agreement which would have been subject to registration under this Part of this Act if the approval had not been given, or that such a recommendation as is mentioned in section 6(7) of this Act has been made by or on behalf of the society, and

(*b*) that the agreement or recommendation has such adverse effects on competition that it should not be precluded from being investigated by the Court under the following provisions of this part of this Act.

(5) On the expiry or withdrawal of an approval given in respect of a society under this section, the provisions of this Part of this Act shall have effect in relation to agreements and recommendations made by the society during the currency of the approval as if the society had not been approved under this section.

(6) In this section—

"industrial and provident society" means a society registered or deemed to be registered under the Industrial and Provident Societies Act 1965 or under the corresponding law in Northern Ireland;

"retail society" means a society which carries on business in the sale by retail of goods for the domestic or personal use of individuals dealing with the society, or in the provision of services for such individuals;

"the corresponding law in Northern Ireland" means the law for the time being in force in Northern Ireland for purposes corresponding to those of the Industrial and Provident Societies Act 1965". [**198**]

COMMENCEMENT

See s. 140 (3), *post*, and the note to s. 1, *ante*.

DEFINITIONS

"agreement": see the Restrictive Trade Practices Act 1956, s. 6 (3), 37 Halsbury's Statutes (3rd Edn.) 82.

"the Court": see s. 2 (1) of that Act, *ibid.*, p. 80.

"goods" and "supply": see s. 36 (1) of that Act, *ibid.*, p. 112.

Note also the definitions in sub-s. (6) of the new s. 6A of the Act of 1956 contained in s. 98 above.

"Act of 1956": the Restrictive Trade Practices Act 1956; see s. 137 (1), *post*.

GENERAL NOTE

Under this section certain bodies may be approved by the Secretary of State and will then cease to be treated as a trade association within the meaning of ss. 6 and 8 of the Act of 1956. Previously co-operative wholesale societies and various other bodies such as some grocers' voluntary groups, not being interconnected bodies corporate within the meaning of s. 154 of the Companies Act 1948 were not treated as a single person (see s. 6 (8) and s. 36 (1) of the Act of 1956, 37 Halsbury's Statutes (3rd Edn.) 83 and 112). Frequently there was in consequence a difficulty in such bodies arranging their business. Often the supplier society was a trade association since it was formed to promote the interests of its members, the retailers (see s. 6 (8) of the Act of 1956). If it then recommended a price at which its members should sell, *e.g.*, by supplying promotion material, an agreement registrable within s. 6 (1) was made by virtue of s. 6 (7) of the Act of 1956. S. 11 of the Act of 1968 effected relief in respect of agreements but not of recommendations by preventing s. 6 (6) of the Act of 1956 from applying to societies approved under s. 11 of the Act of 1968. Section 98 of the 1973 Act takes approved societies out of the ambit of s. 6 of the Act of 1956 altogether both as to agreements under s. 6 (6) and recommendations under s. 6 (7).

The procedure is for the Secretary of State to give exemptions lasting for a maximum of two years. There can also be earlier revocation on the grounds specified in s. 6A (4). An approval, once given, is capable of extension any number of times, though each extension cannot be for longer than two years.

Transactions by co-operative societies and other groups which do not obtain exemption may well not come within Part I of the Act of 1956 on other grounds because of the effect of s. 106, *post*, under which an industrial and provident society and its subsidiaries will now be treated as a single person.

"Secretary of State." One of Her Majesty's Principal Secretaries of State for the time being: see the Interpretation Act 1889, s. 12 (3). The Secretary of State responsible for the administration of the Restrictive Trade Practices Act 1956 is the Secretary of State for Trade.

"Wholly or mainly." See the note to s. 57, *ante*.

"Two years beginning with, etc." See the note "Three months beginning with, etc." to s. 20, *ante*.

"This Part of this Act." *I.e.*, Part I (ss. 1–23) of the Restrictive Trade Practices Act 1956, 37 Halsbury's Statutes (3rd Edn.) 78.

"Sale by retail." A sale by retail is a sale to a person buying for his own use or consumption, and a sale by wholesale is a sale to a person who buys for re-sale in the course of trade; see *Chappell & Co., Ltd.* v. *Nestle Co., Ltd.*, [1958] 2 All E.R. 155, A.C., at pp. 159, 161, 166; on appeal [1959] 2 All E.R. 701, H.L., at p. 704, and *Treacher & Co., Ltd.* v. *Treacher*, [1874] W.N. 4.

"Industrial and Provident Societies Act 1965." See 17 Halsbury's Statutes (3rd Edn.) 333.

Transitional provision. See s. 139 (2) and Sch. 11, para. 13, *post*.

99. Agreements relating to coal or steel

In section 7 of the Act of 1956, before subsection (2) there shall be inserted the following subsections:—

"(1A) In determining whether an agreement is an agreement to which this Part of this Act applies, where—

(*a*) the parties to the agreement are or include two or more bodies to which this subsection applies, and

(*b*) restrictions relating to coal or steel, or relating to both coal and steel, are accepted under the agreement by two or more such bodies, whether the restrictions so accepted by those bodies are the same restrictions or different restrictions,

no account shall be taken of any such restriction which is accepted under the agreement by a body to which this subsection applies, whether that restriction is also accepted by any other party to the agreement or not.

(1B) Subsection (1A) of this section applies to any body which, in accordance with Article 80 of the E.C.S.C. Treaty, constitutes an undertaking for the purposes of Articles 65 and 66 of that Treaty, and in that subsection "coal" and "steel" have the meanings assigned to them respectively by Annex I to that Treaty." **[199]**

COMMENCEMENT

See s. 140 (3), *post*, and the note to s. 1, *ante*.

DEFINITIONS

"This Part of this Act": Part I (ss. 1–23) of the Restrictive Trade Practices Act 1956.

"E.C.S.C. Treaty": the Treaty establishing the European Coal and Steel Community signed at Paris on 18th April 1951; see the European Communities Act 1972, s. 1 (2), Sch. 1, Part I. For art. 80 of, and Annex I to, that Treaty, see 42A Halsbury's Statutes (3rd Edn.) 1288, 1289.

"agreement" and "restriction": see the Restrictive Trade Practices Act 1956, s. 6 (3), 37 Halsbury's Statutes (3rd Edn.) 82.

Note as to "coal" and "steel" the new sub-s. (1B) to s. 7 of the Act of 1956 contained in s. 99 above.

"Act of 1956": the Restrictive Trade Practices Act 1956; see s. 137 (1), *post*. For s. 7 of the Act of 1956, see 37 Halsbury's Statutes (3rd Edn.) 86.

GENERAL NOTE

This section drafts two new subsections into s. 7 of the Act of 1956. The effect is to exempt from the operation of Part I of the Act of 1956, agreements insofar as they contain restrictions relating to coal and/or steel provided the restrictions are accepted by two or more bodies which are within the description in the new s. 7 (1B).

100. Agreements to comply with standards of performance

In section 7(3) of the Act of 1956 (which makes provision as to agreements to comply with standards of dimension, design or quality) in paragraph (*a*), for the words "or quality" there shall be substituted the words "quality or performance". [**200**]

COMMENCEMENT

See s. 140 (3), *post*, and the note to s. 1, *ante*.

DEFINITIONS

"Act of 1956": Restrictive Trade Practices Act 1956; see s. 137 (1), *post*.

For s. 7 of that Act, see 37 Halsbury's Statutes (3rd Edn.) 86.

GENERAL NOTE

The Department of Trade approves from time to time standards of performance as well as of dimension, design or quality. In future, agreements to conform with such standards of performance cannot be taken into account in determining whether a registrable agreement exists.

101. Patent or design pooling agreements

In section 8 of the Act of 1956, at the beginning of subsection (4) there shall be inserted the words "Subject to section 8A of this Act"; and after that section there shall be inserted the following section:—

"**8A.**—(1) No licence, assignment or agreement shall by virtue of section 8(4) of this Act be precluded from being an agreement to which Part I of this Act applies if—

(*a*) in the case of an agreement, it is a patent or design pooling agreement, or

(*b*) whether being a licence, assignment or agreement, it is a licence, assignment or agreement granted or made in pursuance (directly or indirectly) of a patent or design pooling agreement.

(2) In this section (subject to subsection (4)) 'patent or design pooling agreement' means an agreement to which the parties are or include at least three persons (in this subsection referred to as 'principal parties') each of whom has an interest in one or more patents or

registered designs, whereby each of the principal parties agrees, in respect of patents or registered designs in which he has an interest, or in respect of patents or registered designs in which he has or may during the currency of the agreement acquire an interest,—

(*a*) to grant an interest in one or more such patents or registered designs to one or more of the other principal parties, or to one or more of those parties and to other persons, or

(*b*) to grant an interest in at least one such patent or registered design to a third person for the purpose of enabling that person to grant an interest in it to one or more of the other principal parties, or to one or more of those parties and to other persons,

and 'interest', in relation to a patent or registered design, mean an interest as proprietor or licensee of the patent or registered design of an interest consisting of such rights as a person has by virtue of having applied for a patent or for the registration of a design or by virtue of having acquired the right to apply for a patent or for the registration of a design.

(3) For the purposes of this section a licence, assignment or agreement—

(*a*) shall be taken to be granted or made directly in pursuance of a patent or design pooling agreement if it is granted or made in pursuance of provisions of that agreement such as are mentioned in paragraph (*a*) of subsection (2) of this section, and

(*b*) shall be taken to be granted or made indirectly in pursuance of a patent or design pooling agreement if it is granted or made by a third person to whom an interest has been granted in pursuance of provisions of that agreement such as are mentioned in paragraph (*b*) of that subsection.

(4) In relation to any interest held by or granted to any two or more persons jointly, subsection (2) of this section shall apply as if those persons were one person by whom the interest is held or to whom it is granted, and accordingly those persons shall be treated for the purposes of that subsection as together constituting one party". [**201**]

COMMENCEMENT

See s. 140 (3), *post*, and the note to s. 1, *ante*.

DEFINITIONS

"agreement": see the Restrictive Trade Practices Act 1956, s. 6 (3), 37 Halsbury's Statutes (3rd Edn.) 82.

"patent or design pooling agreement", "principal parties" and "interest": note sub-s. (2) of the new s. 8A to the Act of 1956 contained in s. 101 above.

"Act of 1956": Restrictive Trade Practices Act 1956; see s. 137 (1), *post*. For s. 8 of that Act, see 37 Halsbury's Statutes (3rd Edn.) 87.

GENERAL NOTE

Under s. 8 (4) of the Act of 1956 patent licences and agreements for such licences could be so drafted as to bring them within the exemption provided in s. 8 (4) even though the parties had accepted restrictions relating both to the invention and to articles made by the use of that invention. In this way patent pools to which many firms were party to the exclusion of others could survive unregistered. Various methods have been used such as for a company to be formed and patents assigned to it and authority given to it to assign licences. Licences were then granted to the parties to the agreement under which the company was set up. Provided that it was only in relation to the patented inventions or articles made by its use any imposition of price-fixing or of territorial or other limitations came within the exemption provided that actual operation of the agreement did not constitute a registrable arrangement within s. 6 (1) of the Act of 1956.

Under s. 101, a new s. 8A is drafted into the Act of 1956 taking out of the exemption of s. 8 design or patent pooling agreements and licences made pursuant to such agreements. Patent or design pooling agreement is defined in sub-s. (2) of the new s. 8A very widely, although any agreement to which only two persons are party is outside the definition and therefore is capable of being within the exemption of s. 8 of the Act of 1956. However where more than two persons are party a wide variety of agreements qualify. The "interest" of a person granting an interest in a patent is not restricted to ownership so that, for example, if more than one licensee exists in relation to a patent, then if one of the licensees grants the original licensor a sole and exclusive licence under any improvement patent that licensee took out, there would probably be held to be a registrable patent pool agreement.

APPLICATION

S. 8A (2)–(4) of the Act of 1956 contained in s. 101 above are applied by s. 115 (8), *post*, for the purposes of that section.

102. Particulars of export agreements to be furnished to Director

(1) The following subsection shall be added at the end of section 10 of the Act of 1956:—

"(8) Subsections (1) to (6) of this section shall have effect in relation to any agreement which—

(*a*) relates to exports from the United Kingdom, and

(*b*) would, but for section 8(8) of this Act, be an agreement subject to registration under this Part of this Act,

as if, in those subsections, any reference to an agreement being or becoming subject to such registration were a reference to its being or becoming an agreement which, but for section 8(8) of this Act, would be subject to such registration."

(2) The following subsection shall be added at the end of section 14 of the Act of 1956:—

"(4) In subsection (1) of this section the reference to an agreement subject to registration under this Part of this Act shall be construed as including a reference to any agreement which—

(*a*) relates to exports from the United Kingdom, and

(*b*) would, but for section 8(8) of this Act, be an agreement subject to registration under this Part of this Act."

(3) Subsection (1) of section 31 of the Act of 1956 (which requires particulars of agreements relating to exports to be furnished to the Secretary of State) shall cease to have effect. [**202**]

COMMENCEMENT

See s. 140 (3), *post*, and the note to s. 1, *ante*.

DEFINITIONS

"Agreement": see the Restrictive Trade Practices Act 1956, s. 6, (3), 37 Halsbury's Statutes (3rd Edn.) 82.

"This part of this Act": Part I (ss. 1–23) of the Restrictive Trade Practices Act 1956.

"Act of 1956": the Restrictive Trade Practices Act 1956; see s. 137 (1), *post*. For ss. 8 (8), 10, 14 and 31 of the Act of 1956, see 37 Halsbury's Statutes (3rd Edn.) 88, 90, 94, 110. Section 31 of the Act of 1956 is repealed by s. 139 (1) and Sch. 13, *post*.

GENERAL NOTE

Under s. 8 (8) of the Act of 1956 agreements in which the only registrable restrictions related to the supply of goods by export, or the delivery of goods, from the U.K. or the production or processing of goods outside the U.K. or the acquisition of goods to be delivered outside the U.K. are exempt from registration.

S. 102 provides that particulars of such restrictive export agreements which, but for s. 8 (8) would be registrable shall in future be given to the Director General of Fair Trading and not to the Secretary of State as s. 31 of the Act of 1956, now repealed, formerly provided.

The Director's powers under ss. 14 and 15 of the Act of 1956 now extend to such agreements.

If the Director is appointed a competent authority within the meaning of Article 11 of Regulation 17/62 of the Council of Ministers of the EEC then the Commission of the EEC will be able to insist on Director providing any information held by him necessary for them to enforce Articles 85 or 86 of the EEC Treaty. Such information would include information on export agreements held by the Director. For Reg. 17/62, see 42A Halsbury's Statutes (3rd Edn.) 1195; for EEC Treaty, arts. 85, 86, see *ibid.*, pp. 1178, 1183.

103. Examination on oath of certain employees of bodies corporate and unincorporated trade associations

(1) In subsection (3) of section 15 of the Act of 1956 (which in certain cases enables an order to be made for the attendance and examination on oath of an officer of a body corporate), after the words "director, manager, secretary or other officer of that body corporate" there shall be inserted the words "or of any person who (not being such a director, manager, secretary or other officer) is employed by the body corporate and appears to the Court to be likely to have particular knowledge of any of the matters in respect of which the notice was given".

(2) After that subsection there shall be inserted the following subsections:—

"(3A) The provisions of subsection (3) of this section shall have effect in relation to a trade association which is not incorporated as they have effect in relation to a body corporate.

(3B) Nothing in this section shall be taken to compel the disclosure by a barrister, advocate or solicitor of any privileged communication made by or to him in that capacity, or the production by him of any document containing any such communication." [**203**]

COMMENCEMENT

See s. 140 (3), *post*, and the note to s. 1, *ante*.

DEFINITIONS

"the Court": *i.e.*, the Restrictive Practices Court, see the Restrictive Practices Act 1956, s. 2 (1).

"trade association": see the Restrictive Trade Practices Act 1956, s. 6 (8), 37 Halsbury's Statutes (3rd Edn.) 83, as amended by s. 97, *ante*.

"Act of 1956": the Restrictive Trade Practices Act 1956, see s. 137 (1), *post*. For s. 15 (3) of the Act of 1956, see 37 Halsbury's Statutes (3rd Edn.) 95.

GENERAL NOTE

Under s. 14 of the Act of 1956 the Director has power to require of certain persons the production of information. This power may be exercised by examination under oath in accordance with s. 15 of that Act. The words "director, secretary or other officer" of a body corporate in s. 15 (3) of the Act of 1956 were narrowly construed by the Court of Appeal in *Registrar of Restrictive Trading Agreements* v. *Smith* (1969), L.R. 1 R.P. 122. Section 103 extends the ambit of s. 15 to cover any employee of a corporation likely to have knowledge of matters covered by the notice issued under s. 15.

The new sub-s. 3A of s. 15 of the Act of 1956, contained in s. 103 (2), extends the operation of s. 15 to cover unincorporated trade associations, their officers and employees in the same way that it covers bodies corporate.

The new sub-s. (3B) of s. 15 of the Act of 1956, contained in s. 103 (2) gives effect to the general law as to the privilege of legal advisers but does not go beyond it. Thus participation by a legal employee in discussions and arrangements does not *ipso facto* render records of the discussions privileged and that employee may in circumstances not covered by privilege be examinable under s. 15 of the Act of 1956.

104. Extension of certain powers of Restrictive Practices Court

(1) In section 20 of the Act of 1956 (jurisdiction and powers of Restrictive Practices Court), in subsection (3) (which enables the Court to make orders imposing certain restraints on parties to an agreement in respect of restrictions found by the Court to be contrary to the public interest), after the words "United Kingdom" there shall be inserted the words "any trade association of which any such person is a member or any person acting on behalf of such a trade association"; and at the end of that subsection there shall be added the words "or

(*c*) where such an agreement as is mentioned in paragraph (*b*) of this subsection has already been made, from giving effect to that agreement or enforcing or purporting to enforce it;

and, where any of the parties to the agreement against whom the order is made is a member of a trade association, the order may include provisions for restraining the trade association, and any person acting on its behalf, from procuring or assisting any such party to do anything which would be a contravention of the order in its application to him".

(2) In section 7 of the Act of 1968 (consequences of failure to register), in subsection (3) (which enables the Restrictive Practices Court to make orders imposing certain restraints on parties to an agreement of which particulars have not been duly furnished), after the words "United Kingdom" there shall be inserted the words "any trade association of which any such person is a member or any person acting on behalf of such a trade association" and for the word "him" there shall be substituted the words "that person or association" and after that subsection there shall be inserted the following subsection:—

"(3A) Where an order is made under subsection (3) of this section against any party to an agreement and that party is a member of a trade association, the order may include provisions for restraining the trade association, and any person acting on its behalf, from procuring or assisting that party to do anything which would be a contravention of the order in its application to him". [**204**]

COMMENCEMENT

See s. 140 (3), *post*, and the note to s. 1, *ante*.

DEFINITIONS

"trade association": see s. 6 (8) of the Act of 1956, 37 Halsbury's Statutes (3rd Edn.) 83, as amended by s. 97, *ante*.

"agreement": see s. 6 (3) of the Act of 1956, *ibid*., p. 82.

"Act of 1956": the Restrictive Trade Practices Act 1956; see s. 137 (1), *post*. For s. 20 (3) of that Act, see 37 Halsbury's Statutes (3rd Edn.) 99.

Act of 1968: the Restrictive Trade Practices Act 1968; see s. 137 (1), *post*. For s. 7 (3) of that Act, see 37 Halsbury's Statutes (3rd Edn.) 323.

GENERAL NOTE

Sub-s. (1). Under s. 20 (3) of the Act of 1956 the Restrictive Practices Court has power to act on a restrictive agreement which has been found to be contrary to the public interest. The court can now, with the amendment to s. 20 (3) of the Act of 1956 contained in s. 104, restrain a trade association and anyone acting on its behalf whether or not such a person was a party to the offending agreement. This is so whether or not the trade association is incorporated: s. 6 (8) of the Act of 1956 as amended by s. 97, *ante*. The consequence of this amendment is that it will not be possible for an order of the Restrictive Practices Court to be outflanked after it has been made by making and giving effect to a new agreement in the terms of the one proscribed but with different parties.

Sub-s. (2). Under s. 7 of the Act of 1968 powers are given to the Restrictive Practices Court to restrain parties to an agreement, registrable under Part I of the Act of 1956, who have failed to give the Director adequate particulars of the agreement from giving effect to such an agreement or agreements.

These powers can now be exercised against trade associations of which the person party to the agreement is a member, or any other member acting on behalf of the trade association.

This again has the effect, where a member of a trade association is party to the agreement in question, of extending the Court's restraining powers to agreements similar in terms to the one in question but to which the parties are other members of the trade association.

105. Interim orders of Restrictive Practices Court

After section 21 of the Act of 1956 there shall be inserted the following section:—

"**21A.**—(1) Where the Director has made an application in respect of an agreement under subsection (1) of section 20 of this Act, then at any time, whether before or after the Court has made a declaration under that subsection in respect of the agreement, but before the Court has made an order in respect of it under subsection (3) of that section, the Director may apply to the Court for an interim order under this section.

(2) An application under this section shall specify the restrictions which appear to the Director, in relation to the agreement to which the application relates,—

(*a*) to be restrictions such as are mentioned in section 20(1) of this Act, and

(*b*) to be contrary to the public interest, and

(*c*) to be restrictions in respect of which, in accordance with the following provisions of this section, it would be appropriate for an interim order to be made.

(3) If on an application under this section the Court is satisfied that the following conditions are fulfilled in relation to all or any of the restrictions specified in the application, that is to say—

(*a*) that they are restrictions such as are mentioned in section 20(1) of this Act;

(*b*) that they could not reasonably be expected to be shown to fall within any of paragraphs (*a*) to (*h*) of section 21(1) of this Act; and

(*c*) that the operation of the restrictions, during the period likely to elapse before an order can be made in respect of them under section 20(3) of this Act, is likely to cause material detriment to the public or a section of the public generally, or to a particular person who is not a party to the agreement,

the Court may, if it thinks fit, make an interim order specifying the restrictions in relation to which the Court is satisfied that those conditions are fulfilled.

(4) Any such interim order may exercise, in respect of the restrictions specified in the order, any powers which could be exercised in respect of them by an order under section 20(3) of this Act if those restrictions had been found by the Court to be contrary to the public interest.

(5) At any time when any such interim order is in force the Court, on the application of the Director or of any person who is subject to or entitled to the benefit of any restriction specified in the order, may discharge the order and substitute for it any interim order which could have been made on the original application under this section.

(6) An interim order made under this section in respect of an agreement shall cease to have effect on the occurrence of whichever of the following first occurs, that is to say—

(*a*) the termination of such period, or the happening of such event, as may be specified for that purpose in the order;

(*b*) the discharge of the order by the Court;

(*c*) a declaration by the Court that the restrictions specified in the interim order are not contrary to the public interest;

(*d*) the final determination by the Court of an application under section 20(3) of this Act in respect of that agreement." [**205**]

COMMENCEMENT

See s. 140 (3), *post*, and the note to s. 1, *ante*.

DEFINITIONS

"the Court": see s. 2 (1) of the Act of 1956, 37 Halsbury's Statutes (3rd Edn.) 80.

"agreement" and "restriction": see s. 6 (3) of the Act of 1956, *ibid.*, p. 82.

"the Director": see s. 36 (1) of the Act of 1956, *ibid.*, p. 112, as amended by s. 139 (1) and Sch. 12, *post*.

"Act of 1956": the Restrictive Trade Practices Act 1956; see s. 137 (1), *post*. For ss. 20 (1), (3) and 21 of the Act of 1956, see 37 Halsbury's Statutes (3rd Edn.) 99, 101.

GENERAL NOTE

This section empowers the Restrictive Practices Court on the application of the Director to make interim orders in relation to agreements which the Court is satisfied could not reasonably be shown to be defensible within any of the so-called "gateways" of s. 21 of the Act of 1956 provided that the Court is satisfied also that the operation of the restrictions during the time before an order under s. 20 (3) of the Act of 1956 can be made is likely to have the consequence specified in sub-s. (3) (*c*) of the new s. 21A of the Act of 1956 contained in this section.

Rules for the procedure in such interim proceedings will be made under s. 23 of the Act of 1956.

Although a substantial case that the public interest is affected adversely must be made before the interim order can be made there is a possibility that where an interim order has been made the Court might in the subsequent main action come to the view that the application ought not to have been brought by the Director. The Court should then order costs to be paid by the Director to the person affected. It is doubtful whether the aggrieved party in such a case would be awarded compensation. The Director is a public official acting on behalf of the public interest under a statutory authority. As such he is not liable to pay compensation if a successful interim application is not subsequently upheld, just as the Attorney-General, when acting on behalf of the public, obtains an injunction of the kind contemplated by the new s. 21A of the Act of 1956, has never been held liable to give an undertaking in damages or to compensate if ultimately unsuccessful: see *Hoffman-La Roche & Co., A.G.* v. *Secretary of State for Trade and Industry*, [1974] 2 All E.R. 1128, H.L.

106. Industrial and provident societies and their subsidiaries

In section 36 (1) of the Act of 1956, in the definition of "inter-connected bodies corporate", after the words "all other bodies corporate which are its subsidiaries within the meaning of section one hundred and fifty-four of the Companies Act 1948" there shall be inserted the words "or (in the case of an industrial and provident society) within the meaning of section 15 of the Friendly and Industrial and Provident Societies Act 1968". [**206**]

COMMENCEMENT

See s. 140 (3), *post*, and the note to s. 1, *ante*.

DEFINITIONS

"Act of 1956": the Restrictive Trade Practices Act 1956; see s. 137 (1), *post*. For s. 36 (1) of that Act see 37 Halsbury's Statutes (3rd Edn.) 112. S. 36 (1) is also amended by s. 139 (1) and Sch. 12, *post*, and it is partly repealed by s. 139 (1) and Sch. 13, *post*.

GENERAL NOTE

See the General Note to s. 98, *ante*.

Companies Act 1948. See 5 Halsbury's Statutes (3rd Edn.) 234.

Friendly and Industrial and Provident Societies Act 1968. For s. 15, see 17 Halsbury's Statutes (3rd Edn.) 393.

PART X

EXTENSION OF ACT OF 1956 TO AGREEMENTS RELATING TO SERVICES

107. Order bringing under control restrictive agreements relating to services

(1) The Secretary of State may by statutory instrument make an order in respect of a class of services described in the order (in this Act referred to, in relation to an order under this section, as "services brought under control by the order") and direct by the order that, subject to the following provisions of this Part of this Act, the agreements to which Part I of the Act of 1956 applies shall include agreements, whether made before or after the passing of this Act and whether before or after the making of the order, which—

(*a*) are agreements between two or more persons carrying on business within the United Kingdom in the supply of services brought under control by the order, or between two or more such persons together with one or more other parties, and

(*b*) are agreements under which restrictions, in respect of matters specified in the order for the purposes of this paragraph, are accepted by two or more parties.

(2) A class of services described in an order under this section, as being the services brought under control by the order, may consist—

(*a*) of services of one or more descriptions specified in that behalf in the order, or

(*b*) of all services except services of one or more descriptions so specified, or

(*c*) of all services without exception.

(3) The matters which may be specified in such an order for the purposes of subsection (1)(*b*) of this section are any of the following, that is to say—

(*a*) the charges to be made, quoted or paid for designated services supplied, offered or obtained;

(*b*) the terms or conditions on or subject to which designated services are to be supplied or obtained;

(*c*) the extent (if any) to which, or the scale (if any) on which, designated services are to be made available, supplied or obtained;

(*d*) the form or manner in which designated services are to be made available, supplied or obtained;

(*e*) the persons or classes of persons for whom or from whom, or the areas or places in or from which, designated services are to be made available or supplied or are to be obtained. [**207**]

COMMENCEMENT

See s. 140 (3), *post,* and the note to s. 1, *ante.*

DEFINITIONS

"This Part of this Act": *I.e.,* Part X (ss. 107–117) of this Act.

"Act of 1956": *I.e.,* the Restrictive Trade Practices Act 1956; see s. 137 (1), *post.* For Part I of that Act, see 37 Halsbury's Statutes (3rd Edn.) 78 and note the amendments to that Part made by Part IX (ss. 94–106) of this Act, *ante.*

"Designated services": s. 109 (1), *post.*

"services": s. 117 (1), *post.*

"business": s. 117 (2), *post.*

"agreement" and "restriction": by virtue of s. 117 (3), *post,* see the Restrictive Trade Practices Act 1956, s. 6 (3), 37 Halsbury's Statutes (3rd Edn.) 82.

"supply": by virtue of s. 117 (3), *post,* see s. 36 (1) of the Act of 1956, *ibid.,* p. 112.

"scale": s. 137 (1), *post.*

"services brought under control by the order": note sub-s. (1) above.

GENERAL NOTE

Under s. 107 agreements relating to the supply of services may become registrable under Part I of the Act of 1956. These provisions are similar to, but quite separate from, those relating to the supply or processing of goods.

Only agreements coming within an order made by the Secretary of State under powers conferred by s. 107 are registrable.

There will be three main elements in framing an order under s. 107:

1. First it will be necessary to bring classes of service under control, that is to set out in the order those services in which suppliers of the services are operating restrictive agreements. Not all services will be selected and in relation to those not selected restrictive agreements will not be registrable.

2. Secondly it will be necessary to identify the services affected by restrictive agreements between suppliers of the services in the classes brought under control. This will be done by describing them in the order as "designated services". For "designated services", see s. 109, *post.*

3. Thirdly it will be necessary to specify what restrictions can be taken into account in rendering registrable an agreement relating to the designated services.

Examples: (1) Suppose an order is made bringing window cleaning services under control and designating the acquisition of insurance for the window cleaning business. The effect would be to make registrable any agreement between two or more window cleaners about the terms on which they will take out insurance.

(2) Suppose an order is made bringing insurance services under control and designating all restrictions that affect the acquisition of reinsurance of specified risks. The effect would be to make registrable any agreement between two or more insurers about the terms on which they will take out reinsurance on those risks.

It is not known how many orders will be issued under s. 107 or the particularity with which they will be drafted. Under s. 107 (2) the drafting may specify the descriptions of services that are to be brought under control or it may specify the ones that are not to be or it may include all services (as to the meaning of "services", see s. 117 (1), *post*).

FURTHER PROVISIONS

See s. 109 and Sch. 4, *post,* for designated services.

See s. 110, *post,* for supplementary provisions as to orders under s. 107.

See s. 111, *post,* for procedure in relation to such orders.

See s. 112, *post,* for provisions as to certain associations.

See s. 113, *post,* for matters to be treated as equivalent to restrictions for the purposes of s. 107.

See s. 114, *post,* for provisions to be disregarded in determining whether an agreement is brought under control by s. 107.

See s. 115, *post,* for excepted agreements.

See s. 116 and Sch. 10, *post,* for applications of the Acts of 1956 and 1968 to agreements brought under control by order under s. 107.

See also s. 108, *post,* concerning orders bringing under control information agreements relating to services.

108. Order bringing under control information agreements relating to services

(1) The Secretary of State may by statutory instrument make an order in respect of a class of services described in the order (in this Act referred to, in relation to an order under this section, as "services brought under control by the order") and direct by the order that, subject to the following provisions of this Part of this Act, the agreements to which Part I of the Act of 1956 applies shall include agreements, whether made before or after the passing of this Act and whether before or after the making of the order, which—

(*a*) are agreements between two or more persons carrying on business within the United Kingdom in the supply of services brought under control by the order, or between two or more such persons together with one or more other parties, and

(*b*) are agreements under which provision is made for or in relation to the furnishing by two or more parties to each other or to other persons (whether parties or not) of information with respect to matters specified in the order for the purposes of this paragraph.

(2) A class of services described in an order under this section, as being the services brought under control by the order may consist—

(*a*) of services of one or more descriptions specified in that behalf in the order, or

(*b*) of all services except services of one or more descriptions so specified, or

(*c*) of all services without exception.

(3) The matters which may be specified in such an order for the purposes of subsection (1)(*b*) of this section are any of the following, that is to say—

(*a*) the charges made, quoted or paid or to be made, quoted or paid for designated services which have been or are to be supplied, offered or obtained;

(*b*) the terms or conditions on or subject to which designated services have been or are to be supplied or obtained;

(*c*) the extent (if any) to which, or the scale (if any) on which, designated services have been or are to be made available, supplied or obtained;

(*d*) the form or manner in which designated services have been or are to be made available, supplied or obtained;

(*e*) the costs incurred or to be incurred in making available, supplying or obtaining designated services;

(*f*) the persons or classes of persons for whom or from whom, or the areas or places in or from which, designated services have been or are to be made available or supplied or have been or are to be obtained. [**208**]

COMMENCEMENT

See s. 140 (3), *post*, and the note to s. 1, *ante*.

DEFINITIONS

"This part of this Act": *I.e.*, Part X of this Act (ss. 107–117).

"designated services": s. 109 (1), *post*; and see the General Note to s. 107, *ante*.

"services": s. 117 (1), *post*.

"business": s. 117 (2), *post*.

"agreement"; "supply": by virtue of s. 117 (3), *post*, for "agreement", see s. 6 (3) of Restrictive Practices Act 1956, 37 Halsbury's Statutes (3rd Edn.) 82; for "supply", see s. 36 (1) of that Act, *ibid.*, p. 112.

"scale": s. 137 (1), *post*.

"services brought under control by the order", note sub-s. (1), above.

"Act of 1956": the Restrictive Trade Practices Act 1956, see s. 137 (1), *post*. For Part I of that Act see 37 Halsbury's Statutes (3rd Edn.) 78, and note the amendments to that Part made by Part IX of this Act (ss. 94–106), *ante*.

GENERAL NOTE

Under this section an order may be made by statutory instrument introducing registration of agreements for the exchange of information about any of the matters listed in sub-s. (3).

This section is similar to s. 5 of the Restrictive Trade Practices Act 1968 providing for orders for the registration of information agreements relating to the supply of goods. The contents of an order made under s. 108 have the same structure as one made under s. 107 with the specification of classes of "services brought under control" in relation to which other services may be described as "designated". The order must specify "matters" such as the charges for designated services and it is only agreements providing for the giving of information relating to such matters that are registrable. Such matters must be within s. 108 (3).

109. Designated services

(1) In relation to any order made under section 107 or section 108 of this Act, "designated services" in this Part of this Act means services of any class described in the order as being designated services.

(2) Subject to the next following subsection, a class of services described in any such order as being designated services may consist wholly or partly of services brought under control by the order or wholly or partly of other services, and may be described so as to consist—

(*a*) of services of one or more descriptions specified in that behalf in the order, or

(*b*) of all services except services of one or more descriptions so specified,

and different classes of services may be so described in relation to different matters specified in the order for the purposes of section 107(1)(*b*) or section 108(1)(*b*) of this Act as the case may be.

(3) A class of services described in such an order as being designated services shall not include any of the services specified in Schedule 4 to this Act. [**209**]

COMMENCEMENT

See s. 140 (3), *post*, and the note to s. 1, *ante*.

DEFINITIONS

"This Part of this Act": Part X (ss. 107–117) of this Act.
"services brought under control by the order": s. 107 (1) or s. 108 (1), *ante*.
"services": s. 117 (1), *post*.

GENERAL NOTE

The relation of the idea of "designated service" to that of "service brought under control" has been outlined in the notes to ss. 107 and 108, *ante*.

Under sub-s. (2) above an order made under ss. 107 or 108 can describe as a "designated service" any service at all whether or not it is also a "service brought under control" by the order provided it is not a service specified in Schedule 4, *post*.

As under s. 107 (2), *ante*, the drafting may be inclusive or exclusive and in addition the order may describe as "designated services" different services according to the different restrictions specified in the order as rendering the agreement registrable.

110. Supplementary provisions as to orders under s. 107 or s. 108

(1) An order under section 107 or section 108 of this Act may limit the operation of the order to agreements fulfilling such conditions (in addition to those mentioned in section 107 or section 108, as the case may be) as may be specified in the order.

(2) In particular, but without prejudice to the generality of the preceding subsection, an order under section 108 of this Act may limit the operation of the order to agreements under which the provision for the furnishing of information (as mentioned in subsection (1)(*b*) of that section) is provision of a kind specified in the order or provides for the furnishing of information of a kind so specified.

(3) Subject to subsection (1) of this section—

(*a*) for the purposes of any order under section 107 of this Act it is immaterial whether any restrictions accepted by parties to an agreement relate to the same or to different matters specified in the order for the purposes of subsection (1)(*b*) of that section, or have the same or a different effect in relation to any matter to specified, and

(*b*) for the purposes of any order under section 108 of this Act it is immaterial whether any provision made by an agreement for or in relation to the furnishing of information relates to the same or to different matters specified in the order for the purposes of subsection (1)(*b*) of that section,

and it is immaterial for those purposes whether the parties accepting any restrictions, or the parties by whom any information is to be furnished, as the case may be, carry on the same class or different classes of business.

(4) Where, at a time when an order under section 107 or section 108 of this Act (in this subsection referred to as "the earlier order") is in force, another order (in this subsection referred to as "the subsequent order") is made under the same section, the subsequent order may provide that—

(*a*) for the purposes of the earlier order, or
(*b*) for the purposes of the subsequent order, or
(*c*) for the purposes of both orders,

the condition specified in subsection (1)(*a*) of section 107 or in subsection (1)(*a*) of section 108 of this Act, as the case may be, shall be treated as fulfilled in relation to an agreement if it is an agreement to which the parties are or include one person carrying on business in the United Kingdom in the supply of services brought under control by the earlier order and one person carrying on business within the United Kingdom in the supply of services brought under control by the subsequent order.

(5) Subsection (4) of this section shall have effect without prejudice to any power to vary any order made under section 107 or section 108 of this Act.

(6) In the following provisions of this Part of this Act "the relevant enactments", in relation to an order under section 107 or section 108 of this Act, means the provisions of this Part of this Act (including whichever of those sections is applicable) as they have effect in relation to that order and the provisions of the Act of 1956 and of the Act of 1968 as applied in relation to that order by the following provisions of this Part of this Act. [**210**]

COMMENCEMENT

See s. 140 (3), *post*, and the note to s. 1, *ante*.

DEFINITIONS

"services brought under control by the order": s. 107 (1) or s. 108 (1), *ante*.
"services": s. 117 (1), *post*.
"business": s. 117 (2), *post*.
"agreement" and "restriction": by virtue of s. 117 (3), *post*, see Restrictive Trade Practices Act 1956, s. 6 (3).
"supply": by virtue of s. 117 (3), *post*, see the Restrictive Trade Practices Act 1956, s. 36 (1), 37 Halsbury's Statutes (3rd Edn.) 112.

"Act of 1956": the Restrictive Trade Practices Act 1956, see s. 137 (1), *post.* Provisions of that Act are applied by s. 115 (1), (8) and 116 (1)–(3) and Sch. 10, Part I, *post.*
"Act of 1968": *I.e.*, the Restrictive Trade Practices Act 1968; see s. 137 (1), *post.* Provisions of that Act are applied by s. 116 (4), (5) and Sch. 10, Part II, *post.*

GENERAL NOTE

This section allows for further refinement of an order made under ss. 107 or 108. Under s. 110 (1) the Secretary of State has a general discretion as to the scope of any such further refinements or limitations. Under s. 110 (2), without prejudice to the general discretion under s. 110 (1), an order under s. 108 may be limited in operation to specified types of provision as to information in agreements or to specified types of information. Under s. 110 (3) (*a*) an agreement may be subject to an order under s. 107 even though under it more than one of the matters specified in the order is affected by the agreement and the agreement these various matters in different ways and still be subject to the order.

Under s. 110 (3) (*b*) an agreement which makes provision as to the furnishing of information where the provision affects more than one item specified in the order may still be within an order under s. 108, *e.g.*, an agreement which provides for the circulation of information both on price to the consumer as well as costs to the supplier of the services. Further, an agreement may be registrable under an order under s. 107 or s. 108 even though the parties to it do not carry on the same class of business.

Under s. 110 (4) above the Secretary of State may aggregate services designated in different orders.

111. Procedure in relation to orders under s. 107 or s. 108

(1) No order shall be made under section 107 or section 108 of this Act unless a draft of the order has been laid before Parliament and approved by a resolution of each House of Parliament.

(2) Before laying before Parliament a draft of any such order, the Secretary of State shall publish in such manner as he thinks appropriate a notice—

(*a*) describing the classes of services which, if the order is made, will be services brought under control by the order and will be designated services in relation to the order respectively;

(*b*) indicating the nature of any limitation to be imposed by the order under subsection (1) or subsection (2) of section 110 of this Act; and

(*c*) specifying a period (not being less than twenty-eight days) within which representations with respect to the proposed order may be made to the Secretary of State.

(3) In settling the draft to be laid before Parliament the Secretary of State shall take into consideration any representations with respect to the proposed order which may be received by him within the period specified in the notice in accordance with subsection (2)(*c*) of this section. [**211**]

COMMENCEMENT

See s. 140 (3), *post*, and the note to s. 1, *ante*.

DEFINITIONS

"services brought under control by the order": s. 107 (1) or s. 108 (1), *ante*.
"designated services": s. 109 (1), *ante*.
"services": s. 117 (1), *post*.

GENERAL NOTE

This section contains the procedure for issuing an order under either s. 107 or s. 108. The provisions are similar to those of s. 5 of the Restrictive Trade Practices Act 1968. The classes of service to be brought under control and those to be designated, and any limitations to be imposed under s. 110 must be published. Not less than 28 days should be allowed for representations from the public which must be taken into account before a draft of the order is laid before Parliament where it must be approved by affirmative resolution of both Houses.

112. Provisions as to certain associations

(1) For the purposes of any order made under section 107 or section 108 of this Act, and for the purposes of the operation of the relevant enactments in relation to any such order, subsections (2) to (5) of this section shall have effect in relation to any association (whether incorporated or not) if—

(*a*) its membership consists wholly or mainly of persons (in this subsection referred to as "members affected by the order") who are either engaged in the supply of services brought under control by the order or are employed by or represent persons so engaged, and

(*b*) its objects or activities include the promotion of the interests of persons engaged in the supply of those services who are either members affected by the order or are persons represented by such members, and

(*c*) it is not a society which is for the time being approved under section 6A of the Act of 1956.

(2) The relevant enactments shall have effect in relation to any agreement made by the association—

(*a*) as if the agreement were made between all persons who are members of the association or are represented on it by members of the association, and

(*b*) where any restriction is accepted under the agreement by the association, or provision is made in the agreement for or in relation to the furnishing of information by the association, as if the like restriction were accepted by, or (as the case may be) the like provision were made for or in relation to the furnishing of information by, each of the persons who are members of the association or are so represented.

(3) Where the order is one made under section 107 of this Act, and specific recommendations (whether express or implied) are made by or on behalf of the association to its members, or to any class of its members, as to the action to be taken or not to be taken by them in relation to any particular class of services in respect of any matters specified in the order for the purposes of subsection (1)(*b*) of that section, the relevant enactments shall have effect in relation to the agreement for the constitution of the association as if it contained a term by which each such member, and any person represented on the association by any such member, agreed to comply with those recommendations and with any subsequent recommendations made to them by or on behalf of the association as to the action to be taken by them in relation to the same class of services and in respect of the same matters.

(4) Where the order is one made under section 108 of this Act, and specific recommendations (whether express or implied) are made by or on behalf of the association to its members, or to any class of its members, as to the furnishing of information in relation to any particular class of services in respect of any matters specified in the order for the purposes of subsection (1)(*b*) of that section, the relevant enactments shall have effect in relation to the agreement for the constitution of the association as if it contained a term by which each such member, and any person represented on the association by any such member, agreed to comply with those recommendations and with any subsequent recommendations made to them by or on behalf of the association as to the furnishing of information in relation to the same class of services and in respect of the same matters.

(5) Subsection (3) or subsection (4) of this section (where applicable) shall have effect in relation to the agreement for the constitution of an association notwithstanding any provision to the contrary in that agreement.

(6) In relation to a society which is for the time being approved under section 6A of the Act of 1956, but which, in consequence of an order made under section 107 or section 108 of this Act, is a society to which the preceding provisions of this section would apply if it were not so approved, subsection (4) of that section (which confers power on the Secretary of State to withdraw any such approval) shall have effect as if in that subsection—

(*a*) any reference to an agreement which would have been subject to registration under Part I of the Act of 1956 if the approval had not been given included a reference to an agreement which would in those circumstances have been subject to such registration by virtue of the order, and

(*b*) any reference to such a recommendation as is mentioned in section 6(7) of that Act included a reference to such a recommendation as is mentioned in subsection (3) or subsection (4) of this section. [**212**]

COMMENCEMENT

See s. 140 (3), *post*, and the note to s. 1, *ante*.

DEFINITIONS

"services brought under control by the order": s. 107 (1) or s. 108 (1), *ante*.
"relevant enactments": s. 110 (6), *ante*.
"services": s. 117 (1), *post*.
"agreement" and "restriction": by virtue of s. 117 (3), *post*, see the Restrictive Trade Practices Act 1956, s. 6 (3), 37 Halsbury's Statutes (3rd Edn.) 82.
"supply": by virtue of s. 117 (3), *post*, see s. 36 (1) of 1956 Act, *ibid.*, p. 112.
"members affected by the order": note sub-s. (1) (*a*) above.
"Act of 1956": *I.e.*, the Restrictive Trade Practices Act 1956; see s. 137 (1), *post*. For Part I of that Act see 37 Halsbury's Statutes (3rd Edn.) 78, and for s. 6A, see s. 98, *post*. Note also the other amendments made by Part IX (ss. 94–106) of this Act, *ante*.

GENERAL NOTE

Ss. 107 and 108, *ante*, apply only to "agreements between two or more persons carrying on business within the United Kingdom in the supply of services". If such persons form themselves into an association an agreement between that association and another person not engaged in the supply of the same services would *prima facie* not be caught by ss. 107 or 108. The effect of s. 112 (2) above is to "pierce the veil" of the association and treat such an agreement as being with all the members individually so allowing the agreement to come within s. 107 or s. 108.

Recommendations made by an association of suppliers of services to its members or to any class of members as to how they should cope with an order under s. 107 are themselves brought within s. 107 by s. 112 (3) above and such recommendations as to an order under s. 108 are themselves brought within s. 108 by s. 112 (4) above.

By virtue of s. 112 (1) (*a*) an association where the greater part of the membership is not engaged in the supply of services in question and is not employed by or does not represent persons so engaged is not covered by s. 112.

An association may fortuitously contain as a majority of its membership persons described in s. 112 (1) (*a*) but the objects or activities of the association may not consist of the promotion of the interests of its members in their work of supplying such services or of persons represented by those members. If so the association is not covered by s. 112, by virtue of s. 112 (1) (*b*).

By virtue of s. 112 (1) (*c*) an association approved for the time being by the Secretary of State as an industrial and provident society within s. 6A of the Act of 1956 (see the General Note to s. 98, *ante*) is not subject to s. 112. S. 112 (6) allows the Secretary of State to withdraw approval given under s. 6A of the Act of 1956.

113. Matters to be treated as equivalent to restrictions for purposes of s. 107

(1) For the purposes of any order made under section 107 of this Act, and for the purposes of the operation of the relevant enactments in relation to any such order, an agreement which—

(*a*) confers privileges or benefits only upon such parties as comply with conditions as to any such matters as are mentioned in subsection (3) of that section, or

(*b*) imposes obligations upon parties who do not comply with such conditions,

shall be treated as an agreement under which restrictions are accepted by each of the parties in respect of those matters.

(2) Without prejudice to the preceding subsection, an obligation on the part of any party to an agreement to make payments calculated by reference to the extent to which, or the scale on which,—

(*a*) any designated services are made available or supplied by him, or

(*b*) any services are obtained by him for the purpose of making available or supplying any designated services,

if the payments are calculated, or calculated at an increased rate, in respect of an extent or scale exceeding an extent or scale specified in or ascertained in accordance with the agreement, shall, subject to the next following subsection, be treated for the purposes mentioned in the preceding subsection as a restriction in respect of the extent or scale of the designated services to be made available or supplied.

(3) Subsection (2) of this section shall not apply to any obligation on the part of any person to make payments to an association of which he is a member, if it is such an association as is mentioned in section 112(1) of this Act and the payments are to consist only of bona fide subscriptions for membership of the association. [213]

COMMENCEMENT

See s. 140 (3), *post*, and the note to s. 1, *ante*.

DEFINITIONS

"designated services": s. 109 (1), *ante*.

"relevant enactments": s. 110 (6), *ante*.

"services": s. 117 (1), *post*.

"agreement" and "restriction": by virtue of s. 117 (3), *post*, see the Restrictive Trade Practices Act 1956, s. 6 (3), 37 Halsbury's Statutes (3rd Edn.) 82.

"supply": by virtue of s. 117 (3), *post*, see s. 36 (1) of the Act of 1956, *ibid*., p. 112.

GENERAL NOTE

This section amplifies the meaning of "agreement under which . . . restrictions . . . are accepted" in s. 107 (1) (*b*), *ante*, to include the acceptance of obligations of the sort described in sub-ss. (1) and (2) above.

Because of sub-s. (3) above an obligation to pay *bona fide* subscriptions to an association of a kind within s. 112 (1), *ante*, does not operate as the acceptance of a restriction for these purposes.

114. Provisions to be disregarded

(1) The following provisions of this section shall have effect for the purpose of determining whether an agreement is one to which Part I of the Act of 1956 applies by virtue of an order made under section 107 or section 108 of this Act.

(2) Subject to subsections (3) and (4) of this section, no account shall for that purpose be taken of any term which relates exclusively to the services supplied in pursuance of the agreement in question.

(3) Where the order referred to in subsection (1) of this section is an order under section 107 of this Act, and any of the restrictions accepted as mentioned

in subsection (1)(*b*) of that section are accepted as between two or more persons by whom designated services are to be supplied, or as between two or more persons for whom designated services are to be supplied, in pursuance of the agreement, subsection (2) of this section shall not apply to any term of the agreement which imposes those restrictions unless those restrictions are accepted in pursuance of a previous agreement in respect of which particulars have been registered under Part I of the Act of 1956 as applied by this Part of this Act.

(4) Where the order referred to in subsection (1) of this section is an order made under section 108 of this Act, and the term referred to in subsection (2) of this section is a term by which provision is made for the furnishing of information as mentioned in subsection (1)(*b*) of that section by two or more persons by whom designated services are to be supplied, or by two or more persons for whom designated services are to be supplied, in pursuance of the agreement, subsection (2) of this section shall not apply to that term unless it was included in the agreement in pursuance of a previous agreement of which particulars have been registered under Part I of the Act of 1956 as applied by this Part of this Act.

(5) For the purpose mentioned in subsection (1) of this section no account shall be taken of any term by which the parties or any of them agree to comply with or apply, in respect of making available, supplying or obtaining any designated services,—

(*a*) any standards (whether being standards of performance in the provision of the services or standards of dimension, design, quality or performance in respect of goods used in providing them) which are either standards approved for the time being by the British Standards Institution or standards prescribed or adopted by an association or other body and for the time being approved by an order made by the Secretary of State by statutory instrument, or

(*b*) any arrangements either approved by the British Standards Institution, or prescribed or adopted and approved by an order of the Secretary of State, as mentioned in the preceding paragraph, as to the provision of information or advice to persons for whom designated services are supplied or agreed to be supplied.

(6) For the purpose mentioned in subsection (1) of this section no account shall be taken of any restriction which affects or relates to any of the matters mentioned in section 7(4) of the Act of 1956 (which relates to employment and to terms and conditions of employment) or of any provision for or in relation to the furnishing of information with respect to any of those matters. [**214**]

COMMENCEMENT

See s. 140 (3), *post*, and the note to s. 1, *ante*.

DEFINITIONS

"designated services": s. 109 (1), *ante*.

"services": s. 117 (1), *post*.

"agreement" and "restriction": by virtue of s. 117 (3), *post*, see the Restrictive Trade Practices Act 1956, s. 6 (3), 37 Halsbury's Statutes (3rd Edn.) 82.

"goods": by virtue of s. 117 (3), *post*, see s. 36 (1) of the Act of 1956, *ibid*., p. 112.

"Act of 1956": *I.e.*, the Restrictive Trade Practices Act 1956; see s. 137 (1), *post*. For Part I and s. 7 (4) of that Act, see 37 Halsbury's Statutes (3rd Edn.) 78, 86, and note the amendments made to that Part by Part IX (ss. 94–106) of this Act, *ante*.

GENERAL NOTE

Ss. 114 and 115 provide in respect of services for most of the exceptions from registration contained in ss. 7 and 8 of the Restrictive Trade Practices Act 1956 relating to goods. As to the framing of orders under this Part, see the notes to ss. 107–110, *ante*.

115. Excepted agreements

(1) Subsection (1) of section 8 of the Act of 1956 (which relates to agreements expressly authorised by or under an enactment) and subsection (2) of that section (which relates to agreements constituting or forming part of a scheme certified under provisions of the Income and Corporation Taxes Act 1970 relating to schemes for rationalising industry) shall have effect in relation to any agreement notwithstanding any order under section 107 or section 108 of this Act.

(2) Part I of the Act of 1956 shall not apply by virtue of any such order to an agreement to which there are no parties other than one person who agrees to supply services and another person for whom they are to be supplied, where neither of those persons is, in relation to that order, such an association as is mentioned in section 112(1) of this Act and, except in respect of the supply of services of the same description to, or obtaining services of the same description from, other persons,—

(*a*) in the case of an order under section 107 of this Act, no restrictions are accepted under the agreement by those parties in respect of matters specified in the order for the purposes of subsection (1)(*b*) of that section, or

(*b*) in the case of an order under section 108 of this Act, no provision is made under the agreement for or in relation to the furnishing of information with respect to matters specified in the order for the purpose of subsection (1)(*b*) of that section.

(3) Subject to the next following subsection, Part I of the Act of 1956 shall not apply by virtue of any such order to any licence granted by the proprietor or any licensee of a patent or by a person who has applied for a patent to any assignment of a patent or of the right to apply for a patent, or to any agreement for such a licence or assignment, if it is a licence, assignment or agreement under which—

(*a*) in the case of an order under section 107 of this Act, no restrictions in respect of matters specified in the order for the purposes of subsection (1)(*b*) of that section are accepted except in respect of the invention to which the patent or application for a patent relates, or

(*b*) in the case of an order under section 108 of this Act, no provision for or in relation to the furnishing of information with respect to matters specified in the order for the purposes of subsection (1)(*b*) of that section is made except in respect of that invention.

(4) No licence, assignment or agreement shall by virtue of subsection (3) of this section be precluded from being an agreement to which Part I of the Act of 1956 applies if—

(*a*) in the case of an agreement, it is a patent or design pooling agreement, or

(*b*) whether being a licence, assignment or agreement, it is a licence, assignment or agreement granted or made in pursuance (directly or indirectly) of a patent or design pooling agreement.

(5) Part I of the Act of 1956 shall not apply by virtue of any order section 107 of this Act to an agreement between two persons, neither of whom is such an association as is mentioned in section 112(1) of this Act, for the exchange of information relating to techniques or processes to be applied in the provision of designated services where—

(*a*) no other person is party to the agreement, and

(*b*) all such restrictions as are mentioned in section 107(1)(*b*) of this Act which are accepted under the agreement relate exclusively to the form or manner in which services incorporating those techniques or processes are to be made available or supplied.

(6) Part I of the Act of 1956 shall not apply by virtue of any such order to any agreement where—

(*a*) in the case of an order under section 107 of this Act all such restrictions as are accepted under the agreement in respect of matters specified in the order for the purposes of subsection (1)(*b*) of that section (or, in a case falling within subsection (3) of section 112 of this Act, all the recommendations referred to in that subsection) relate to the supply of services outside the United Kingdom or to the supply of services to persons or in relation to property outside the United Kingdom, or

(*b*) in the case of an order under section 108 of this Act, all such provision as is made under the agreement for or in relation to the furnishing of information with respect to matters specified in the order for the purposes of subsection (1)(*b*) of that section (or, in a case falling within subsection (4) of section 112 of this Act, every such recommendation as is referred to in that subsection) relates to the supply of services as mentioned in the preceding paragraph.

(7) Any reference in this section to restrictions accepted in respect of matters specified in an order under section 107 of this Act for the purposes of subsection (1)(*b*) of that section, or to provision made for or in relation to the furnishing of information with respect to matters specified in an order under section 108 of this Act for the purposes of subsection (1)(*b*) of that section, shall be construed, in relation to any agreement, as not including anything of which, by virtue of section 114 of this Act, account cannot be taken for the purpose mentioned in subsection (1) of that section.

(8) Subsections (2) to (4) of section 8A of the Act of 1956 shall have effect for the purposes of this section as they have effect for the purposes of that section.

(9) In this section "property" means property of any description, whether movable or immovable. [**215**]

COMMENCEMENT

See s. 140 (3), *post*, and the note to s. 1, *ante*.

DEFINITIONS

"designated service": s. 109 (1), *ante*.

"services": s. 117 (1), *post*.

"agreement" and "restriction": by virtue of s. 117 (3), *post*, see the Restrictive Trade Practices Act 1956, s. 6 (3), 37 Halsbury's Statutes (3rd Edn.) 82.

"supply": by virtue of s. 117 (3), *post*, see s. 36 (1) of the Act of 1956, *ibid*., p. 112.

"patent or design pooling agreement": see s. 8A (2) of the Act of 1956 as inserted by s. 101, *ante*.

"licence, assignment or agreement granted or made in pursuance of such a pooling agreement": see s. 8A (3) of the Act of 1956 inserted by s. 101, *ante*. Note also the definitions in s. 115 (7) and (9) above.

"Act of 1956": *I.e.*, the Restrictive Trade Practices Act 1956; see s. 137 (1), *post*. For Part I and s. 8 (1), (2) of that Act, see 37 Halsbury's Statutes (3rd Edn.) 78, 87, and for s. 8A (2)–(4), see s. 101, *ante*. Note also the other amendments to that Part made by Part IX (ss. 94–106) of this Act, *ante*.

GENERAL NOTE

See the General Note to s. 114, *ante*.

Income and Corporation Taxes Act 1970. The relevant provisions of that Act are contained in ss. 406–410 thereof, 33 Halsbury's Statutes (3rd Edn.) 524–528.

116. Application of provisions of Acts of 1956 and 1968

(1) Subject to the following provisions of this section, sections 9 to 23 of the Act of 1956 shall have effect in relation to agreements to which Part I of that Act applies by virtue of an order under section 107 or section 108 of this Act as they have effect in relation to agreements to which Part I of that Act applies apart from any such order.

(2) For the purposes of the application of those sections in relation to an agreement to which Part I of that Act applies by virtue of such an order, such of those sections as are specified in the first column of Part I of Schedule 10 to this Act shall have effect subject to the modifications specified in relation to them in the second column of that Part of that Schedule.

(3) For the purposes of the application of section 21 of that Act in relation to an agreement to which Part I of that Act applies by virtue of such an order, that section shall have effect subject to the following modifications, that is to say—

(*a*) with the substitution, for paragraphs (*a*) and (*b*) of subsection (1), of the following paragraphs:—

"(*a*) that the restriction is reasonably necessary, having regard to the character of the services to which it applies, to protect the public against injury (whether to persons or to premises) in connection with the use of those services or in connection with the consumption, installation or use of goods in relation to which those services are supplied;

(*b*) that the removal of the restriction would deny to the public as users of any services, or as purchasers, consumers or users of any goods in relation to which any services are supplied, other specific and substantial benefits or advantages enjoyed or likely to be enjoyed by them as such, whether by virtue of the restriction itself or of any arrangements or operations resulting therefrom";

(*b*) with the substitution, for paragraph (*d*) of subsection (1), of the following paragraph:—

"(*d*) that the restriction is reasonably necessary to enable the persons party to the agreement to negotiate fair terms for the supply of services to, or for obtaining services from, any one person not party thereto who controls a preponderant part of the trade or business of supplying such services, or for the supply of services to any person not party to the agreement and not carrying on such a trade or business who, either alone or in combination with any other such person, controls a preponderant part of the market for such services"; and

(*c*) with the substitution, in the provisions of that subsection after paragraph (*h*), for the words "(being purchasers, consumers or users of goods produced or sold by such parties, or persons engaged or seeking to become engaged in the trade or business of selling such goods or of producing or selling similar goods)" of the words "(being users of services supplied by such parties, or persons engaged or seeking to become engaged in any business of supplying such services or of making available or supplying similar services, or being purchasers, consumers or users of goods in relation to which any such services or similar services are supplied)".

(4) Sections 1 to 3 and sections 6 and 7 of the Act of 1968 shall have effect in relation to agreements to which Part I of the Act of 1956 applies by virtue

of an order under section 107 or section 108 of this Act, but, in the case of such of those sections as are specified in the first column of Part II of Schedule 10 to this Act, shall have effect in relation to such agreements subject to the modifications specified in relation to them in the second column of that Part of that Schedule.

(5) In section 9 of the Act of 1968 any reference to particulars entered or filed in the register pursuant to Part I of the Act of 1956 shall be construed as including a reference to particulars so entered or filed pursuant to any provisions of Part I of the Act of 1956 as applied by subsection (1) of this section.

(6) Any reference in this section to any provisions of the Act of 1956 shall be construed as including a reference to those provisions as applied by section 5(2) of the Act of 1968 (which relates to information agreements); and the modifications of section 21 of the Act of 1956 made by subsection (3) of this section shall be construed accordingly.

(7) Where by virtue of subsection (2) or subsection (4) of this section any provisions of the Act of 1956 or of the Act of 1968 are to have effect subject to modifications specified in Schedule 10 to this Act for the purposes of their application to an agreement to which Part I of the Act of 1956 applies by virtue of an order under section 107 or section 108 of this Act—

(*a*) that order shall be taken to be "the relevant order" referred to in those modifications, and

(*b*) in those modifications "the Act of 1973" means this Act and "services brought under control by the relevant order" means services of the class described in that order in accordance with section 107(1) or section 108(1) of this Act. [**216**]

COMMENCEMENT

See s. 140 (3), *post*, and the note to s. 1, *ante*.

DEFINITIONS

"services": s. 117 (1), *post*.

"business": s. 117 (2), *post*.

"agreement" and "restriction": by virtue of s. 117 (3), *post*, see the Restrictive Trade Practices Act 1956, s. 6 (3), 37 Halsbury's Statutes (3rd Edn.) 82.

"goods" and "supply": by virtue of s. 117 (3), *post*, see s. 36 (1) of that Act, *ibid*., p. 112.

"purchasers", "consumers" and "users" and "any one person": by virtue of s. 117 (3), *post*, see s. 21 (2) of the Act of 1956, *ibid*., p. 102.

"Act of 1956": *I.e.*, the Restrictive Trade Practices Act 1956; see s. 137 (1), *post*. For Part I and ss. 9–23 of that Act, see 37 Halsbury's Statutes (3rd Edn.) 78, 89–103, and note the amendments made to that Part by Part IX (ss. 94–106) of this Act, *ante*.

"Act of 1968": *I.e.*, the Restrictive Trade Practices Act 1968; see s. 137 (1), *post*. For ss. 1–3, 5 (2), 6, 7 and 9 of that Act, see 37 Halsbury's Statutes (3rd Edn.) 317–319, 321, 322, 323, 325. S. 6 of the Act of 1968 is amended by s. 139 (1) and Sch. 12, *post*, and s. 7 is amended by s. 104 (2), *ante*.

GENERAL NOTE

This section applies the various provisions of the Restrictive Trade Practices Act 1956 and 1968 (listed under Definitions above) to agreements made registrable by orders under s. 107 or s. 108 of this Act.

In addition under s. 116 (3) above the criteria of the public interest (the gateways to validation by the Restrictive Practices Court of a registered agreement) contained in s. 21 of the Act of 1956 are modified in ways relevant to restrictions on the supply of services.

117. Interpretation of Part X and Schedule 10

(1) In this Part of this Act, and in the modifications made by it, "services" does not include the application to goods of any process of manufacture or any

services rendered to an employer under a contract of employment, but, with those exceptions, includes engagements (whether professional or other) which for gain or reward are undertaken and performed for any matter other than the production or supply of goods, and any reference to the supply of services or to supplying, obtaining or offering services or to making services available shall be construed accordingly.

(2) In this Part of this Act and in the modifications made by it "business" includes a professional practice.

(3) Subsection (3) of section 6 (which relates to the meaning of "agreement" and "restriction") and subsections (1) to (3) of section 36 (interpretation) of the Act of 1956 shall have effect for the purposes of this Part of this Act and of the modifications made by it.

(4) For the purposes of this Part of this Act any two or more interconnected bodies corporate, or any two or more individuals carrying on business in partnership with each other, shall be treated as a single person.

(5) In this section any reference to the modifications made by this Part of this Act is a reference to any provisions which by virtue of section 116 of this Act (whether they are provisions set out in that section or in Schedule 10 to this Act) are to be treated, for purposes mentioned in that section, as substituted for provisions of the Act of 1956 or of the Act of 1968. [**217**]

COMMENCEMENT

See s. 140 (3), *post*, and the note to s. 1, *ante*.

DEFINITIONS

"This Part of this Act": *I.e.*, Part X (ss. 107–117) of this Act.

"shall be treated as a single person": the meaning of the corresponding provision in the Restrictive Trade Practices Act 1956, s. 8 (9), 37 Halsbury's Statutes (3rd Edn.) 88, was considered in *Re Schweppes Ltd's. Agreement* (*No.* 2), *Registrar of Restrictive Trading Agreements* v. *Schweppes, Ltd.*, [1971] 2 All E.R. 1473, at 1487, 1488.

"contract of employment": s. 137 (1), *post*.

"goods", "interconnected bodies corporate" and "supply", see, by virtue of sub-s. (3) above, the Restrictive Trades Practices Act 1956, s. 36 (1), 37 Halsbury's Statutes (3rd Edn.) 112, as amended by s. 106, *ante*.

Note sub-s. (5) above on "modification made by this Part of this Act".

PART XI

PYRAMID SELLING AND SIMILAR TRADING SCHEMES

118. Trading schemes to which Part XI applies

(1) This Part of this Act applies to any trading scheme which includes the following elements, that is to say—

(*a*) goods or services, or both, are to be provided by the person promoting the scheme (in this Part of this Act referred to as "the promoter") or, in the case of a scheme promoted by two or more persons acting in concert (in this Part of this Act referred to as "the promoters"), are to be provided by one or more of those persons;

(*b*) the goods or services so provided are to be supplied to or for other persons under transactions effected by persons (other than the promoter or any of the promoters) who participate in the scheme (each of whom is in this Part of this Act referred to as a "participant");

(*c*) those transactions, or most of them, are to be effected elsewhere than at premises at which the promoter or any of the promoters or the participant effecting the transaction carries on business; and (*d*) the prospect is held out to participants of receiving payments or other benefits in respect of any one or more of the matters specified in the next following subsection.

(2) The matters referred to in paragraph (*d*) of subsection (1) of this section are—

(*a*) the introduction of other persons who become participants;
(*b*) the promotion, transfer or other change of status of participants within the trading scheme;
(*c*) the supply of goods to other participants;
(*d*) the supply of training facilities or other services for other participants;
(*e*) transactions effected by other participants under which goods are to be supplied to, or services are to be supplied for, other persons.

(3) For the purposes of this Part of this Act a trading scheme shall be taken to include the element referred to in paragraph (*b*) of subsection (1) of this section whether the transactions referred to in that paragraph are to be effected by participants in the capacity of servants or agents of the promoter or of one of the promoters or in any other capacity.

(4) In determining, for the purposes of paragraph (*c*) of subsection (1) of this section, whether any premises are premises at which a participant in a trading scheme carries on business, no account shall be taken of transactions effected or to be effected by him under that trading scheme.

(5) For the purposes of this Part of this Act such a prospect as is mentioned in paragraph (*d*) of subsection (1) of this section shall be taken to be held out to a participant—

(*a*) whether it is held out so as to confer on him a legally enforceable right or not, and
(*b*) in so far as it relates to the introduction of new participants, whether it is limited to the introduction of new participants by him or extends to the introduction of new participants by other persons.

(6) In this Part of this Act "trading scheme" includes any arrangements made in connection with the carrying on of a business, whether those arrangements are made or recorded wholly or partly in writing or not.

(7) In this section any reference to the provision of goods or services by a person shall be construed as including a reference to the provision of goods or services under arrangements to which that person is a party. [**218**]

COMMENCEMENT

See s. 140 (3), *post*, and the note to s. 1, *ante*.

DEFINITIONS

"business", "goods" and "supply": s. 137 (2).
"supply of services": s. 137 (3).
"services": s. 137(4).
"promoter", "promoters", "participant", "trading scheme" and "provision of goods or services by a person". Note the definitions in sub-ss. (1) (*a*), (*b*), (6), (7) above.

GENERAL NOTE

Sub-s. (1): "*Trading scheme.*" "Trading scheme" is defined in sub-s. (6) above. The most significant word in the definition appears to be "arrangements". This word is undoubtedly wider than the word "agreements" and appears to include mutual rights and obligations which are not enforceable by legal process; see *Re Austin Motor Car Co. Ltd.'s Agreements* (1957), L.R. 1 R.P. 6, and *Re British Basic Slag, Ltd.'s Agreements*, (1962), L.R. 3 R.P. 178.

"*Which includes.*" A "trading scheme" need not therefore be confined to the matters itemised in paragraphs (*a*)–(*d*) of sub-s. (1).

Para. (*a*): "*Provided by the person.*" This expression receives an extended definition from sub-s. (7) above. It is, apparently, not necessary for the "promoter" to be the person by whom those goods or services were directly provided.

Para. (*b*): "*Effected.*" The use of the word "effected" in sub-s. (1) (*b*) suggests that the "participant" is required to play an active role in the transaction. It would not appear to be sufficient that the participant is merely a party to those transactions.

Para. (*c*): "*Or most of them.*" The use of these words would appear to require a proportion considerably in excess of one half.

"*Carries on business.*" Cf. the note "Carrying on a business" to s. 29, *ante*.

Para. (*d*): "*The prospect is held out.*" For definition, note sub-s. (5) above.

"*Or other benefits.*" This provision, which is in general terms, appears to cover all benefits other than those payable in money or money's worth.

Sub-s. (2): "*Of participants.*" This expression appears to include the promotion, transfer or other change of status of the relevant participant himself.

119. Regulations relating to such trading schemes

(1) Regulations made by the Secretary of State by statutory instrument may make provision with respect to the issue, circulation or distribution of documents, whether being advertisements, prospectuses, circulars or notices, which—

(*a*) contain any invitation to persons to become participants in a trading scheme to which this Part of this Act applies, or

(*b*) contain any information calculated to lead directly or indirectly to persons becoming participants in such a trading scheme,

and may prohibit any such document from being issued, circulated or distributed unless it complies with such requirements as to the matters to be included or not included in it as may be prescribed by the regulations.

(2) Regulations made by the Secretary of State by statutory instrument may prohibit the promoter or any of the promoters of, or any participant in, a trading scheme to which this Part of this Act applies from—

(*a*) supplying any goods to a participant in the trading scheme, or

(*b*) supplying any training facilities or other services for such a participant, or

(*c*) providing any goods or services under a transaction effected by such a participant, or

(*d*) being a party to any arrangements under which goods or services are supplied or provided as mentioned in any of the preceding paragraphs, or

(*e*) accepting from any such participant any payment, or any undertaking to make a payment, in respect of any goods or services supplied or provided as mentioned in any of paragraphs (*a*) to (*d*) of this subsection or in respect of any goods or services to be so supplied or provided,

unless (in any such case) such requirements are as prescribed by the regulations are complied with.

(3) Any requirements prescribed by regulations under subsection (2) of this section shall be such as the Secretary of State considers necessary or expedient for the purpose of preventing participants in trading schemes to which this Part of this Act applies from being unfairly treated; and, without prejudice to the generality of this subsection, any such requirements may include provisions—

(*a*) requiring the rights and obligations of every participant under such a trading scheme to be set out in full in an agreement in writing made between the participant and the promoter or (if more than one) each of the promoters;

(*b*) specifying rights required to be conferred on every such participant, and obligations required to be assumed by the promoter or promoters, under any such trading scheme; or

(*c*) imposing restrictions on the liabilities to be incurred by such a participant in respect of any of the matters mentioned in paragraphs (*a*) to (*e*) of subsection (2) of this section.

(4) Regulations made under subsection (2) of this section—

(*a*) may include provision for enabling a person who has made a payment as a participant in a trading scheme to which this Part of this Act applies, in circumstances where any of the requirements prescribed by the regulations were not complied with, to recover the whole or part of that payment from any person to whom or for whose benefit it was paid, and

(*b*) subject to any provision made in accordance with the preceding paragraph, may prescribe the degree to which anything done in contravention of the regulations is to be treated as valid or invalid for the purposes of any civil proceedings.

(5) The power to make regulations under this section may be exercised so as to make different provision—

(*a*) in relation to different descriptions of trading schemes to which this Part of this Act applies, or

(*b*) in relation to trading schemes which are or were in operation on a date specified in the regulations and trading schemes which are or were not in operation on that date,

or in relation to different descriptions of participants in such trading schemes.

[219]

COMMENCEMENT

See s. 140 (3), *post*, and the note to s. 1, *ante*.

DEFINITIONS

"the promoter", "the promoters", "participant", "trading scheme": s. 118.
"goods", "supply", "supply of services" and "services": s. 137.

GENERAL NOTE

Sub-s. (1): *"Regulations."* The Pyramid Selling Schemes Regulations 1973, S.I. 1973 No. 1740, which came into operation on the 15th November 1973, have been made under this section. The Regulations are set out in Division 3, *post*.

"Secretary of State." See the note to s. 1, *ante*.

"Statutory instrument." See the note to s. 3, *ante*.

"Issue." It is not clear whether such a document becomes issued when delivered to the first recipient or when the document is initially signed and completed. It is suggested that issue does not take place until the document is actually delivered to a recipient; but see *Chong* v. *Fairfield Municipal Council* (1968), 89 W.N. (Pt. 1) (N.S.W.) 194.

"Circulation." This implies that the relevant document is already passing from hand to hand, see *Bank of Africa, Ltd.* v. *Colonial Government* (1888), 57 L.J.P.C. 66.

"Distribution." This word appears to be similar to "circulation" but, perhaps, implies the simultaneous delivery of the document to a number of persons; see *R.* v. *McNiven*, [1944] 1 W.W.R. 127.

"Documents." This undoubtedly includes written material conveying or containing information and, probably, extends to tape recordings, computer print outs and cinema films; see *e.g.*, *Cassidy* v. *Engwirda Construction Co.*, [1967] Q.W.N. 16, and *Grant* v. *South Western and County Properties*, [1974] 2 All E.R. 465.

"Advertisements." For a case dealing with a similar provision of the Protection of Depositors Act 1963, see *R.* v. *Delmayne*, [1970] 2 Q.B. 170.

"Prospectuses." See the definition in the Companies Act 1948, s. 455, read in the light of s. 55 of that Act.

"*Circulars.*" This word has not been defined judicially but would appear to extend to a document sent, or intended to be sent, to a number of persons.

"*Notices.*" This word is used in a number of Statutes and appears to include any document containing a direct and definite statement of the requisite material.

"*Any invitation.*" These words would appear to be equivalent to the expression "invitation to treat" in contractual usage. It would not therefore appear to be necessary for the relevant document to be capable of creating legal obligations simply on acceptance by the would-be "participant".

"*Calculated.*" This word is not free from ambiguity as it may mean either "likely" or "intended". It is submitted that, in the present context, the word has the former meaning. For relevant authorities, see *Eno* v. *Dunn* (1890), 15 App. Cas. 252; *Re McGlennon's Application for Registration of Shamrock* (1908), 25 T.L.R. 23; *Re Royal Worcester Corset Co.'s Application*, [1909] 1 Ch. 459; *North Cheshire and Manchester Brewery Co.* v. *Manchester Brewery Co.*, [1899] A.C. 83, and *McDowell* v. *Standard Oil Co. (New Jersey)*, [1927] A.C. 632.

Sub-s. (2). The material set out in paras. (*a*)–(*e*) obviously relates back to s. 118, *ante*.

Sub-s. (3): "*Such as the Secretary of State considers.*" The Secretary of State is thus entrusted with a discretion which must, probably, be exercised reasonably; cf. the note "If it appears to him" to s. 15, *ante*.

"*Necessary or expedient.*" These are alternative conditions. The word "expedient"— can probably be paraphrased as "practically desirable".

"*Unfairly treated.*" This expression which is general and which imports a value judgement is nowhere defined in the Act.

"*Without prejudice to the generality.*" Paragraphs (*a*)–(*c*) in no way detract from the general force of the words "unfairly treated".

Para. (a): "*Agreement in writing.*" This is narrower than the expression "arrangement". The agreement must be legally binding and must be in writing within the meaning of the Interpretation Act 1889, s. 20.

Sub-s. (4): "*May include.*" This is therefore a permissive provision.

"*A payment.*" This is thus narrower than the expression "payments or other benefits" referred to in s. 118.

"*To whom or for whose benefit.*" The provision thus includes a person who derives an indirect benefit from a payment made.

120. Offences under Part XI

(1) Subject to the next following section, any person who issues, circulates or distributes, or causes another person to issue, circulate or distribute, a document in contravention of any regulations made under subsection (1) of section 119 of this Act shall be guilty of an offence.

(2) Any person who contravenes any regulations made under subsection (2) of that section shall be guilty of an offence.

(3) If any person who is a participant in a trading scheme to which this Part of this Act applies, or has applied or been invited to become a participant in such a trading scheme,—

(*a*) makes any payment to or for the benefit of the promoter or (if there is more than one) any of the promoters, or to or for the benefit of a participant in the trading scheme, and

(*b*) is induced to make that payment by reason that the prospect is held out to him of receiving payments or other benefits in respect of the introduction of other persons who become participants in the trading scheme,

any person to whom or for whose benefit that payment is made shall be guilty of an offence.

(4) If the promoter or any of the promoters of a trading scheme to which this Part of this Act applies, or any other person acting in accordance with such a trading scheme, by holding out to any person such a prospect as is mentioned in subsection (3)(*b*) of this section, attempts to induce him—

(*a*) if he is already a participant in the trading scheme, to make any payment to or for the benefit of the promoter or any of the promoters or to or for the benefit of a participant in the trading scheme, or

(*b*) if he is not already a participant in the trading scheme, to become such a participant and to make any such payment as is mentioned in the preceding paragraph,

the person attempting to induce him to make that payment shall be guilty of an offence.

(5) In determining, for the purposes of subsection (3) or subsection (4) of this section, whether an inducement or attempt to induce is made by holding out such a prospect as is therein mentioned, it shall be sufficient if such a prospect constitutes or would constitute a substantial part of the inducement.

(6) Where the person by whom an offence is committed under subsection (3) or subsection (4) of this section is not the sole promoter of the trading scheme in question, any other person who is the promoter or (as the case may be) one of the promoters of the trading scheme shall, subject to the next following section, also be guilty of that offence.

(7) Nothing in subsections (3) to (6) of this section shall be construed as limiting the circumstances in which the commission of any act may constitute an offence under subsection (1) or subsection (2) of this section.

(8) In this section any reference to the making of a payment to or for the benefit of a person shall be construed as including the making of a payment partly to or for the benefit of that person and partly to or for the benefit of one or more other persons. [**220**]

COMMENCEMENT

See s. 140 (3), *post*, and the note to s. 1, *ante*.

DEFINITIONS

"the promoter", "the promoters", "participant" and "trading scheme": s. 118.

GENERAL NOTE

Sub-s. (1): *"Issues, circulates or distributes."* Cf. the notes "Issue", "Circulation", "Distribution" to s. 119, *ante*.

"Causes another person." The guilty person must, so to speak, be the *causa causans* of the offending act.

"Document." See the note to s. 119, *ante*.

"Guilty of an offence." For defences, see s. 121, *post*; for penalties, see s. 122, *post*; and for enforcement, see s. 123, *post*.

Sub-s. (3). Note that the requirements of paras. (*a*) and (*b*) are cumulative.

Para. (a): *"To or for the benefit of."* Note the definition of this expression in sub-s. (8) above.

Para. (b): *"In respect of."* Although these words have been described as colourless (see *Cunard's Trustees* v. *Inland Revenue Commissioners* (1946), 174 L.T. 133), it is clear that the expression includes benefits having any connection, whether direct or indirect, with the introduction of a participant.

"To whom or for whose benefit." Note the definition in sub-s. (8), above.

Sub-s. (4): *"Attempts to induce."* It is sufficient that the offending person holds out a prospect such as is mentioned in sub-s. (3) (*b*) above—the prospect is not required to have had any effect.

"To make any payment." This expression, as used in paras. (*a*) and (*b*) seems confined to benefits in money or money's worth and does not extend to other benefits—cf. the "other benefits" mentioned in s. 118 (1) (*d*), *ante*.

Sub-s. (5): *"Constitutes or would constitute."* The two limbs of this provision cover inducing and attempting to induce as set out in sub-ss. (3) and (4) above.

"Substantial part." Although it is, probably, not possible to evaluate this requirement in quantitative terms, it is apparent that the prospect must constitute a significant part of the inducement.

Sub-s. (7): *"Nothing in subsections* (3) *to* (6)." This provision makes it clear that sub-ss. (3)–(6) merely contain examples of possible offences under sub-ss. (1) and (2).

121. Defences in certain proceedings under Part XI

(1) Where a person is charged with an offence under subsection (1) of section 120 of this Act in respect of an advertisement, it shall be a defence for him to prove that he is a person whose business it is to publish or arrange for the publication of advertisements, and that he received the advertisement for publication in the ordinary course of business and did not know, and had no reason to suspect, that its publication would amount to an offence under that subsection.

(2) Where a person is charged with an offence by virtue of subsection (6) of section 120 of this Act, it shall be a defence for him to prove—

(*a*) that the trading scheme to which the charge relates was in operation before the commencement of this Act, and

(*b*) that the act constituting the offence was committed without his consent or connivance. [**221**]

COMMENCEMENT

See s. 140 (3), *post*, and the note to s. 1, *ante*.

GENERAL NOTE

Sub-s. (1). For a similar provision, see s. 25 (3), *ante*, and the notes thereto.

"Be a defence." See the note to s. 25 (1), *ante*.

Sub-s. (2): *"Was in operation."* This must presumably require that a scheme of the like, or similar, nature was in operation at the relevant time.

"Consent; connivance." See the notes to s. 38 (1), *ante*.

122. Penalties for offences under Part XI

A person guilty of an offence under this Part of this Act shall be liable—

(*a*) on summary conviction, to a fine not exceeding £400 or to imprisonment for a term not exceeding three months or to both;

(*b*) on conviction on indictment, to a fine or to imprisonment for a term not exceeding two years or to both. [**222**]

COMMENCEMENT

See s. 140 (3), *post*, and the note to s. 1, *ante*.

GENERAL NOTE

"Person"; "summary conviction"; "conviction on indictment"; "fine"; "not exceeding two years." See the notes to s. 23, *ante*.

"Guilty of an offence." For offences, see s. 120, *ante*; for defences, see s. 121, *ante*; and for enforcement, see s. 123, *post*.

123. Enforcement provisions

(1) The provisions of sections 29 to 32 of this Act shall have effect for the purposes of this Part of this Act as if in those provisions—

(*a*) references to a weights and measures authority or a duly authorised officer of such an authority were omitted, and

(*b*) any reference to an offence under section 23 of this Act were a reference to an offence under this Part of this Act.

(2) For the purposes of the application to Northern Ireland of those provisions as applied by the preceding subsection—

(*a*) any reference to the Secretary of State shall be construed as a reference to the Ministry of Commerce for Northern Ireland, and (*b*) paragraphs (*c*) and (*d*) of section 33(2) of this Act shall have effect for the purposes of the application of Part II of this Act to Northern Ireland. [**223**]

COMMENCEMENT

See s. 140 (3), *post*, and the note to s. 1, *ante*.

GENERAL NOTE

"*Sections 29 to 32 of this Act shall have effect.*" Thus this section incorporates most of the enforcement machinery applicable to Orders under s. 22, *ante*.

"*This Part.*" *I.e.*, Part XI (ss. 118–123).

"*Part II.*" *I.e.*, ss. 13–33, *ante*.

PART XII

MISCELLANEOUS AND SUPPLEMENTARY PROVISIONS

124. Publication of information and advice

(1) With respect to any matter in respect of which the Director has any duties under section 2(1) of this Act, he may arrange for the publication, in such form and in such manner as he may consider appropriate, of such information and advice as it may appear to him to be expedient to give to consumers in the United Kingdom.

(2) In arranging for the publication of any such information or advice, the Director shall have regard to the need for excluding, so far as that is practicable,—

(*a*) any matter which relates to the private affairs of an individual, where the publication of that matter would or might, in the opinion of the Director, seriously and prejudicially affect the interests of that individual, and

(*b*) any matter which relates specifically to the affairs of a particular body of persons, whether corporate or unincorporate, where publication of that matter would or might, in the opinion of the Director, seriously and prejudicially affect the interests of that body.

(3) Without prejudice to the exercise of his powers under subsection (1) of this section, it shall be the duty of the Director to encourage relevant associations to prepare, and to disseminate to their members, codes of practice for guidance in safeguarding and promoting the interests of consumers in the United Kingdom.

(4) In this section "relevant association" means any association (whether incorporated or not) whose membership consists wholly or mainly of persons engaged in the production or supply of goods or in the supply of services or of persons employed by or representing persons so engaged and whose objects or activities include the promotion of the interests of persons so engaged. [**224**]

COMMENCEMENT

See s. 140 (3), *post*, and the note to s. 1, *ante*.

DEFINITIONS

"The Director", "consumer", "goods" and "supply": s. 137 (2); and for "consumer" also s. 137 (6).

"supply of services": s. 137 (3).

"services": 137 (4).

As to "relevant association": s. 124 (4).

GENERAL NOTE

Sub-s. (1): "*Duty under Section* 2 (1)." See the note "Duty of the Director" to s. 2 (1) (*a*), *ante*.

"*May arrange.*" These words are permissive.

"*Publication, in such form and in such manner as he may consider appropriate.*" These words confer on the Director a wide power which presumably includes the power to sell literature and to distribute it without charge.

"*Expedient.*" It is suggested that this involves something in the nature of public interest.

"*United Kingdom.*" See the note to s. 2, *ante.*

Sub-s. (2). This subsection is applied by s. 125 (5), *post.*

"*Shall have regard.*" The Director is obliged to consider both paras. (*a*) and (*b*), but is not inately entrusted with a discretion which must be exercised reasonably.

"*So far as that is practicable.*" Cf. *Lee* v. *Nursery Furnishings, Ltd.*, [1945] 1 All E.R. 387; *Adsett* v. *K and L Steelfounders and Engineers, Ltd.*, [1953] 1 W.L.R. 773, 779; *Knight* v. *Demolition and Construction Co., Ltd.*, [1953] 2 All E.R. 508; [1953] 1 W.L.R. 981; affirmed, [1954] 1 All E.R. 711, n.; [1954] 1 W.L.R. 563; *Re Farquhar's Affairs*, [1943] 2 All E.R. 781.

Para. (*a*): "*Private affairs.*" It is unclear what "private" is intended to add to "affairs". In the context of deciding whether someone is of unsound mind and incapable of managing himself and his affairs, "affairs" has been defined as including "the problems of work, society and marriage". The word "private" does not appear in sub-s. (2) (*b*); however it is suggested that "private" does not exclude business affairs. The subsection is not designed to put an individual in a worse position than a "body of persons".

"*In the opinion of the Director.*" These words qualify both "would" and "might". The test is subjective; but cf. the note "If it appears to him" to s. 15, *ante.*

"*Seriously and prejudicially.*" Note that these words are cumulative.

"*Interests.*" It is suggested that the word "interests" is not confined to proprietary interests but has its natural wider meaning.

Para. (*b*): "*Specifically.*" It is suggested that information or advice will only fall within para. (*b*) if its main or principal purpose is to draw attention to the affairs of a "particular body of persons".

"*Whether corporate or unincorporate.*" These words qualify "body" not "persons".

"*Where publication.*" The word "the" is omitted from para. (*b*). It seems therefore that the Director must consider under para. (*b*) a wider question than he must consider under para. (*a*).

Sub-s. (3): "*Encourage.*" The opening words of the section envisage that the Director will exercise his powers under sub-s. (1) with a view to encouragement under sub-s. (3). The Director cannot require the preparation and dissemination of codes of practice.

"*Codes of practice for guidance.*" There is no provision *requiring* the introduction of these codes. Nevertheless, they will have to be registered under the Restrictive Trade Practices Act 1956 (see s. 6 (3) of that Act). The constitutions of the "relevant associations" must also be registered under that Act (see s. 6 (7) thereof).

"*Safeguarding and promoting.*" Note that these words are cumulative.

"*Objects or activities include.*" A relevant association may therefore be principally concerned with other activities and objectives.

125. Annual and other reports of Director

(1) The Director shall, as soon as practicable after the end of the year 1974 and of each subsequent calendar year, make to the Secretary of State a report on his activities, and the activities of the Advisory Committee and of the Commission, during that year.

(2) Every such report shall include a general survey of developments, during the year to which it relates, in respect of matters falling within the scope of the Director's duties under any enactment (including any enactment contained in this Act, other than this section) [and shall set out any directions given to the Director under section 2(2) of the Consumer Credit Act 1974 during that year].

(3) The Secretary of State shall lay a copy of every report made by the Director under subsection (1) of this section before each House of Parliament, and shall arrange for every such report to be published in such manner as he may consider appropriate.

(4) The Director may also prepare such other reports as appear to him to

be expedient with respect to such matters as are mentioned in subsection (2) of this section, and may arrange for any such report to be published in such manner as he may consider appropriate.

(5) In making any report under this Act the Director shall have regard to the need for excluding, so far as that is practicable, any such matter as is specified in paragraph (*a*) or paragraph (*b*) of section 124(2) of this Act.

(6) For the purposes of this section any period between the commencement of this Act and the end of the year 1973 shall be treated as included in the year 1974. [**225**]

COMMENCEMENT

See s. 140 (3), *post*, and the note to s. 1, *ante*.

AMENDMENT

The words in square brackets were added by the Consumer Credit Act 1974, s. 5.

DEFINITIONS

"The Director", "the Advisory Committee", "the Commission", "enactment": s. 137 (2).

GENERAL NOTE

Sub-s. (1): *"Secretary of State."* See the note to s. 1, *ante*.

"Activities." I.e., the exercise of powers and rights and the performance of duties.

Sub-s. (2): *"Within the scope of the Directors duties."* But not apparently within the scope of his powers and rights.

Sub-s. (3): *"Lay . . . before . . . Parliament."* For meaning, see the Laying of Documents before Parliament (Interpretation) Act 1948.

"Published." Cf. the note "Publication, in such form, etc." to s. 124, *ante*.

Sub-s. (4). Unlike the rest of the section this is permissive. These reports do not have to be laid before Parliament.

"Expedient." See the note to s. 124 (1), *ante*.

Sub-s. (5): *Shall have regard; so far as that is practicable*. See the notes to s. 124 (2), *ante*.

126. Special provisions relating to patents

The following subsections shall be substituted for subsections (3) and (4) of section 40 of the Patents Act 1949 (which confer certain powers on the comptroller where a report of the Commission relates to patented articles or processes):—

"(3) Where, on a reference under section 50 or section 51 of the Fair Trading Act 1973, a report of the Monopolies and Mergers Commission, as laid before Parliament, contains conclusions to the effect—

(*a*) that a monopoly situation (within the meaning of that Act) exists in relation to a description of goods which consists of or includes patented articles, or consists of or includes articles to which a patented process has been applied, or that such a situation exists in relation to a description of services in which a patented process is used, and

(*b*) that facts found by the Commission in pursuance of their investigations under section 49 of that Act operate, or may be expected to operate, against the public interest,

the appropriate Minister or Ministers, subject to subsection (3B) of this section, may apply to the comptroller for an order under subsection (4) of this section in respect of the patent.

(3A) Where, on a reference under section 64 or section 75 of the Fair Trading Act 1973, a report of the Monopolies and Mergers Commission, as laid before Parliament, contains conclusions to the effect—

(*a*) that a merger situation qualifying for investigation has been created;

(*b*) that one of the elements which constitute the creation of that situation is that the condition specified in subsection (2) or in subsection (3) of section 64 of that Act prevails (or does so to a greater extent) in respect of a description of goods which consists of or includes patented articles, or consists of or includes articles to which a patented process has been applied, or in respect of a description of services in which a patented process is used; and

(*c*) that the creation of that situation, or particular elements in or consequences of it specified in the report, operate, or may be expected to operate, against the public interest,

the Secretary of State, subject to the next following subsection, may apply to the comptroller for an order under subsection (5) of this section in respect of the patent.

(3B) Before making an application under subsection (3) or subsection (3A) of this section, the appropriate Minister or Ministers shall publish, in such manner as he or they think appropriate, a notice describing the nature of the proposed application, and shall consider any representations which, within the period of thirty days from the date of publication of the notice, may be made to him or them by persons whose interests appear to the appropriate Minister or Ministers to be likely to be affected by the proposed application.

(4) If, on an application under subsection (3) of this section, it appears to the comptroller that the facts specified in the report of the Monopolies and Mergers Commission as being those which, in the opinion of the Commission, operate or may be expected to operate against the public interest include—

(*a*) any conditions in a licence or licences granted by the patentee under the patent restricting the use of the invention by the licensee or the right of the patentee to grant other licences under the patent, or

(*b*) a refusal by the patentee to grant licences under the patent on reasonable terms,

the comptroller may by order cancel or modify any such condition or may, if he thinks fit, instead of making such an order or in addition to making such an order, order the patent to be endorsed with the words 'licences of right'.

(5) If on an application under subsection (3A) of this section it appears to the comptroller that the particular matters indicated in the report of the Monopolies and Mergers Commission as being those which, in the opinion of the Commission, operate or may be expected to operate against the public interest (whether those matters are so indicated in pursuance of a requirement imposed under section 69(4) or section 75(3) of the Fair Trading Act 1973 or otherwise) include any such condition or refusal as is mentioned in paragraph (*a*) or paragraph (*b*) of subsection (4) of this section, the comptroller may by order cancel or modify any such condition or may, if he thinks fit, instead of making such an order or in addition to making such an order, order the patent to be endorsed with the words 'licences of right'.

(6) In this section 'the appropriate Minister or Ministers' in relation to a report of the Monopolies and Mergers Commission, means the Minister or Ministers to whom the report is made." [**226**]

COMMENCEMENT

See s. 140 (3), *post*, and the note to s. 1, *ante*.

DEFINITIONS

"article", "comptroller", "patent" and "patentee", see the Patents Act 1949, s. 101 (1).

Appropriate minister or ministers: note sub-s. (6) above.

"the Commission": s. 137 (2).

"monopoly situation": s. 137 (2) and s. 5 (3).

"merger situation qualifying for investigation": ss. 64 (8) and 137 (2).

GENERAL NOTE

This section substitutes new provisions for the Patents Act 1949, s. 40 (3), (4), consequent upon the replacement by Parts IV (ss. 44–56) and V (ss. 57–77) of this Act of the provisions relating to monopoly and merger references to the Monopoly Commission. There is no longer a requirement of a resolution by both Houses of Parliament declaring the monopoly situation against the public interest. However the Minister must publish his intention to apply to the comptroller and must consider representations.

"*Monopolies and Mergers Commission.*" See s. 4, *ante*, and Sch. 3, *post* (especially para. 16 (2) thereof).

"*As laid before Parliament.*" *I.e.*, under s. 83, *ante*.

"*Conclusions to the effect.*" It is submitted that the conclusions required by (*a*) and (*b*) must be expressed or implicit in the report, and it is not sufficient if the report adverts to a chain of inference or reasoning tending towards such conclusions.

Sub-s. (3) (*b*): "*Operate . . . against the public interest.*" For factors taken into account, see s. 84, *ante*.

Sub-s. (3B): "*Shall publish.*" Publication is obligatory but there is a discretion about the manner of publication. The test is subjective; see, however, the note "If it appears to him" to s. 15, *ante*.

"*Notice describing the nature of the proposed application.*" It would not be sufficient if the notice merely stated whether the application was under sub-s. (3) or (3A). The facts and findings on which the application is made should be included in the licence.

"*Shall consider any representations.*" There is thus a duty to act judicially and fairly, but there is no express obligation on the Minister to hear oral representations.

"*Interests.*" See the note to s. 124 (2), *ante*.

"*Appear to the appropriate Minister or Ministers.*" The test is thus basically subjective; cf. the note "If it appears to him" to s. 15, *ante*.

"*If on an application.*" The report of the Commission is prima facie evidence, on an application, of certain matters stated in the report; see the Patents Act 1949, s. 43 (6), as amended by s. 139 (1), *post*.

"*Any conditions in a licence.*" As to conditions on sale or lease of patented articles which are void, see the Patents Act 1949, s. 57.

"*Licences of right.*" See generally as to endorsement in this manner, the Patents Act 1949, s. 35.

127. Additional power to make orders under Agricultural Marketing Act 1958

The following section shall be inserted in the Agricultural Marketing Act 1958 after section 19:—

"**19A.**—(1) The provisions of this section shall have effect where a report made by the Monopolies and Mergers Commission under section 54 of the Fair Trading Act 1973, as laid before Parliament, contains conclusions to the effect—

(*a*) that certain matters indicated in the report operate, or may be expected to operate, against the public interest, and

(*b*) that those matters consist of or include any provision of a scheme or any act or omission of a board administering a scheme.

(2) In the circumstances mentioned in subsection (1) of this section, the Minister shall have the like power to make orders under section 19 of this Act as if those conclusions of the Monopolies and Mergers Commission—

(*a*) had been to the effect that the provision of the scheme in question, or the act or omission of the board to which those conclusions relate, were contrary to the interests of consumers of the regulated product, and

(*b*) had been contained in a report of a committee of investigation." **[227]**

COMMENCEMENT

See s. 140 (3), *post*, and the note to s. 1, *ante*.

DEFINITIONS

"committee of inspection": Agriculture Marketing Act 1958, s. 19 (1).
"regulated product", "scheme", "board": *ibid.*, s. 52 (1).

GENERAL NOTE

The section inserted in the Agricultural Marketing Act 1958 allows an order to be made under s. 19 of that Act amending or revoking a marketing scheme or directing a marketing board to take certain steps to rectify a scheme, on the basis of an adverse report of the Monopolies and Mergers Commission.

"*Monopolies and Mergers Commission.*" See s. 4, *ante*, and Sch. 3, *post* (in particular para. 16 (2) thereof).

"*As laid before Parliament.*" *I.e.*, under s. 83, *ante*.

"*Conclusions to the effect.*" See the note to s. 126, *ante*.

"*Against the public interest.*" For factors taken into account, see s. 84, *ante*.

128. Order superseded by declaration of Restrictive Practices Court

Where an application is made to the Restrictive Practices Court under subsection (2) of section 30 of the Act of 1956 (which in certain circumstances enables an application to be made to that Court to declare whether proposed restrictions are contrary to the public interest) and—

(*a*) on that application the Court makes a declaration under that subsection in relation to a restriction proposed to be accepted under an agreement, and

(*b*) by virtue of an order under section 56 of this Act which is for the time being in force, the making or carrying out of an agreement under which that restriction was accepted would be unlawful,

the order under section 56 of this Act shall cease to have effect in so far as it renders unlawful the making or carrying out of an agreement under which that restriction is accepted. **[228]**

COMMENCEMENT

See s. 140 (3), *post*, and the note to s. 1, *ante*.

GENERAL NOTE

This section provides that an order of a Minister made under s. 56, *ante*, consequent upon a report on a monopoly reference is to cease to have effect in so far as it is superseded by a declaration made by the Restrictive Practices Court under the Restrictive Trade Practices Act 1956, s. 30 (2).

Restrictive Practices Court. See the Restrictive Trade Practices Act 1956, s. 2 (1).

Section 30 (2) of the Act of 1956. That subsection is amended by s. 139 and Sch. 12, *post*.

The Act of 1956. I.e., the Restrictive Trade Practices Act 1956; see s. 137 (1), *post*.

Restriction; agreement. These words are defined by the Restrictive Trade Practices Act 1956, s. 6 (3).

Proposed restrictions. I.e., those to which Part I of the Restrictive Trade Practices Act applies; see s. 30 (2) of that Act (as amended by s. 139, Sch. 12, *post*).

Paras. (a) and (b). Note that these provisions are cumulative.

Contrary to the public interest. See the Restrictive Trade Practices Act 1956, s. 30 (5) and the criteria set out in s. 21 of that Act.

Restriction is accepted. See the Restrictive Trade Practices Act 1956, s. 6.

129. Time-limit for prosecutions

(1) No prosecution for an offence under this Act shall be commenced after the expiration of three years from the commission of the offence or one year from its discovery by the prosecutor, whichever is the earlier.

(2) Notwithstanding anything in section 104 of the Magistrates' Courts Act 1952, a magistrates' court may try an information for an offence under this Act if the information was laid within twelve months from the commission of the offence.

(3) Notwithstanding anything in section 23 of the Summary Jurisdiction (Scotland) Act 1954, summary proceedings in Scotland for an offence under this Act may be commenced within twelve months from the commission of the offence, and subsection (2) of the said section 23 shall apply for the purposes of this subsection as it applies for the purposes of that section.

(4) In the application of this section to Northern Ireland, for the references in subsection (2) to section 104 of the Magistrates' Courts Act 1952 and to the trial and laying of an information there shall be substituted respectively references to section 34 of the Magistrates' Courts Act (Northern Ireland) 1964 and to the hearing and determination and making of a complaint. **[229]**

COMMENCEMENT

See s. 140 (3), *post*, and the note to s. 29, *ante*.

GENERAL NOTE

The normal time limit of 6 months for bringing summary proceedings is extended to 12 months by sub-s. (2). Sub-s. (1) imposes a time limit on proceedings on indictment.

"Offence under this Act." See ss. 23, 24, 30, 46, 62, 85, 120, *ante*, and s. 132, *post*.

"Commenced." Proceedings are commenced when the information is laid; *Abraham* v. *Jutson* (1962), 106 Sol. Jo. 880; *Beardsley* v. *Giddings*, [1904] 1 K.B. 847. It is the duty of the magistrates' clerk and not of the defendant to see that the proceedings have been properly instituted and the time limits complied with; *Price* v. *Humphries*, [1958] 2 Q.B. 353. A failure to observe the time limits is an incurable defect which cannot be waived; *Dixon* v. *Wells* (1890), 25 Q.B.D. 249.

"Discovery." Authority suggests that there is no discovery if the prosecutor is under a misapprehension of law, until the misapprehension is discovered; see *Cenlon Finance Co., Ltd.* v. *Ellwood*, [1962] A.C. 782.

"The prosecutor." Presumably the prosecutor will normally be the Director or a local weights and measures department, however it should be noted that the knowledge of one of these does not create a time bar operating against other prosecutors.

Section 104 of the Magistrates' Courts Act. That section, so far as relevant, runs as follows: "104. Limitation of time. Except as otherwise expressly provided by any enactment, a magistrates' court shall not try an information or hear a complaint unless the information was laid or the complaint made within six months from the time when the offence was committed, or the matter of complaint arose: . . ."

"Information was laid." See the Magistrates' Courts Act 1952, s. 1, and the Magistrates' Court Rules 1968, r. 1.

130. Notice to Director of intended prosecution

(1) Where a local weights and measures authority in England or Wales proposes to institute proceedings for an offence under section 23 of this Act, or for an offence under the Trade Descriptions Act 1968, other than an offence under section 28(5) or section 29 of that Act, it shall, as between the authority and the

Director, be the duty of the authority to give to the Director notice of the intended proceedings, together with a summary of the facts on which the charges are to be founded, and to postpone institution of the proceedings until either—

(*a*) twenty-eight days have elapsed since the giving of that notice, or
(*b*) the Director has notified the authority that he has received the notice and the summary of the facts.

(2) In relation to offences under the Trade Descriptions Act 1968, the preceding subsection shall have effect subject to the transitional provisions having effect by virtue of section 139 of this Act. **[230]**

COMMENCEMENT
See s. 140 (3), *post*, and the note to s. 1, *ante*.

DEFINITION
The Director: s. 137 (2).

GENERAL NOTE
This section replaces the Trade Descriptions Act 1968, s. 30 (2)–(4 (repealed by s. 139 (1), Sch. 13, *post*, subject to the transitional provisions in s. 139 (2), Sch. 11, para. 16, *post*).

"*Local weights and measures authority*." See the note to s. 27, *ante*.

"*Institute proceedings*." Cf. the note "Commenced" to s. 129, *ante*.

Section 28 (5). The Trade Descriptions Act 1968, s. 28 (5), imposes restrictions on the disclosure of information obtained in premises entered by virtue of that section, or obtained in pursuance of that Act.

Section 29. The Trade Descriptions Act 1968, s. 29, creates offences relating to the obstruction of officers and the making of false declarations.

Postpone institution of proceedings. The Trade Descriptions Act 1968, s. 30 (2), (3) (repealed) which were differently worded imposed a condition precedent to a prosecution by a weights and measures authority and not of course by any other prosecutor. It was for the defendant to raise the question of whether the condition had been complied with; *Hastings* v. *Tesco Supermarkets* (unreported; see O'Keefe, *Trade Descriptions Act*, s. 30, page 75). It is suggested that the new wording probably has the same effect.

"*Transitional provisions*." See s. 139 (2) and Sch. 11, para. 16, *post*.

131. Notification of convictions and judgments to Director

(1) Where in any criminal proceedings a person is convicted of an offence by or before a court in the United Kingdom, or a judgment is given against a person in civil proceedings in any such court, and it appears to the court—

(*a*) having regard to the functions of the Director under Part III of this Act, that it would be expedient for the conviction or judgment to be brought to his attention, and
(*b*) that it may not be brought to his attention unless arrangements for the purpose are made by the court,

the court may make arrangements for that purpose notwithstanding that the proceedings have been finally disposed of by the court.

(2) In this section "judgment" includes any order or decree, and any reference to the giving of a judgment shall be construed accordingly. **[231]**

COMMENCEMENT
See s. 140 (3), *post*, and the note to s. 1, *ante*.

DEFINITIONS
"Director": s. 137 (2).
"judgment": note sub-s. (2) above.

GENERAL NOTE
"*Criminal proceedings . . . civil proceedings*." For the evidentiary value of the decisions of such proceedings, see s. 36, *ante*.

"*United Kingdom*." See the note to s. 2, *ante*.

"*Part III.*" *I.e.*, ss. 34–43, *ante*.
"*Expedient.*" See the note to s. 124, *ante*.
Paras. (*a*) *and* (*b*). Note that these paragraphs are cumulative.
"*Judgment.*" There is apparently no obligation to send with the notification a summary of the facts on which the judgment was based.

132. Offences by bodies corporate

(1) Where an offence under section 23, section 46, section 85(6) or Part XI of this Act, which has been committed by a body corporate, is proved to have been committed with the consent or connivance of, or to be attributable to any neglect on the part of, any director, manager, secretary or other similar officer of the body corporate, or any person who was purporting to act in any such capacity, he as well as the body corporate shall be guilty of that offence and be liable to be proceeded against and punished accordingly.

(2) Where the affairs of a body corporate are managed by its members, subsections (1) of this section shall apply in relation to the acts and defaults of a member in connection with his functions of management as if he were a director of the body corporate. [**232**]

COMMENCEMENT

See s. 140 (3), *post*, and the note to s. 129, *ante*.

GENERAL NOTE

"*Which has been committed.*" The guilt of the body corporate is thus a condition precedent of the liability of the officer. A body corporate may be guilty of an offence notwithstanding an absence of mens rea; see the note "Contravenes a prohibition etc." to s. 23, *ante*.

"*Proved.*" A fact is proved if a court finds, in this case beyond a reasonable doubt, that it has occurred.

"*With the consent.*" Consent involves knowledge; see *Re Caughey, Ex parte Ford* (1876), 1 Ch. D. 521, 528 C.A.; *Lamb* v. *Wright & Co.*, [1924] 1 K.B. 857, at 864. However constructive knowledge is probably sufficient; cf. *Knox* v. *Boyd*, 1941 S.C.(J.) 82, at 86; *Taylors Central Garages* (*Exeter*), *Ltd.* v. *Roper* (1951), 115 J.P. 455 at 449–50; *Mallon* v. *Allon*, [1964] 1 Q.B. 385 at 394.

"*Connivance.*" Connivance involves knowledge and acquiescence in the offence which has been committed; see *Boulting* v. *Boulting* (1864), 3 Sw. & Tr. 329. Actual knowledge is probably not necessary and suspicion will do although mere negligence or inattention is insufficient; see *e.g.*, *Rogers* v. *Rogers* (1830), 3 Hag. Ecc. 57. Connivance must precede the offence (*Churchman* v. *Churchman*, [1945] P. 44) and may lapse by passage of time or by lack of causal connection between the connivance and the offence (*Godfrey* v. *Godfrey*, [1965] A.C. 444). Mere silence is not always sufficient to establish acquiescence.

"*Attributable.*" This word imposes a causative test. The offence must be wholly or to a material extent caused by the neglect.

"*Neglect.*" This involves a breach of duty of which the defendant knows or ought to know; see *Re Hughes, Rea* v. *Black*, [1943] Ch. 296 at 298.

"*Director, manager, secretary or other similar officer.*" This means a central officer not a branch manager; cf. *Tesco Supermarkets, Ltd.* v, *Nattrass*, [1972] A.C. 153; *Registrar of Rrestrictive Trading Agreements* v. *W. H. Smith & Son, Ltd.*, [1969] 3 All E.R. 1065; [1969] 1 W.L.R. 1460. It is suggested that the officers are confined to officers with managerial roles and it is in that capacity that the secretary is in the section; cf. *Panorama Developments* (*Guildford*), *Ltd.* v: *Fidelis Furnishing Fabrics, Ltd.*, [1971] 2 Q.B. 711, C.A. It has been suggested, however (O'Keefe, *op. cit.*), that an auditor might be included as *eiusdem generis* with the secretary.

"*Purporting to act.*" This is included as the result of the decision in *Dean* v. *Hiesler*, [1942] 2 All E.R. 340, but see the note "which has been committed" above.

"*Accordingly.*" It is wrong in principal to impose a fine on the individual defendant on the basis that the fine will be met by the body corporate.

"*Are managed by its members.*" This includes the nationalised corporations.

"*Acts and defaults.*" This is theoretically narrower than consent, connivance and neglect. A member's acts and defaults must amount to consent, connivance and neglect.

"*In connections with his functions of management.*" The acts and defaults must be committed by the member *qua* manager and not *qua* member.

133. General restrictions on disclosure of information

(1) Subject to subsections (2) to (4) of this section, no information with respect to any particular business which has been obtained under or by virtue of the provisions (other than Part II) of this Act or under or by virtue of the Act of 1956 or the Act of 1968 shall, so long as that business continues to be carried on, be disclosed without the consent of the person for the time being carrying on that business.

(2) The preceding subsection does not apply to any disclosure of information which is made—

(*a*) for the purpose of facilitating the performance of any functions of the Director, the Commission, the Secretary of State or any other Minister under this Act, the Act of 1956 or the Act of 1968, or

(*b*) in pursuance of a Community obligation within the meaning of the European Communities Act 1972.

(3) Subsection (1) of this section does not apply to any disclosure of information which is made for the purposes of any proceedings before the Restrictive Practices Court or of any other legal proceedings, whether civil or criminal, under this Act, the Act of 1956 or the Act of 1968.

(4) Nothing in subsection (1) of this section shall be construed—

(*a*) as limiting the matters which may be included in, or made public as part of, a report of the Advisory Committee or of the Commission;

(*b*) as limiting the particulars which may be entered or filed in, or made public as part of, the register under Part I of the Act of 1956; or

(*c*) as applying to any information which has been made public as part of such a report or as part of that register.

(5) Any person who discloses any information in contravention of this section shall be guilty of an offence and shall be liable—

(*a*) on summary conviction, to a fine not exceeding £400;

(*b*) on conviction on indictment, to imprisonment for a term not exceeding two years or to a fine or to both.

(6) In this section references to this Act shall be construed as including references to any enactment repealed by this Act. [233]

COMMENCEMENT

See s. 140 (3), *post*, and the note to s. 1, *ante*.

DEFINITIONS

"The Act of 1956", "the Act of 1968": s. 137 (1).

"The Advisory Committee", "business", "the Commission", "the Director", "enactment", "Minister": s. 137 (2).

GENERAL NOTE

This section replaces the Monopolies and Restrictive Practices (Inquiry and Control) Act 1948, s. 17, the Restrictive Trade Practices Act 1956, s. 33, and the Monopolies and Mergers Act 1965, s. 11 (3).

Sub-s. (1): *"Information."* Only "information" is protected. It would appear that information does not include advice and opinions; cf. s. 124, *ante*.

"Business." The wording in the earlier legislation was "trade or business". This is now covered by the definition of business in s. 137 (2), *post*. Normally speaking business is synonymous with trade; *Delany* v. *Delany* (1885), 15 L.R.Ir. 55.

"Particular." This presumably imports the idea of a business operated by one person or group of persons. How wide the group must be before it ceases to be protected by the section is unclear.

"*(Other than Part II)*." The provisions of Part II referred to are ss. 29 and 30, *ante*.

"*Continues to be carried on.*" See *South Behar Rail. Co., Ltd.* v. *Inland Revenue Commissioners*, [1925] A.C. 476, as to the time at which a business ceases to be carried on.

"*Disclosed.*" "Disclosure" is not necessarily confined to public disclosure.

"*Person for the time being carrying on that business.*" In most cases this person will not be difficult to identify. It is suggested, however, that the consent should be obtained both from the *de facto* controller of the business (*e.g.*, the general manager) and the *de jure* controller (*e.g.* the board of directors).

"*Community obligation.*" The European Communities Act 1972, s. 1, Sch. 1, Part II, defines a community obligation as "any obligation created or arising by or under the Treaties whether an enforceable community obligation or not".

"*Reports.*" See ss. 21, 54, 61 and 72, *ante*.

"*Summary conviction*", etc. See the notes to s. 23, *ante*.

"*Enactment repealed by this Act.*" See s. 139 (1), *post*.

134. Provisions as to orders

(1) Any statutory instrument whereby any order is made under any of the preceding provisions of this Act, other than a provision which requires a draft of the order to be laid before Parliament before making the order, or whereby any regulations are made under this Act, shall be subject to annulment in pursuance of a resolution of either House of Parliament.

(2) Any power conferred by any provision of this Act to make an order by statutory instrument shall include power to revoke or vary the order by a subsequent order made under that provision. **[234]**

COMMENCEMENT

See s. 140 (3), *post*, and the note to s. 29, *ante*.

GENERAL NOTE

The negative resolution procedure for statutory instruments is to be found in the Statutory Instruments Act 1946, s. 5.

"*Power to revoke*", etc. This power must be expressly given since the general power in the Interpretation Act 1889, s. 32 (3) does not apply to orders.

135. Financial provisions

(1) The Secretary of State shall pay all remuneration, allowances or other sums payable under this Act to or in respect of persons who are or have been members of the Advisory Committee or the Commission, and shall defray—

(*a*) all expenses duly incurred by the Commission in the payment of remuneration or allowances payable under this Act to staff of the Commission, and

(*b*) to such amount as the Secretary of State with the approval of the Minister for the Civil Service may determine, all other expenses duly incurred by the Advisory Committee or the Commission.

(2) There shall be defrayed out of moneys provided by Parliament—

(*a*) all expenses incurred by the Secretary of State in consequence of the provisions of this Act;

(*b*) any expenses incurred in consequence of those provisions by any other Minister of the Crown or government department, not being a Minister or department of the Government of Northern Ireland;

(*c*) the remuneration of, and any travelling or other allowances payable under this Act to, the Director and any staff of the Director, any other sums payable under this Act to or in respect of the Director, and any expenses duly incurred by the Director or by any of his staff in consequence of the provisions of this Act;

(*d*) any increase attributable to this Act in the sums payable out of moneys so provided under the Superannuation Act 1972.

(3) (*Rep. by the Northern Ireland (Modification of Enactments—No.* 1) *Order* 1973, *S.I.* 1973 *No.* 2163, *art.* 14 (2), *Sch.* 6.) [**235**]

COMMENCEMENT

Sub-s. (2) (*a*) and (*b*) was brought into force on 14th September 1973; see s. 140 (3), *post*, and the note to s. 29, *ante*. The remainder of the section was brought into operation on 1st November 1973; see the note to s. 1, *ante*.

DEFINITIONS

"The Director", "Advisory Committee", "Commission", "Minister": s. 137 (2).
"financial year": *I.e.*, the twelve months ending 31st March; see the Interpretation Act 1889, s. 22.

136. Powers of Parliament of Northern Ireland

The Parliament of Northern Ireland shall have the same power to pass Acts with respect to any matter as they would have had if this Act had not been passed; and, in the event of any inconsistency between any Act of the Parliament of Northern Ireland passed after the passing of this Act and any provision of this Act or any order or other instrument having effect by virtue of this Act, the Act of the Parliament of Northern Ireland shall, in Northern Ireland, prevail. [**236**]

137. General interpretation provisions

(1) In this Act—

"the Act of 1948" means the Monopolies and Restrictive Practices (Inquiry and Control) Act 1948;
"the Act of 1956" means the Restrictive Trade Practices Act 1956;
"the Act of 1964" means the Resale Prices Act 1964;
"the Act of 1965" means the Monopolies and Mergers Act 1965;
"the Act of 1968" means the Restrictive Trade Practices Act 1968;
"assignment", in relation to Scotland, means assignation;
"contract of employment" means a contract of service or of apprenticeship, whether it is express or implied, and (if it is express) whether it is oral or in writing;
"scale" (where the reference is to the scale on which any services are, or are to be, made available, supplied or obtained) means scale measured in terms of money or money's worth or in any other manner.

(2) Except in so far as the context otherwise requires, in this Act, except in Part X, the following expressions have the meanings hereby assigned to them respectively, that is to say—

"the Advisory Committee" means the Consumer Protection Advisory Committee;
"agreement" means any agreement or arrangement, in whatever way and in whatever form it is made, and whether it is, or is intended to be, legally enforceable or not;
"business" includes a professional practice and includes any other undertaking which is carried on for gain or reward or which is an undertaking in the course of which goods or services are supplied otherwise than free of charge;
"commercial activities in the United Kingdom" means any of the following, that is to say, the production and supply of goods in the

United Kingdom, the supply of services in the United Kingdom and the export of goods from the United Kingdom;

"the Commission" means the Monopolies and Mergers Commission;

"complex monopoly situation" has the meaning assigned to it by section 11 of this Act;

"consumer" (subject to subsection (6) of this section) means any person who is either—

(*a*) a person to whom goods are or are sought to be supplied (whether by way of sale or otherwise (in the course of a business carried on by the person supplying or seeking to supply them, or

(*b*) a person for whom services are or are sought to be supplied in the course of a business carried on by the person supplying or seeking to supply them,

and who does not receive or seek to receive the goods or services in the course of a business carried on by him;

"the Director" means the Director General of Fair Trading;

"enactment" includes an enactment of the Parliament of Northern Ireland;

"goods" includes buildings and other structures, and also includes ships, aircraft and hovercraft, but does not include electricity;

"group" (where the reference is to a group of persons fulfilling specified conditions, other than the condition of being interconnected bodies corporate) means any two or more persons fulfilling those conditions, whether apart from fulfilling them they would be regarded as constituting a group or not;

"merger reference" has the meaning assigned to it by section 5(3) of this Act;

"merger situation qualifying for investigation" has the meaning assigned to it by section 64(8) of this Act;

"Minister" includes a government department but shall not by virtue of this provision be taken to include the establishment consisting of the Director and his staff, and, except where the contrary is expressly provided, does not include any Minister or department of the Government of Northern Ireland;

"monopoly reference" and "monopoly situation" have the meanings assigned to them by section 5(3) of this Act;

"newspaper merger reference" has the meaning assigned to it by section 59(3) of this Act;

"practice" means any practice, whether adopted in pursuance of an agreement or otherwise;

"price" includes any charge or fee, by whatever name called;

"produce", in relation to the production of minerals or other substances, includes getting them, and, in relation to the production of animals or fish, includes taking them;

"supply", in relation to the supply of goods, includes supply by way of sale, lease, hire or hire-purchase, and, in relation to buildings or other structures, includes the construction of them by a person for another person;

"uncompetitive practices" means practices having the effect of preventing, restricting or distorting competition in connection with any commercial activities in the United Kingdom;

"worker" (subject to subsection (7) of this section) has the meaning assigned to it by section 167 of the Industrial Relations Act 1971.

(3) In the provisions of this Act other than Part X (and without prejudice to the construction of that Part in accordance with section 117 of this Act) "the supply of services" does not include the rendering of any services under a contract of employment but, with that exception,—

(*a*) includes the undertaking and performance for gain or reward of engagements (whether professional or other) for any matter other than the supply of goods, and

(*b*) includes both the rendering of services to order and the provision of services by making them available to potential users;

and any reference in those provisions to services supplied or to be supplied, or to services provided or to be provided, shall be construed accordingly.

(4) For the purposes of this Act, except Part X, "services" includes electricity.

(5) For the purposes of the provisions of this Act other than Part X, any two bodies corporate are to be treated as interconnected if one of them is a body corporate of which the other is a subsidiary (within the meaning of section 154 of the Companies Act 1948) or if both of them are subsidiaries (within the meaning of that section) of one and the same body corporate; and in those provisions "interconnected bodies corporate" shall be construed accordingly, and "group of interconnected bodies corporate" means a group consisting of two or more bodies corporate all of whom are interconnected with each other.

(6) For the purposes of the application of any provision of this Act in relation to goods or services of a particular description or to which a particular practice applies, "consumers" means persons who are consumers (as defined by subsection (2) of this section) in relation to goods or services of that description or in relation to goods or services to which that practice applies.

(7) For the purposes of the application of this Act to Northern Ireland, the definition of "worker" in subsection (2) of this section shall apply as if the Industrial Relations Act 1971 extended to Northern Ireland but, in section 167(2)(*a*) of that Act, references to general medical services, pharmaceutical services, general dental services or general ophthalmic services provided under the enactments mentioned in that subsection were references to the corresponding services provided in Northern Ireland under the corresponding enactments there in force.

(8) Except in so far as the context otherwise requires, any reference in this Act to an enactment shall be construed as a reference to that enactment as amended or extended by or under any other enactment, including this Act.

[237]

COMMENCEMENT

See s. 140 (3), *post*, and the note to s. 29, *ante*.

GENERAL NOTE

Sub-s. (1): *"Contract of service."* The distinction between a contract of service and a contract for services is a question of fact depending on the terms of the contract; *Pauley* v. *Kenaldo, Ltd.*, [1953] 1 All E.R. 226, C.A., at p. 228; *Whittaker* v. *Minister of Pensions and National Insurance*, [1966] 3 All E.R. 531, at 536; *Argent* v. *Minister of Social Security*, [1968] 3 All E.R. 208; and *Global Plant, Ltd.* v. *Secretary of State for Social Services*, [1972] 1 Q.B. 139.

"Writing." See the Interpretation Act 1889, s. 20.

Sub-s. (2): "*Part X.*" Special provisions for the interpretation of Part X (ss. 107–117) are contained in s. 117, *ante*.

"*Consumer Protection Advisory Committee.*" See s. 3, *ante*.

"*Agreement.*" See the interpretation of "agreement" in the Restrictive Trade Practices Act 1956, s. 6.

"*Business.*" As at common law the profit motive is not necessarily an element in the definition.

"*Any other undertaking which is carried on.*" These words do not involve a full time activity but import some idea of continuity which is not necessarily implied in the normal meaning of business; cf. *Re Abenheim* (1913), 109 L.T. 219.

"*United Kingdom.*" See the note to s. 2, *ante*.

"*The Monopolies and Mergers Commission.*" See s. 4, *ante*.

"*Consumer.*" Note the limitation imposed by sub-s. (6) above in respect of particular goods.

"*In the course of a business carried on by him.*" It is by these words that the consumer is distinguished from the man of trade or commerce. Note that the latter will be a consumer when not receiving goods in the course of his trade or business.

"*The Director.*" See s. 2, *ante*.

"*Enactment.*" This means an Act or section or subsection of an Act. It may also mean orders; see *Rathbone* v. *Bundock*, [1962] 2 Q.B. 260.

"'*Goods' includes buildings.*" The definition of "goods" is not exhaustive, but it is suggested that despite the inclusion of buildings, goods does not include land.

"*Electricity.*" Note sub-s. (4).

"*Practice.*" This concept involves a regular and accepted method of conducting business.

"*Produce.*" The definitions of "produce" in relation to the production of minerals etc. and to the production of animals or fish are not exhaustive.

"*Includes taking them.*" Rearing and slaughtering animals are also doubtless included.

"*Supply . . . in relation to buildings.*" Buildings does not, presumably, include land; cf. the note "'Goods' includes buildings" above.

"*Uncompetitive practices*": "*preventing, restricting distorting.*" See s. 6, *ante*.

"*Worker.*" See *Broadbent* v. *Crisp*, [1974] 1 All E.R. 1052; *Writers' Guild of Great Britain* v. *British Broadcasting Corporation*, [1974] 1 All E.R. 574.

Sub-s. (3): "*Potential users.*" There is no need for a supplier of services to have any customers; potential users are those envisaged by the supplier even if looking objectively none can be found.

Sub-s. (5): "*Section* 154 *of the Companies Act.*" For the application of s. 154 (2) to the nationalised industries, see *Southern Electricity Board* v. *Collins*, [1970] 1 Q.B. 83, 89.

138. Supplementary interpretation provisions

(1) This section applies to the following provisions of this Act, that is to say, section 2(4), Parts II and III, section 137(6), and the definition of "consumer" contained in section 137(2).

(2) For the purposes of any provisions to which this section applies it is immaterial whether any person supplying goods or services has a place of business in the United Kingdom or not.

(3) For the purposes of any provisions to which this section applies any goods or services supplied wholly or partly outside the United Kingdom, if they are supplied in accordance with arrangements made in the United Kingdom, whether made orally or by one or more documents delivered in the United Kingdom or by correspondence posted from and to addresses in the United Kingdom, shall be treated as goods supplied to, or services supplied for, persons in the United Kingdom.

(4) In relation to the supply of goods under a hire-purchase agreement, a credit-sale agreement or a conditional sale agreement, the person conducting any antecedent negotiations, as well as the owner or seller, shall for the purposes of any provisions to which this section applies be treated as a person supplying or seeking to supply the goods.

(5) *Subsection* (4) *of this section shall be construed—*

(*a*) *in relation to England and Wales, in accordance with subsections* (1), (3), (4) *and* (5) *of section* 58 *of the Hire-Purchase Act* 1965;

(*b*) *in relation to Scotland, in accordance with subsections* (1), (3), (4) *and* (5) *of section* 54 *of the Hire-Purchase* (*Scotland*) *Act* 1965; *and*

(*c*) *in relation to Northern Ireland, in accordance with subsections* (1), (3), (4) *and* (5) *of section* 65 *of the Hire-Purchase Act* (*Northern Ireland*) 1966.

[(5) In subsection (4) of this section, the following expressions have the meanings given by, or referred to in, section 189 of the Consumer Credit Act 1974—

"antecedent negotiations",
"conditional sale agreement",
"credit-sale agreement",
"hire-purchase agreement".]

(6) In any provisions to which this section applies—

(*a*) any reference to a person to or for whom goods or services are supplied shall be construed as including a reference to any guarantor of such a person, and

(*b*) any reference to the terms or conditions on or subject to which goods or services are supplied shall be construed as including a reference to the terms or conditions on or subject to which any person undertakes to act as such a guarantor;

and in this subsection "guarantor", in relation to a person to or for whom goods or services are supplied, includes a person who undertakes to indemnify the supplier of the goods or services against any loss which he may incur in respect of the supply of the goods or services to or for that person.

(7) For the purposes of any provisions to which this section applies goods or services supplied by a person carrying on a business shall be taken to be supplied in the course of that business if payment for the supply of the goods or services is made or (whether under a contract or by virtue of an enactment or otherwise) is required to be made. [**238**]

COMMENCEMENT

See s. 140 (3), *post*, and the note to s. 1, *ante*.

AMENDMENT

Sub-s. (5), printed in italics, is substituted by the words in square brackets by the Consumer Credit Act 1974, s. 192 (3) (*a*), Sch. 4, Part I, para. 37, as from a day to be appointed.

DEFINITIONS

"business", "goods", "supply": s. 137 (2).
"supply of services": s. 13 (3).
"services": s. 137 (4).

GENERAL NOTE

Sub-s. (2): "*Place of business.*" See *Grant* v. *Anderson & Co.*, [1892] 1 Q.B. 108, for the sort of supplier who would escape but for this section. There remains the problem of establishing jurisdiction.

"*United Kingdom.*" See the note to s. 2, *ante*.

Sub-s. (3): "*In accordance with.*" It is submitted that this should not be construed as having a narrower meaning than "pursuant to".

"*Arrangements.*" These are not limited to enforceable contracts and therefore presumably do not include all the terms for the supply of the goods or services.

"Arrangement" is a word which has to be given its ordinary popular meaning; *Re British Basic Slag, Ltd.'s Application, British Basic Slag* v. *Registrar of Restrictive Trading Agreements*, [1963] 2 All E.R. 807; [1963] 1 W.L.R. 727, C.A. See further the note "Trading scheme" to s. 118 (1), *ante*.

"*Documents*." There seems no reason why this should not include correspondence. The provisions as to correspondence therefore seem superfluous.

"*From and to addresses in the United Kingdom*." These words restrict correspondence to inland mail; but see the note "Documents" above. It may be that "and" is used alternatively rather than conjunctively in which case the provisions for correspondence are wider than those for other documents.

Sub-s. (4): "*Hire purchase agreement, credit sale agreement, or a conditional sale agreement*." By virtue of sub-s. (5) above and the Hire-Purchase Act 1965, s. 58 (1), for meanings, see s. 1 of the Act of 1965; or by virtue of sub-s. (5) above as substituted from a day to be appointed, see the Consumer Credit Act 1974, s. 189.

"*Antecedent negotiations*." By virtue of sub-s. (5) above, for meaning, see the Hire-Purchase Act 1965, s. 58 (3) and (5); or, as from a day to be appointed, the Consumer Credit Act 1974, s. 189. See also *Re Galvanised Tank Manufacturers Association's Agreement*, [1965] 2 All E.R. 1003; [1965] 1 W.L.R. 1074; *Re Mileage Conference Group of Tyre Manufacturers' Conference Ltd.'s Agreement*, [1966] 2 All E.R. 849; [1966] 1 W.L.R. 1137.

"*Owner or seller*." By virtue of sub-s. (5) above, for meaning, see the Hire-Purchase Act 1965, s. 58 (1) (prospectively repealed by the Consumer Credit Act 1974, s. 192 (3), Sch. 51).

Sub-s. (6): "*Indemnify*." "Guarantor" is widely defined to avoid the distinction between an indemnity and a guarantee.

Sub-s. (7): "*Required*." It is submitted that this does not involve a demand.

139. Amendments, repeals and transitional provisions

(1) Subject to the transitional provisions and savings contained in Schedule 11 to this Act—

(*a*) the enactments specified in Schedule 12 to this Act shall have effect subject to the amendments specified in that Schedule (being minor amendments or amendments consequential upon the preceding provisions of this Act), and

(*b*) the enactments specified in Schedule 13 to this Act are hereby repealed to the extent specified in the third column of that Schedule.

(2) The provisions of Schedule 11 to this Act shall have effect for the purposes of this Act. [**239**]

COMMENCEMENT

See s. 140 (3), *post*, and the note to s. 1, *ante*.

DEFINITION

"enactment": s. 137 (2).

GENERAL NOTE

See the notes to the Schedules, *post*.

140. Short title, citation, commencement and extent

(1) This Act may be cited as the Fair Trading Act 1973.

(2) The Restrictive Trade Practices Act 1956, the Restrictive Trade Practices Act 1968, Parts IX and X of this Act, Schedules 4 and 10 to this Act and so much of Schedules 12 and 13 to this Act as relates to those Acts may be cited together as the Restrictive Trade Practices Acts 1956 to 1973.

(3) This Act shall come into operation on such day as the Secretary of State may by order made by statutory instrument appoint: and different dates may be so appointed for, or for different purposes of, any one or more of the provisions of this Act (including, in the case of section 139 of this Act, the amendment or

repeal of different enactments specified in Schedule 12 or Schedule 13 to this Act or of different provisions of any enactment so specified).

(4) Where any provision of this Act, other than a provision contained in Schedule 11, refers to the commencement of this Act, it shall be construed as referring to the day appointed under this section for the coming into operation of that provision.

(5) This Act extends to Northern Ireland. **[240]**

ORDERS UNDER THIS SECTION

The Fair Trading Act 1973 (Commencement No. 1) Order 1973, S.I. 1973 No. 1545 (bringing the following provisions of the Act into force on 14th September 1973: ss. 29–32, 33 (2) (*c*), (*d*), Part XI (ss. 118–123), ss. 129, 132, 134, 135 (2) (*a*), (*b*), 137, 140); the Fair Trading Act 1973 (Commencement No. 2) Order 1973, S.I. 1973 No. 1652 (bringing the remainder of the Act into force on 1st November 1973).

SCHEDULES

Section 1

SCHEDULE 1

DIRECTOR GENERAL OF FAIR TRADING

1. There shall be paid to the Director such remuneration, and such travelling and other allowances, as the Secretary of State with the approval of the Minister for the Civil Service may determine.

2. In the case of any such holder of the office of the Director as may be determined by the Secretary of State with the approval of the Minister for the Civil Service, there shall be paid such pension, allowance or gratuity to or in respect of him on his retirement or death, or such contributions or payments towards provision for such a pension, allowance or gratuity, as may be so determined.

3. If, when any person ceases to hold office as the Director, it appears to the Secretary of State with the approval of the Minister for the Civil Service that there are special circumstances which make it right that he should receive compensation, there may be paid to him a sum by way of compensation of such amount as may be so determined.

4. In the House of Commons Disqualification Act 1957, in Part III of Schedule 1 (other disqualifying offices) there shall (at the appropriate place in alphabetical order) be inserted the following entry:—

"Director General of Fair Trading";

and the like amendment shall be made in the Part substituted for the said Part III by Schedule 3 to that Act in its application to the Senate and House of Commons of Northern Ireland.

5. The Director shall have an official seal for the authentication of documents required for the purposes of his functions.

6. The Documentary Evidence Act 1868 shall have effect as if the Director were included in the first column of the Schedule to that Act, as if the Director and any person authorised to act on behalf of the Director were mentioned in the second column of that Schedule, and as if the regulations referred to in that Act included any document issued by the Director or by any such person.

7. Anything authorised or required by or under this Act or any other enactment to be done by the Director, other than the making of a statutory instrument, may be done by any member of the staff of the Director who is authorised generally or specially in that behalf in writing by the Director. **[241]**

COMMENCEMENT

See s. 140 (3), *post*, and the note to s. 1, *ante*.

DEFINITION

"The Director": ss. 1 (1) and s. 137 (2).

GENERAL NOTE

This Schedule establishes the status of the Director and makes provision for his remuneration and other incidents of his employment.

Para. 1: *Secretary of State.* See the note to s. 1, *ante.*

Para. 3. Crown servants are not entitled to redundancy payments; see the Redundancy Payments Act 1965, s. 16.

Para. 4. The Director is thus disqualified from being or becoming a member of the House of Commons.

Para. 6. This paragraph provides for a mode of proving documents issued by the Director.

Para. 7. This paragraph clarifies the Director's powers of delegation.

"Statutory instruments." See the note to s. 3, *ante.*

Section 3

SCHEDULE 2

CONSUMER PROTECTION ADVISORY COMMITTEE

Status of Committee

1. Members of the Advisory Committee in their capacity as such shall not be regarded as servants or agents of the Crown or as enjoying any status, immunity or privilege of the Crown. [242]

Tenure of office of members

2.—(1) Subject to the following provisions of this paragraph, a member of the Advisory Committee shall hold and vacate office as such in accordance with the terms of his appointment.

(2) A person shall not be appointed to the Advisory Committee for a term exceeding three years; but previous membership shall not affect eligibility for re-appointment.

(3) A member of the Advisory Committee may at any time resign his membership by notice in writing addressed to the Secretary of State.

(4) The Secretary of State may remove a member of the Advisory Committee on the ground of incapacity or misbehaviour. [243]

Tenure of office of chairman and deputy chairman

3.—(1) The chairman or deputy chairman of the Advisory Committee may at any time resign his office as such by notice in writing addressed to the Secretary of State.

(2) The Secretary of State may remove a chairman or deputy chairman of the Advisory Committee on the ground of incapacity or misbehaviour. [244]

Remuneration and allowances

4. There shall be paid to the members of the Advisory Committee such remuneration, and such travelling and other allowances, as in the case of any of those members the Secretary of State may determine with the approval of the Minister for the Civil Service. [245]

General provisions as to sums payable on retirement or death of members

5. As regards any member of the Advisory Committee in whose case the Secretary of State may so determine with the approval of the Minister for the Civil Service, the Secretary of State shall pay such pension, allowance or gratuity to or in respect

of him, or make such payments towards the provision of such a pension, allowance or gratuity, as may be so determined.

6. If, when any person ceases to be a member of the Advisory Committee, it appears to the Secretary of State that there are special circumstances which make it right that he should receive compensation, the Secretary of State may pay him a sum by way of compensation of such amount as he may determine with the approval of the Minister for the Civil Service. [246]

Procedure of Committee

7. In the case of an equality of votes on any question at a meeting of the Advisory Committee the chairman shall have a second or casting vote.

8. At any time when the chairman is absent or otherwise incapable of acting, or there is a vacancy in the office of chairman, the deputy chairman may perform any of the functions of the chairman.

9. At any time when the chairman and deputy chairman of the Advisory Committee are absent or otherwise incapable of acting or there is a vacancy in the office of chairman and of deputy chairman, such member of the Advisory Committee as the Secretary of State may direct, or in default of any such direction such member of the Advisory Committee as the Advisory Committee may agree, may perform any of the functions of the chairman. [247]

COMMENCEMENT

See s. 140 (3) and the note to s. 1, *ante*.

DEFINITION

"Advisory Committee": s. 3 (1) or 137 (2).

GENERAL NOTE

This Schedule makes provision for the status and terms of appointment of members of the Advisory Committee. Provision is also made for certain aspects of the Committee's procedure. For provisions relating to references to the Committee, see ss. 81–83. The effect of these provisions is to give the members of the Committee a greater element of independence than for example the Director.

Paras. 2 (4) *and* 3 (2). The chairman, deputy chairman and members of the Committee are not Crown servants. The appropriate remedy for a removal from office which is not in accordance with the Schedule is presumably a declaration by analogy with such cases as *Abbott* v. *Sullivan*, [1952] 1 K.B. 189, and *Davis* v. *Carew-Pole*, [1956] 2 All E.R. 524. It may be, however, that para. 2 (1) envisages an express contract. Authorities on the meaning of the Industrial Relations Act 1971, s. 24 (2) (*a*) and (*b*) (repealed, but re-enacted in the Trade Union and Labour Relations Act 1974, Sch. 1, Part II, para. 6 (2) (*a*), (*b*)) may be of some assistance in determining what amounts to incapacity and misbehaviour.

Section 4

SCHEDULE 3

THE MONOPOLIES AND MERGERS COMMISSION

PART I

STATUS, TERMS OF OFFICE, AND STAFF

Status of Commission

1. Members of the Commission in their capacity as such shall not be regarded as servants or agents of the Crown or as enjoying any status, immunity or privilege of the Crown. [248]

Tenure of office of regular members

2.—(1) Subject to the following provisions of this paragraph, a regular member of the Commission shall hold and vacate office as such in accordance with the terms of his appointment.

(2) A person shall not be appointed to be a regular member of the Commission for a term exceeding five years; but previous membership shall not affect eligibility for re-appointment.

(3) A regular member of the Commission may at any time resign his membership by notice in writing addressed to the Secretary of State.

(4) The Secretary of State may remove a regular member of the Commission on the ground of incapacity or misbehaviour. [**249**]

Appointment and tenure of office of chairman and deputy chairmen

3.—(1) There shall be a chairman of the Commission appointed from among the regular members by the Secretary of State; and the Secretary of State may appoint not more than three other regular members to be deputy chairmen.

(2) The chairman or a deputy chairman may at any time resign his office as such by notice in writing addressed to the Secretary of State.

(3) The Secretary of State may remove a chairman or deputy chairman of the Commission on the ground of incapacity or misbehaviour.

(4) If the chairman or a deputy chairman of the Commission ceases to be a regular member of the Commission, he shall also cease to be chairman or, as the case may be, a deputy chairman. [**250**]

Staff

4. The Commission shall have a secretary, who shall be a person appointed by the Commission with the approval of the Secretary of State.

5. The Commission may appoint such other staff as the Commission think fit, subject to the approval of the Secretary of State and of the Minister for the Civil Service as to numbers and as to terms and conditions of service. [**251**]

Remuneration and allowances

6. There shall be paid to the members of the Commission such remuneration, and such travelling and other allowances, as in the case of any of those members the Secretary of State may determine with the approval of the Minister for the Civil Service.

7. There shall be paid to the staff of the Commission such remuneration, and such travelling and other allowances, as the Commission may determine with the approval of the Secretary of State and of the Minister for the Civil Service. [**252**]

General provisions as to sums payable on retirement or death of members

8. As regards any member of the Commission in whose case the Secretary of State may so determine with the approval of the Minister for the Civil Service, the Secretary of State shall pay such pension, allowance or gratuity to or in respect of him, or make such payments towards the provision of such a pension, allowance or gratuity, as may be so determined.

9. If, when any person ceases to be a member of the Commission, it appears to the Secretary of State that there are special circumstances which make it right that he should receive compensation, the Secretary of State may pay him a sum by way of compensation of such amount as he may determine with the approval of the Minister for the Civil Service. [**253**]

Part II

Performance of Functions of Commission

10.—(1) If the chairman of the Commission so directs—

(*a*) the functions of the Commission in relation to any investigation under this

Act, in so far as those functions have not been performed before the direction is given, or

(*b*) the functions of the Commission in relation to the making of a report required of them under Part VI of this Act,

shall be performed through a group of not less than five regular members of the Commission selected by the chairman of the Commission.

(2) In the following provisions of this Part of this Schedule "group" means a group of members of the Commission selected under this paragraph, and "the chairman" (except where the reference is expressly to the chairman of a group) means the chairman of the Commission.

11. Where, after a direction under paragraph 10 of this Schedule has been given with respect to the investigations on a monopoly reference or on a merger reference, the reference is varied under section 52 of this Act or, in the case of a merger reference, under section 71 of this Act, the functions of the Commission in relation to those investigations shall be performed either through the group specified in that direction, or through another group, or by the Commission as a whole, as the chairman may direct.

12. The chairman may appoint one of the members of a group to act as chairman of the group.

13.—(1) Where during the proceedings of a group—

(*a*) a member of the group ceases to be a member of the Commission, or

(*b*) the chairman is satisfied that a member of the group will be unable for a substantial period to perform his duties as a member of the group,

the chairman may appoint any member of the Commission to be a member of the group in his place.

(2) The chairman may also at any time appoint any member of the Commission to be an additional member of a group, whether the person so appointed was or was not a member of the Commission at the time when the group was originally selected.

14.—(1) At the invitation of the chairman of a group, any member of the Commission who is not a member of the group may attend meetings or otherwise take part in the proceedings of the group, except that such a member shall not be entitled—

(*a*) to vote at any such meeting or in any such proceedings, or

(*b*) to have a statement of his dissent from a conclusion of the group included in a report made by them.

(2) Nothing in the preceding sub-paragraph shall be taken to prevent a group or a member of a group from consulting any member of the Commission with respect to any matter or question with which the group is concerned.

15. In determining their procedure, and in exercising any powers conferred on the Commission by this Act, a group shall comply with any special or general directions which may be given to them by the Commission, as well as with any directions given to the Commission by the Secretary of State.

16.—(1) Subject to the next following sub-paragraph, anything done by or in relation to a group in, or in connection with, the performance of functions required by a direction under paragraph 10 or paragraph 11 of this Schedule to be performed by the group shall have the same effect as if it had been done by or in relation to the Commission.

(2) For the purposes of sections 56 and 75 of this Act, of section 40 of the Patents Act 1949 (which confers on the comptroller certain powers which are exercisable with reference to a report of the Commission) and of section 19A of the Agricultural Marketing Act 1958, a conclusion contained in a report of the Commission shall be disregarded if the report is made through a group and the conclusion is not that of at least two-thirds of the members of the group.

17. The quorum necessary—
  (*a*) for any meeting of the Commission held for the final settling of a report of the Commission shall be not less than two-thirds of the regular members of the Commission, and
  (*b*) for any other meeting of the Commission shall be such as the Commission may from time to time determine.

18. The quorum necessary for a meeting of a group shall be such as the group may from time to time determine.

19. In the case of an equality of votes on any question at a meeting of the Commission or of a group the chairman, or the chairman of the group, as the case may be, shall have a second or casting vote.

20. At any time when the chairman is absent or otherwise incapable of acting, or there is a vacancy in the office of chairman,—
  (*a*) such one of the deputy chairmen of the Commission as the Secretary of State may direct, or in default of any such direction such one of them as they may agree, or
  (*b*) if there is only one deputy chairman of the Commission the deputy chairman,

may perform any of the functions of the chairman.

21. At any time when every person who is chairman or deputy chairman of the Commission is absent or otherwise incapable of acting, or there is no such person, such member of the Commission as the Secretary of State may direct, or in default of any such direction such member of the Commission as the Commission may agree, may perform any of the functions of the chairman.

22. For the purposes of a newspaper merger reference the Secretary of State may appoint three, four, or five additional members of the Commission, from a panel maintained by the Secretary of State for the purpose of making such appointments; and if any functions of the Commission in relation to that reference are performed through a group, any additional members appointed under this paragraph for the purposes of the reference shall be members of the group in addition to the members selected by the chairman. [**254**]

COMMENCEMENT

See s. 140 (3) and the note to s. 1, *ante*.

DEFINITIONS

"The Commission": s. 4 (1) or s. 137 (2).
"monopoly reference" and "merger reference": s. 5 (3).
"newspaper merger reference": s. 59 (3).
"group" and "chairman": note para. 10 (2) above.

GENERAL NOTE

Part I of this Schedule makes provision in respect of the status and appointment of members of the Commission similar to that made in respect of the Committee by Sch. 2, *ante*. Provision is also made for a staff to be appointed to the Commission. See generally the notes to Sch. 2, *ante*.

Part II of this Schedule makes more complex provision for the procedure of the Commission than is made for the Committee. The principal feature is the use of "groups" or subcommittees for some of the major activities of the Commission. The use of groups is within the discretion of the Chairman.

"*Part IV of this Act.*" *I.e.*, ss. 78–80, *ante*.
"*Consulting.*" See the note "After consulting" to s. 20, *ante*.
"*Secretary of State.*" See the note to s. 1, *ante*.
"*Quorum.*" See the note "Quorum necessary" to s. 20, *ante*.
Patents Act 1949, *s.* 40. That section is amended by s. 126, *ante*.
Agricultural Marketing Act 1958, *s.* 19A. That section is inserted by s. 127, *ante*.

SCHEDULE 4

Sections 14 and 109

SERVICES EXCLUDED FROM SECTIONS 14 AND 109

1. Legal services (that is to say, the services of barristers, advocates or solicitors in their capacity as such).

2. Medical services (that is to say, the provision of medical or surgical advice or attendance and the performance of surgical operations).

3. Dental services (that is to say, any services falling within the practice of dentistry within the meaning of the Dentists Act 1957).

4. Ophthalmic services (that is to say, the testing of sight).

5. Veterinary services (that is to say, any services which constitute veterinary surgery within the meaning of the Veterinary Surgeons Act 1966).

6. Nursing services (that is to say, any services which constitute nursing within the meaning of the Nurses Act 1957, the Nurses (Scotland) Act 1951 or the Nurses and Midwives Act (Northern Ireland) 1970).

7. The services of midwives, physiotherapists or chiropodists in their capacity as such.

8. The services of architects in their capacity as such.

9. Accounting and auditing services (that is to say, the making or preparation of accounts or accounting records and the examination, verification and auditing of financial statements).

10. The services of patent agents (within the meaning of the Patents Act 1949), in their capacity as such.

11. The services of parliamentary agents entered in the register in either House of Parliament as agents entitled to practise both in promoting and in opposing Bills, in their capacity as such parliamentary agents.

12. The services of surveyors (that is to say, of surveyors of land, of quantity surveyors, of surveyors of buildings or other structures and of surveyors of ships) in their capacity as such surveyors.

13. The services of professional engineers or technologists (that is to say, of persons practising or employed as consultants in the field of—

(*a*) civil engineering;
(*b*) mechanical, aeronautical, marine, electrical or electronic engineering;
(*c*) mining, quarrying, soil analysis or other forms of minerology or geology;
(*d*) agronomy, forestry, livestock rearing or ecology;
(*e*) metallurgy, chemistry, biochemistry or physics; or
(*f*) any other form of engineering or technology analogous to those mentioned in the preceding sub-paragraphs),

in their capacity as such engineers or technologists.

14. Services consisting of the provision—

(*a*) of primary, secondary or further education within the meaning of the Education Act 1944, the Education (Scotland) Acts 1939 to 1971 or the Education and Libraries (Northern Ireland) Order 1972, or
(*b*) of university or other higher education not falling within the preceding sub-paragraph.

15. The services of ministers of religion in their capacity as such ministers.

[255]

COMMENCEMENT

See s. 140 (3) and the note to s. 1, *ante*.

GENERAL NOTE

This Schedule lists the services excluded from ss. 14 and 109 of the Act. It can be seen that the basic intention is to exclude professional services. See the notes to ss. 14 and 109, *ante*.

Para. 3. For the meaning of "practice of dentistry", see the Dentists Act 1957, s. 33.

Para. 4. Ophthalmic services appear to have been somewhat narrowly defined.

Para. 5. For the meaning of "veterinary surgery", see the Veterinary Surgeons Act 1966, s. 27 (1).

Para. 6. For the meaning of "nursing" in England and Wales, see the Nurses Act 1957, s. 33 (1).

Para. 9. This does not cover all the services provided by professional accountants. It does not for example include advisory or consultancy services. It does however include services provided by accountants and auditors who are not professionally qualified.

Para. 10. For the meaning of "patent agent", see the Patents Act 1949, s. 101 (1).

Para. 14. For meanings of "primary education" and "secondary" education, see the Education Act 1944, s. 8 (1); for the meaning of "further education", see s. 41 of that Act.

SCHEDULE 5

Sections 16, 50 and 51

GOODS AND SERVICES REFERRED TO IN SECTION 16

PART I

GENERAL RESTRICTION

1. Gas supplied through pipes, otherwise than for industrial purposes as mentioned in section 9(4) of the Continental Shelf Act 1964.

2. Natural gas (that is to say, gas derived from natural strata) in so far as it does not fall within the preceding paragraph.

3. Electricity.

4. The carriage of passengers by road or rail.

5. The carriage of goods by rail.

6. The services of conveying, receiving, collecting, despatching and delivering letters.

7. The running of any system for the conveyance, through the agency of electric, magnetic, electro-magnetic, electro-chemical or electro-mechanical energy, of any of the matters specified in paragraphs (*a*) to (*d*) of section 24(1) of the Post Office Act 1969. [256]

PART II

LIMITED RESTRICTION

Description of goods or services	*Form of supply*
8.—(1) Apparatus or equipment used, or constructed or adapted for use, for the purposes of or in association with any such system as is mentioned in paragraph 7 of this Schedule.	Supply to persons who are subscribers to a service provided by the Post Office which constitutes or forms part of any such system, in their capacity as subscribers to such a service.
(2) The installation or maintenance of any such apparatus or equipment. [257]	

COMMENCEMENT

See s. 140 (3) and the note to s. 1, *ante*.

GENERAL NOTE

See, generally, the note to s. 16, *ante*.

Constructed or adapted. This means originally constructed or subsequently altered so as to make apt; cf. *French* v. *Champkin*, [1920] 1 K.B. 76, and *Hubbard* v. *Messenger*, [1938] 1 K.B. 300; see also *Taylor* v. *Mead*, [1961] 1 All E.R. 626; *Maddox* v. *Storer*, [1963] 1 Q.B. 451; *Flower Freight Co., Ltd.* v. *Hammond*, [1963] 1 Q.B. 275; and *Popperwell* v. *Cockerton*, [1968] 1 All E.R. 1038.

SCHEDULE 6

Section 19

Matters Falling Within Scope of Proposals Under Section 17

1. Prohibition of the specified consumer trade practice either generally or in relation to specified consumer transactions.

2. Prohibition of specified consumer transactions unless carried out at specified times or at a place of a specified description.

3. Prohibition of the inclusion in specified consumer transactions of terms or conditions purporting to exclude or limit the liability of a party to such a transaction in respect of specified matters.

4. A requirement that contracts relating to specified consumer transactions shall include specified terms or conditions.

5. A requirement that contracts or other documents relating to specified consumer transactions shall comply with specified provisions as to lettering (whether as to size, type, colouring or otherwise).

6. A requirement that specified information shall be given to parties to specified consumer transactions. [**258**]

COMMENCEMENT

See s. 140 (3) and the note to s. 1, *ante*.

DEFINITIONS

"consumer trade practice": s. 13.

"specified consumer trade practice", "specified consumer transactions", and "specified": s. 19 (3).

GENERAL NOTE

See the note to s. 19, *ante*.

SCHEDULE 7

Sections 50 and 51

Goods and Services (in addition to those in Schedule 5) Wholly or Partly Excluded from Section 50

Part I

Goods and Services Wholly Excluded

1. Raw cane or beet sugar.

2. Sugar beet.

3. Hops.

4. Water.

5. Port facilities (as defined by section 92(1) of the Transport Act 1962).

6. Air navigation services (as defined by section 64(1) of the Civil Aviation Act 1971).

7. The carriage of passengers or goods by air.

8. The provision by programme contractors of programmes for transmission (whether by way of television or of sound broadcasting) by the Independent Broadcasting Authority. [**259**]

Part II

Goods and Services Partly Excluded

Description of goods or services	*Form of supply excluded*
9. Liquid cows' milk.	Supply otherwise than in containers in which milk is put up for purposes of retail sale.

10. Refined sugar.	Supply otherwise than by way of retail sale.
11. Fleece wool.	Supply under a scheme for the time being in force under the Agricultural Marketing Act 1958.
12. Potatoes to which no process of manufacture (other than dressing or dyeing) has been applied.	Supply which is neither— (*a*) supply by way of retail sale, other than any such supply by the producer of the goods, nor (*b*) supply to a person purchasing the goods for the purpose of selling them by retail.
13. Services supplied at aerodromes (as defined by section 64(1) of the Civil Aviation Act 1971) in connection with the landing, housing, parking or taking off of aircraft or the accommodation of passengers or cargo and their transfer to and from aircraft.	Supply at aerodromes which are either— (*a*) aerodromes owned or managed by the Civil Aviation Authority, or (*b*) aerodromes in respect of which a licence for public use (as defined by any Order in Council for the time being in force under section 8 of the Civil Aviation Act 1949) is for the time being in force. [**260**]

PART III

GOODS PARTLY EXCLUDED IN RELATION TO NORTHERN IRELAND ONLY

Description of goods	*Form of supply excluded*
14. Live pigs.	Supply for slaughter.
15. Fresh uncured carcases or parts of carcases of pigs.	Supply otherwise than by way of retail sale. [**261**]

COMMENCEMENT

See s. 140 (3) and the note to s. 1, *ante*.

GENERAL NOTE

See the notes to ss. 50 and 51, *ante*. The goods and services listed in this Schedule may be referred to the Commission only by Ministers; see s. 51 (2), *ante*.

Retail Sale. See the note "Sale by retail" to s. 98, *ante*.

Civil Aviation Authority. See the Civil Aviation Act 1971, s. 1.

Sections 56, 73, 74, 77, 89, and 91

SCHEDULE 8

POWERS EXERCISABLE BY ORDERS UNDER SECTIONS 56 AND 73

PART I

POWERS EXERCISABLE IN ALL CASES

1. Subject to paragraph 3 of this Schedule, an order under section 56 or section 73 of this Act (in this Schedule referred to as an "order") may declare it to be unlawful, except to such extent and in such circumstances as may be provided by or under the order, to make or to carry out any such agreement as may be specified or described in the order.

2. Subject to the next following paragraph, an order may require any party to any such agreement as may be specified or described in the order to terminate the agreement within such time as may be so specified, either wholly or to such extent as may be so specified.

3.—(1) An order shall not by virtue of paragraph 1 of this Schedule declare it to be unlawful to make any agreement in so far as, if made, it would be an agreement to which Part I of the Act of 1956 would apply.

(2) An order shall not by virtue of paragraph 1 or paragraph 2 of this Schedule declare it to be unlawful to carry out, or require any person to terminate, an agreement in so far as it is an agreement to which Part I of the Act of 1956 applies.

(3) An order shall not by virtue of either of those paragraphs declare it to be unlawful to make or to carry out, or require any person to terminate, an agreement in so far as, if made, it would relate, (or as the case may be) in so far as it relates, to the terms and conditions of employment of any workers, or to the physical conditions in which any workers are required to work.

(4) In this paragraph "terms and conditions of employment" has the meaning assigned to it by section 167(1) of the Industrial Relations Act 1971.

4. An order may declare it to be unlawful, except to such extent and in such circumstances as may be provided by or under the order, to withhold or to agree to withhold or to threaten to withhold, or to procure others to withhold or to agree to withhold or threaten to withhold, from any such persons as may be specified or described in the order, any supplies or services so specified or described or any orders for such supplies or services (whether the withholding is absolute or is to be effectual only in particular circumstances).

5. An order may declare it to be unlawful, except to such extent and in such circumstances as may be provided by or under the order, to require, as a condition of the supplying of goods or services to any person,—

(*a*) the buying of any goods, or
(*b*) the making of any payment in respect of services other than the goods or services supplied, or
(*c*) the doing of any other such matter as may be specified or described in the order.

6. An order may declare it to be unlawful, except to such extent and in such circumstances as may be provided by or under the order,—

(*a*) to discriminate in any manner specified or described in the order between any persons in the prices charged for goods or services so specified or described, or
(*b*) to do anything so specified or described which appears to the appropriate Minister to amount to such discrimination,

or to procure others to do any of the things mentioned in sub-paragraph (*a*) or sub-paragraph (*b*) of this paragraph.

7. An order may declare it to be unlawful, except to such extent and in such circumstances as may be provided by or under the order,—

(*a*) to give or agree to give in other ways any such preference in respect of the supply of goods or services, or the giving of orders for goods or services, as may be specified or described in the order, or
(*b*) to do anything so specified or described which appears to the appropriate Minister to amount to giving such preference,

or to procure others to do any of the things mentioned in sub-paragraph (*a*) or sub-paragraph (*b*) of this paragraph.

8. An order may declare it to be unlawful, except to such extent and in such circumstances as may be provided by or under the order, to charge for goods or services supplied prices differing from those in any published list or notification, or to do anything specified or described in the order which appears to the appropriate Minister to amount to charging such prices.

9. An order may require a person supplying goods or services to publish a list of or otherwise notify prices, with or without such further information as may be specified or described in the order.

10.—(1) Subject to the following provisions of this paragraph, an order may, to such extent and in such circumstances as may be provided by or under the order, regulate the prices to be charged for any goods or services specified or described in the order.

(2) An order shall not exercise the power conferred by the preceding sub-paragraph in respect of goods or services of any description unless the matters specified in the relevant report as being those which in the opinion of the Commission operate, or may be expected to operate, against the public interest relate, or include matters relating, to the prices charged for goods or services of that description.

(3) In this paragraph "the relevant report", in relation to an order, means the report of the Commission in consequence of which the order is made, in the form in which that report is laid before Parliament.

11. An order may declare it to be unlawful, except to such extent and in such circumstances as may be provided by or under the order, for any person, by publication or otherwise, to notify, to persons supplying goods or services, prices recommended or suggested as appropriate to be charged by those persons for those goods or services.

12.—(1) An order may prohibit or restrict the acquisition by any person of the whole or part of the undertaking or assets of another person's business, or the doing of anything which will or may have a result to which this paragraph applies, or may require that, if such an acquisition is made or anything is done which has such a result, the persons concerned or any of them shall thereafter observe any prohibitions or restrictions imposed by or under the order.

(2) This paragraph applies to any result which consists in two or more bodies corporate becoming interconnected bodies corporate.

(3) Where an order is made in consequence of a report of the Commission under section 72 of this Act, or is made under section 74 of this Act, this paragraph also applies to any result (other than that specified in sub-paragraph (2) of this paragraph) which, in accordance with section 65 of this Act, consists in two or more enterprises ceasing to be distinct enterprises.

13. In this Part of this Schedule "the appropriate Minister", in relation to an order, means the Minister by whom the order is made. [**262**]

PART II

POWERS EXERCISABLE EXCEPT IN CASES FALLING WITHIN SECTION 56(6)

14. An order may provide for the division of any business by the sale of any part of the undertaking or assets or otherwise (for which purpose all the activities carried on by way of business by any one person or by any two or more interconnected bodies corporate may be treated as a single business), or for the division of any group of interconnected bodies corporate, and for all such matters as may be necessary to effect or take account of the division, including—

- (*a*) the transfer or vesting of property, rights, liabilities or obligations;
- (*b*) the adjustment of contracts, whether by discharge or reduction of any liability or obligation or otherwise;
- (*c*) the creation, allotment, surrender or cancellation of any shares, stock or securities;
- (*d*) the formation or winding up of a company or other association, corporate or unincorporate, or the amendment of the memorandum and articles or other instruments regulating any company or association;
- (*e*) the extent to which, and the circumstances in which, provisions of the order affecting a company or association in its share capital, constitution or other matters may be altered by the company or association, and the registration under any enactment of the order by companies or associations so affected;

(*f*) the continuation, with any necessary change of parties, of any legal proceedings.

15. In relation to an order under section 73 of this Act, the reference in paragraph 14 of this Schedule to the division of a business as mentioned in that paragraph shall be construed as including a reference to the separation, by the sale of any part of any undertaking or assets concerned or other means, of enterprises which are under common control otherwise than by reason of their being enterprises of interconnected bodies corporate. [**263**]

COMMENCEMENT

See s. 140 (3) and the notes to s. 1, *ante*.

DEFINITIONS

"Commission": s. 4 (1) or 137 (2).
"enterprise": s. 63.
"agreement", "business", "enactment", "goods", "Minister", "price", "supply" and "worker": s. 137 (2); also s. 137 (7) as to "worker".
"supply of services": s. 137 (3).
"services": s. 137 (4).
"interconnected bodies corporate", "group of connected bodies corporate": s. 137 (5).
"order": note para. 1 above.
"relevant report": note para. 10 (3) above.
"appropriate minister": note para. 13 above.

GENERAL NOTE

This Schedule provides for the matters on which orders may be made following a report containing an adverse finding. The provisions are along the same lines as the provisions of the Monopolies and Mergers Act 1965, s. 3. There is an additional power in para. 11 to prohibit the recommending of prices. Part II provides for a power to "unscramble" mergers. See the notes to ss. 56, 73, 74, 77, 89 and 91, *ante*.

Para. 3: "*Act of* 1956." See the General Note to s. 10, *ante*.

"*Section* 167 (1) *of the Industrial Relations Act* 1971." That Act was repealed by the Trade Union and Labour Relations Act 1974, s. 1.

Para. 6: "*Discriminate*"; "*discrimination.*" These expressions refer to differences in treatment between two persons; see *Melbourne Corporation* v. *Commonwealth* (1947), 74 C.L.R. 31, 61; *Post Office* v. *Union of Post Office Workers*, [1974] 1 All E.R. 229.

Para. 10: "*Against the public interest.*" See s. 84, *ante*.

"*Report.*" See ss. 54 and 72, *ante*.

"*Laid before Parliament.*" See s. 83, *ante*.

Para. 12: "*Undertaking or assets.*" The shares in a company are not part of its undertaking or assets but the acquisition of shares in a business is covered by the remaining words of the paragraph. So also it seems is the lending of money on the security of the undertaking or assets; for this may have the result at some future time of the lender acquiring the undertaking or assets or part of them.

Para. 12: "*Ceasing to be distinct enterprises.*" See ss. 65 and 66, *ante*.

Para. 14: "*Carried on by way of business by any one person.*" Note the provisions of s. 77, *ante*.

SCHEDULE 9

Section 91

PROCEDURE PRELIMINARY TO LAYING DRAFT OF ORDER TO WHICH SECTION 91(1) APPLIES

1. The provisions of this Schedule shall have effect where the Secretary of State proposes to lay before Parliament a draft of any such order as is mentioned in section 91(1) of this Act.

2. The Secretary of State shall cause notice of his intention to lay a draft of the order before Parliament to be published in the London Gazette, the Edinburgh Gazette and the Belfast Gazette and in two or more daily newspapers (other than local newspapers), and shall not lay a draft of the order until the end of the period

of forty-two days beginning with the day on which the publication of the notice in accordance with this paragraph is completed.

3. A notice under this Schedule shall—

(*a*) state that it is proposed to lay a draft of the order before Parliament;
(*b*) indicate the nature of the provisions to be embodied in the order;
(*c*) name a place where a copy of the draft will be available to be seen at all reasonable times; and
(*d*) state that any person whose interests are likely to be affected by the order, and who is desirous of making representations in respect of it, should do so in writing (stating his interest and the grounds on which he wishes to make the representations) before the date on which the period mentioned in paragraph 2 of this Schedule is due to expire (specifying that date).

4. The Secretary of State shall consider any representation that is duly made with respect to the draft order and is not withdrawn, and, at any time after the date specified in the notice in accordance with sub-paragraph (*d*) of paragraph 3 of this Schedule, may lay the draft order either—

(*a*) in the form in which it was made available as stated in the notice in compliance with sub-paragraph (*c*) of that paragraph, or
(*b*) in that form subject to such modifications as appear to the Secretary of State to be necessary to ensure that the rights and interests of persons likely to be affected by the provisions of the order are so adjusted as to secure an equitable distribution of any burden imposed by, or any benefit accruing from, any provisions of the order. [**264**]

COMMENCEMENT

See s. 140 (3) and the note to s. 1, *ante*.

GENERAL NOTE

This Schedule makes provision for the procedure to be followed before an order can be made under Sch. 8, Part II, *ante*; see the note to s. 91, *ante*.

"*Forty-two days beginning with.*" See the note to s. 20, *ante*.

"*Secretary of State*"; "*writing.*" See the notes to s. 1, *ante*.

"*Lay before Parliament.*" See the Laying of Documents before Parliament (Interpretation) Act 1948.

"*Secretary of State shall consider.*" It seems likely that the Minister has a duty to act judicially.

Sections 116, 117

SCHEDULE 10

MODIFICATIONS OF ACTS OF 1956 AND 1968 IN RELATION TO SERVICES

PART I

MODIFICATIONS OF ACT OF 1956

Section of Act	*Modification*
Section 10 ..	In subsection (1)(*b*), for the words "any such restrictions as are described in subsection (1) of section six of this Act" there shall be substituted the words "restrictions, or provision for or in relation to the furnishing of information, in respect of matters specified in the relevant order for the purposes of section 107(1)(*b*) or section 108(1)(*b*) of the Act of 1973". In subsection (7), for the words "this Part of this Act applies by virtue of subsection (6) of section six of this Act as if it were an agreement made between members of a trade association" there shall be substituted the words "subsection (1) of this section applies by virtue of section 112 of the Act of 1973 as if it were an agreement made between members of an association", and for the words "subsection (7) of the said section six" there shall be substituted the words "subsection (3) or subsection (4) of that section".

Section of Act	*Modification*
Section 14—*cont.*	In subsection (8), paragraph (*a*) shall be omitted, and for the words "section 8(8) of this Act", in each place where they occur, there shall be substituted the words "section 115(6) of the Act of 1973".
Section 11 ..	In subsection (3)(*b*), the words "of manufacture" shall be omitted.
Section 14 ..	In subsection (1), for paragraphs (*a*) and (*b*) there shall be substituted the following: "(*a*) a person carrying on within the United Kingdom any business of supplying services brought under control by the relevant order, or (*b*) an association which, in relation to the relevant order, is such an association as is mentioned in section 112(1) of the Act of 1973", and for the words "any such matters as are described in paragraphs (*a*) to (*e*) of the said subsection (1)" there shall be substituted the words "matters specified in the relevant order for the purposes of section 107(1)(*b*) or section 108(1)(*b*) of the Act of 1973". In subsection (3), the word "trade" shall be omitted. In subsection (4), paragraph (*a*) shall be omitted, and for the words "section 8(8) of this Act" there shall be substituted the words "section 115(6) of the Act of 1973".
Section 15 ..	In subsection (3A), for the words "a trade association which is not incorporated" there shall be substituted the words "an unincorporated association falling within section 112(1) of the Act of 1973".
Section 19 ..	In subsection (1)(*b*), for the word "prices" there shall be substituted the word "charges".
Section 20 ..	In subsection (1), for the words "matters described in paragraphs (*b*) to (*d*) of subsection (8) of section eight of this Act" there shall be substituted the words "the supply of services outside the United Kingdom or the supply of services to persons or in relation to property (as defined by section 115(9) of the Act of 1973) outside the United Kingdom". In subsection (3), for the words "any trade association" there shall be substituted the words "any such association as is mentioned in section 112(1) of the Act of 1973", for the words "such a trade association" and for the words "a trade association" there shall be substituted the words "such an association", and for the words "the trade association" there shall be substituted the words "the association". In subsection (4), for the words "subsection (7) of section six of this Act in an agreement for the constitution of a trade association" there shall be substituted the words "subsection (3) or subsection (4) of section 112 of the Act of 1973 in an agreement for the constitution of an association". [**265**]

PART II

MODIFICATIONS OF ACT OF 1968

Section of Act	*Modification*
Section 1 ..	In subsection (2), for the words "purchasers, consumers or users

Section of Act	*Modification*
Section 1—*cont.*	of any relevant goods" there shall be substituted the words "users of any relevant services".
Section 2 ..	In subsection (1), for the words "prices to be charged" there shall be substituted the words "charges to be made" and for the word "prices", in the second place where it occurs, there shall be substituted the word "charges".
Section 3 ..	In subsection (1), for the words "a trade association" there shall be substituted the words "an association", and for the words "subsection (7) of section 6 of the Act of 1956" and the words in parentheses immediately after those words there shall be substituted the words "subsection (3) or subsection (4) (as the case may be) of section 112 of the Act of 1973". In subsections (2) and (6), for the words "a trade association", in each place where they occur, there shall be substituted the words "an association".
Section 6 ..	In subsection (1), after paragraph (*i*) there shall be inserted the following paragraph:— "(*j*) in the case of an agreement which becomes subject to registration by virtue of an order under section 107 or section 108 of the Act of 1973 coming into force after the making of the agreement, within three months from the day on which the agreement becomes so subject."
Section 7 ..	In subsection (3), for the words "any trade association" there shall be substituted the words "any such association as is mentioned in section 112(1) of the Act of 1973", and for the words "a trade association" there shall be substituted the words "an association". In subsection (3A), for the words "a trade association" there shall be substituted the words "such an association as is mentioned in section 112(1) of the Act of 1973", and for the words "the trade association" there shall be substituted the words "the association". In subsection (4), for the words "a trade association" there shall be substituted the words "an association" and for the words "subsection (7) of section 6 of the Act of 1956" there shall be substituted the words "subsection (3) or subsection (4) of section 112 of the Act of 1973". [**266**]

COMMENCEMENT

See s. 140 (3) and the note to s. 1, *ante*.

DEFINITIONS

"relevant order", "the Act of 1973" and "services brought under control by the relevant order": s. 116 (8).

"services": s. 117 (1).

"business": s. 117 (2) (by virtue of 117 (3)).

"agreement" and "restriction": Restrictive Trade Practices Act 1956, s. 6 (3).

"supply": Restrictive Trade Practices Act 1956, s. 36 (1).

"the Act of 1956": s. 137 (1).

GENERAL NOTE

This Schedule sets out amendments to the 1956 Act and the 1968 Act consequent upon the passing of the 1973 Act. See further the notes to ss. 116 and 117, *ante*.

Sections 139, 140

SCHEDULE 11

TRANSITIONAL PROVISIONS AND SAVINGS

General provisions

1.—(1) Subject to the following provisions of this Schedule, in so far as anything done under an enactment repealed by this Act could have been done under a corresponding provision of this Act, it shall not be invalidated by the repeal but shall have effect as if done under that provision.

(2) In relation to the Commission (by whichever of the names mentioned in section 4(1) of this Act it was for the time being called) sub-paragraph (1) of this paragraph applies, in particular, to any appointment of a member of the Commission (including any appointment, or extension of the term of service, of a chairman or deputy chairman of the Commission) or of any of the staff of the Commission, any reference made to the Commission, any proceedings or report of the Commission on such a reference, and any order made in consequence of any such report.

(3) A provision of this Act shall, for the purposes of this Schedule, be regarded as corresponding to an enactment repealed by this Act if (notwithstanding that it differs, whether to a small extent or substantially, from that enactment) it fulfils in in this Act a purpose similar to that which that enactment fulfilled in the repealed enactments; and any reference in this Schedule to provisions of the repealed enactments corresponding to any provisions of this Act shall be construed accordingly.

(4) In this Schedule "the repealed enactments" means the enactments repealed by this Act, and "the commencement of this Act", where that expression occurs in any provision of this Schedule,—

(*a*) if the same day is appointed under section 140 of this Act for the repeal of all those enactments, means the day so appointed, or

(*b*) if different days are appointed under that section for the repeal of different enactments, means such day as may be specified for the purposes of this sub-paragraph in an order made by the Secretary of State by statutory instrument;

and different days may be so specified in relation to different provisions of this Schedule.

2. For the purposes of the operation of paragraph 1 of this Schedule, anything done by or in relation to the Board of Trade shall be treated as having been done by or in relation to the Secretary of State, whether apart from this paragraph it would fall to be so treated or not.

3. Without prejudice to any express amendment made by this Act, where an Act (whether passed before, or in the same Session as, this Act) or any document refers, either expressly or by implication, to an enactment repealed by this Act, the reference shall, except where the context otherwise requires, be construed as, or as including, a reference to any corresponding provision of this Act.

4. Where any period of time specified in an enactment repealed by this Act is current at the commencement of this Act, and there is a corresponding provision in this Act, this Act shall have effect as if that corresponding provision had been in force when that period began to run.

5. Without prejudice to paragraph 1 of this Schedule, any reference in this Act (whether express or implied) to a thing done or required or authorised to be done, or omitted to be done, or to an event which has occurred, under or for the purposes of or by reference to or in contravention of any provisions of this Act shall, except where the context otherwise requires, be construed as including a reference to the corresponding thing done or required or authorised to be done, or omitted, or to the corresponding event which occurred, as the case may be, under or for the purposes of or by reference to or in contravention of any corresponding provisions of the repealed enactments.

6. Nothing in this Act shall affect the repealed enactments in their operation in relation to offences committed before the commencement of this Act. [**267**]

Reference made to Commission before commencement of Act

7.—(1) Any reference made to the Commission under the repealed enactments, and any report of the Commission made before the commencement of this Act on any such reference, shall have effect in accordance with paragraph 1 of this Schedule if made in accordance with such of the repealed enactments as were applicable to it, and shall so have effect notwithstanding that the reference or report was not made in accordance with the corresponding provisions of this Act.

(2) In the case of any such reference on which the Commission have not made their report before the commencement of this Act—

(*a*) any proceedings of the Commission on that reference after the commencement of this Act shall be conducted in accordance with the repealed enactments as if they had not been repealed, and

(*b*) any report of the Commission on that reference shall be made in accordance with those enactments and not in accordance with any corresponding provisions of this Act;

but nothing in this sub-paragraph shall be construed as excluding the operation of any provisions of this Act relating to any functions of the Director in relation to the Commission, to the transmission to the Director of copies of reports of the Commission, or to any other action authorised or required to be taken in relation to or in consequence of a report made by the Commission.

(3) In particular, but without prejudice to the generality of the preceding sub-paragraphs, any reference, proceedings or report to which either of those sub-paragraphs applies shall have effect, or shall be conducted or made, as mentioned in that sub-paragraph notwithstanding that the reference or report related or relates to the question whether conditions to which the Act of 1948 applied prevailed or prevail, and not to the existence or possible existence of a monopoly situation within the meaning of this Act.

(4) For the purposes of the operation of sub-paragraph (2) of this paragraph in relation to a report made by the Commission after the commencement of this Act, section 29(1) of the Act of 1956 (whereby conditions to which the Act of 1948 applied were not to be considered to prevail by reason of any agreement to which Part I of the Act of 1956 applied) shall be construed as if section 6(1) of the Act of 1956 had been originally enacted as amended by section 95 of this Act. [**268**]

Report of Commission made before 5th August 1965

8. An order made under section 56 of this Act in consequence of a report made by the Commission before the commencement of the Act of 1965 shall not exercise any of the powers specified in Part II of Schedule 8 to this Act; and accordingly the powers conferred by section 89 of this Act shall not be exercisable in consequence of any such report. [**269**]

Undertaking given in consequence of report on reference made under repealed enactments

9.—(1) This paragraph applies to any undertaking given to a Minister which is certified by the Secretary of State to have been given in relation to matters dealt with in a report made by the Commission on a reference under section 2 of the Act of 1948 or on a reference under section 6 of the Act of 1965 and which either—

(*a*) was given before the commencement of this Act, or

(*b*) is given after the commencement of this Act in a case where no request under subsection (1) of section 88 of this Act has been made to the Director to carry out consultations in accordance with that subsection.

(2) A copy of any certificate given by the Secretary of State under the preceding

sub-paragraph shall be furnished to the Director and the Minister to whom any such undertaking was or is given shall furnish particulars of it to the Director.

(3) Subsection (4) of section 88 of this Act shall have effect in relation to any undertaking to which this paragraph applies as if—

(*a*) it were an undertaking of which particulars have been furnished to the Director under subsection (2) of that section, and

(*b*) any reference in subsection (4) of that section to the report of the Director were a reference to a report made by the Commission as mentioned in sub-paragraph (1) of this paragraph.

(4) The preceding provisions of this paragraph shall have effect without prejudice—

(*a*) to the duty of the Commission under section 86 of this Act to transmit to the Director copies of reports which were made by the Commission before the commencement of this Act and which, by virtue of paragraphs 1 and 7 of this Schedule, have effect as if made under this Act, or

(*b*) to any duty of the Director, where requested by the appropriate Minister or Ministers to do so with respect to any such report, to carry out such consultations as are mentioned in section 88(1) of this Act. [**270**]

Functions of Director in relation to orders made under Acts of 1948 *and* 1965

10. Subsection (5) of section 88 of this Act shall have effect in relation to any order which was made under section 10 of the Act of 1948 or under section 3 or section 6 of the Act of 1965 and which, by virtue of paragraph 1 of this Schedule, has effect as if made under this Act, as that subsection has effect in relation to orders made under this Act in the circumstances specified in that subsection. [**271**]

Provisions consequential upon transfer of functions from Registrar to Director

11.—(1) Except as provided by paragraph 15 of this Schedule in, relation to any time after the commencement of this Act, anything which has before the commencement of this Act been done by or in relation to the Registrar shall have effect as if it had been done by or in relation to the Director.

(2) Sub-paragraph (1) of this paragraph applies, in particular, to any regulations made by the Registrar, any register kept or document issued by the Registrar, any particulars furnished to the Registrar, and any application to or proceedings before the Restrictive Practices Court, or any other court, tribunal or authority, made or instituted by or against the Registrar or to which the Registrar was otherwise a party; and any such proceedings, if pending at the commencement of this Act, may accordingly be continued by or against the Director, or with the Director being otherwise treated as a party to them, as the circumstances may require, and for the purpose of so continuing them anything done by or in relation to the Registrar in connection with any such proceedings shall be treated as having been done by or in relation to the Director.

(3) In this Schedule "the Registrar" means the Registrar of Restrictive Trading Agreements. [**272**]

Particulars of export agreements

12. Any particulars furnished to the Board of Trade or to the Secretary of State under section 31(1) of the Act of 1956 shall be treated as if they had been furnished to the Director under section 10 of that Act as amended by sections 94(2) and 102(1) of this Act. [**273**]

Restrictive Trade Practices Act 1968, *s.* 11

13. An agreement which—

(*a*) was made before the commencement of this Act by a society at a time when it was approved for the purposes of section 11 of the Act of 1968 (wholesale co-operative societies), and

(*b*) by virtue of that approval was not subject to registration under Part I of the Act of 1956,

shall, notwithstanding the repeal of that section, not be subject to such registration. **[274]**

Pension benefits

14. The repeal by this Act of the following enactments, that is to say, Part II of Schedule 1 to the Act of 1965 and section 3(4)(*d*) of the Superannuation (Miscellaneous Provisions) Act 1967, shall not affect the operation of those enactments in relation to any person who was appointed to be chairman or deputy chairman of the Commission before the commencement of this Act; and, in relation to any such person, a recommendation made under paragraph 5 of that Schedule shall have effect whether made before or after the commencement of this Act.

15.—(1) The repeal by this Act of subsections (7) and (8) of section 1 of the Act of 1956 shall not affect the operation of those subsections in relation to any person who was appointed to be the Registrar before the commencement of this Act; and, in relation to any such person, a determination made under subsection (7) of that section shall have effect whether made before or after the commencement of this Act.

(2) Paragraph 11 of this Schedule shall not have effect for the purposes of the operation of subsection (7) or subsection (8) of section 1 of the Act of 1956 in accordance with the preceding sub-paragraph. **[275]**

Trade Descriptions Act 1968, *s.* 30

16. The repeal by this Act of subsections (2) to (4) of section 30 of the Trade Descriptions Act 1968 shall not affect the operation of those subsections in their application to any case where a notice under subsection (2) of that section, or a certificate under subsection (4) of that section or a document purporting to be such a certificate, has been given or issued before the commencement of this Act; and the duty imposed by section 130(1) of this Act shall not apply where such a notice has been so given. **[276]**

COMMENCEMENT

See s. 140 (3) and the note to s. 1, *ante*.

DEFINITIONS

"Commission": ss. 4 (1) and 137 (2).
"enactment": s. 137 (2).

GENERAL NOTE

This Schedule contains transitional provisions between the enactments repealed by this Act and the new provisions. For the enactments repealed see s. 139, *ante*, and Sch. 13, *post*.

Section 139

SCHEDULE 12

ENACTMENTS AMENDED

Act	*Amendment*
The Patents Act 1949 (12, 13 & 14 Geo. 6. c. 87).	In section 43, in subsection (6), for the words "Monopolies and Restrictive Practices Commission" there shall be substituted the words "Monopolies and Mergers Commission", and for the words "section nine of the Monopolies and Restrictive Practices (Inquiry and Control) Act 1948" there shall be substituted the words "Part VII of the Fair Trading Act 1973".

Act	*Amendment*
The Restrictive Trade Practices Act 1956 (4 & 5 Eliz. 2. c. 68).	In section 6, in subsection (1), for the words "the two next following sections" there shall be substituted the words "sections 7 and 8 of this Act" In section 22, after subsection (4) there shall be inserted the following subsection:— "(5) The foregoing provisions of this section shall not apply in relation to any order made under section 21A of this Act." In section 23, in subsection (2), after the words "this Part of the Act" there shall be inserted the words "or under Part III of the Fair Trading Act 1973". In section 30, in subsection (2), for the words "the said section ten" there shall be substituted the words section 56 of the Fair Trading Act 1973, or having effect as if made under that section". In section 36, in subsection (1), before the definition of "enactment" there shall be inserted the following:— " 'the Director' means the Director General of Fair Trading appointed under the Fair Trading Act 1973." In the Schedule, at the beginning of paragraph 7 there shall be inserted the words "Except as provided by section 42 of the Fair Trading Act 1973"; at the end of paragraph 8 there shall be inserted the words "but this paragraph shall not apply to appeals under section 42 of the Fair Trading Act 1973"; and in paragraph 10, after the word "Act" there shall be inserted the words "or under Part III of the Fair Trading Act 1973".
The Agricultural Marketing Act 1958 (6 & 7 Eliz. 2. c. 47)	In section 47, in the proviso to subsection (2), after paragraph (*a*) there shall be inserted the following paragraph:— "(*aa*) made to the Monopolies and Mergers commission or to any member, of that Commission, or to any of the staff of that commission, or to the Director General of Fair Trading or any of the staff appointed by that Director General, if it is made for the purpose of enabling the Commission or the Director General to perform any functions of theirs or his under the Fair Trading Act 1973."
The Public Records Act 1958 (6 & 7 Eliz. 2. c. 51).	In Schedule 1, in Part II of the Table set out at the end of paragraph 3, for the words "Registrar of Restrictive Trading Agreements" there shall be substituted the words " the Director General of Fair Trading".
The Agricultural Marketing Act (Northern Ireland) 1964 (c. 13).	In section 23, in subsection (2), after paragraph (*aa*) there shall be inserted the following paragraph:— "(*aaa*) made to the Monopolies and Mergers Commission or to any member of that Commission or to any of the staff of that Commission, or to the Director General of Fair Trading or any of the staff appointed by that Director General, if it is made for the purpose of enabling the Commission or the Director General to perform any functions of theirs or his under the Fair Trading Act 1973."

Act	*Amendment*
The Resale Prices Act 1964 (1964 c. 58).	In section 11(1), after the definition of "dealer" there shall be inserted the following:— " 'the Director' means the Director General of Fair Trading."
The Iron and Steel Act 1967 (c. 17).	In section 33, in subsection (4), for the words "Registrar of Restrictive Trading Agreements" there shall be substituted the words "Director General of Fair Trading" and, in subsection (5), for the word "Registrar" there shall be substituted the word "Director".
The Restrictive Trade Practices Act 1968 (1968 c. 66).	In section 6, in subsection (1), after paragraph (*g*) there shall be inserted the following paragraphs:— "(*h*) in the case of an agreement made before the commencement of the Fair Trading Act 1973 which becomes subject to registration in consequence of section 95 or section 101 of that Act, within three months from the coming into operation of Part IX of that Act; (*i*) in the case of an agreement which becomes subject to registration by virtue of the expiration or withdrawal of an approval given under section 6A of the Act of 1956, within three months from the day on which the agreement become so subject."
	In section 12, in subsection (3), for the words "Section 11 of the Monopolies and Restrictive Practices (Inquiry and Control) Act 1948" there shall be substituted the words "Section 93 of the Fair Trading Act 1973", and for the words "under section 10 of that Act" there shall be substituted the words "to which section 90 of that Act applies" and, in subsection (4), for the words "Board of Trade pursuant to section 31" there shall be substituted the words "Director pursuant to section 10(8)".
The Pensions (Increase) Act 1971 (1971 c. 56).	In Schedule 2, in paragraph 6, for the words from "the Chairman" to the end of the paragraph there shall be substituted the words "widows and children of any chairman or deputy chairman of the Commission which, by virtue of section 4(1) of the Fair Trading Act 1973, is known as the Monopolies and Mergers Commission, or payable out of moneys provided by Parliament in accordance with any recommendation made under paragraph 5 of Schedule 1 to the Monopolies and Mergers Act 1965 (chairman or deputy chairman of the Commission)".
The European Communities Act 1972 (1972 c. 68).	In section 10, for the word "Registrar", in each place where it occurs, there shall be substituted the word "Director"; and after subsection (2) there shall be inserted the following subsection:— "(2A) In this section 'the Director' means the Director General of Fair Trading."
The Local Government Act 1972 (1972 c. 70).	In section 201, in subsection (6)(*a*), after the words "Trade Descriptions Acts 1968 and 1972" there shall be inserted the words "or the Fair Trading Act 1973". [277]

COMMENCEMENT

See s. 140 (3) and the note to s. 1, *ante*.

SCHEDULE 13

Enactments Repealed

Chapter	Short Title	Extent of Repeal
11 & 12 Geo. 6. c. 66.	The Monopolies and Restrictive Practices (Inquiry and Control) Act 1948.	The whole Act.
4 & 5 Eliz. 2. c. 68.	The Restrictive Trade Practices Act 1956.	In section 1, subsection (1), and subsections (3) to (8). In section 11(7), the words "assistant registrar or other". In section 23, subsection (4). In section 24, subsection (8). Section 29. In section 30, in subsection (3), the words from the beginning of the subsection to the word "and", and subsections (4), (6) and (7). Section 31. Section 33. In section 35, paragraph (*a*) of subsection (1). In section 36(1), the definition of "the Registrar".
5 & 6 Eliz. 2. c. 20.	The House of Commons Disqualification Act 1957.	In Part III of Schedule 1, and in the Part substituted for the said Part III by Schedule 3, the words "Registrar of Restrictive Trading Agreements".
6 & 7 Eliz. 2. c. 51	The Public Records Act 1958.	In Schedule 2, the entries relating to section 17 of the Monopolies and Restrictive Practices (Inquiry and Control) Act 1948 and section 33 of the Restrictive Trade Practices Act 1956.
1964 c. 58.	The Resale Prices Act 1964.	In section 8, subsection (4). In section 11(1), the definition of "the Registrar".
1965 c. 50.	The Monopolies and Mergers Act 1965.	The whole Act.
1967 c. 28.	The Superannuation (Miscellaneous Provisions) Act 1967.	In section 3, paragraph (*d*) of subsection (4).
1968 c. 29.	The Trade Descriptions Act 1968.	In section 30, subsections (2) to (4).
1968 c. 66.	The Restrictive Trade Practices Act 1968.	Section 11.
1972 c. 68.	The European Communities Act 1972.	In section 10, subsection (3).

[278]

COMMENCEMENT

See s. 140 (3) and the notes to s. 1, *ante*.

DIVISION 3

REGULATIONS

THE PYRAMID SELLING SCHEMES REGULATIONS 1973

(S.I. 1973 No. 1740)

Made	..	*22nd October* 1973
Laid before Parliament	..	*25th October* 1973
Coming into Operation	..	*15th November* 1973

The Secretary of State in exercise of his powers under section 119 of the Fair Trading Act 1973 hereby makes the following Regulations:—

General

1.—(1) These Regulations may be cited as the Pyramid Selling Schemes Regulations 1973 and shall come into operation on 15th November 1973.

(2) In these Regulations "trading scheme" means a scheme to which Part XI of the Fair Trading Act 1973 applies other than a scheme under which—

(*a*) the prospect of receiving payments or other benefits in respect of all or any of the matters specified in section 118(2) of that Act is held out to only one participant in the United Kingdom; or

(*b*) the only prospect held out to any participant of receiving payments or other benefits in respect of matters so specified is the prospect of receiving a sum not exceeding £10 in respect of the introduction by him of another person who becomes a participant.

(3) The Interpretation Act 1889 shall apply to the interpretation of these Regulations as it applies to the interpretation of an Act of Parliament. [**279**]

GENERAL NOTE

These Regulations apply to all "trading schemes" (as defined in s. 118 of the Act) other than schemes under which the prospect of payments or benefits are held out to only one participant in the United Kingdom or, alternatively, under which the only prospect of benefit is the receipt of a sum not exceeding £10 in respect of the introduction of another participant.

The Regulations prescribe the contents of advertisements etc. relating to "trading schemes". The requirements are both positive and negative: such advertisements etc. are required to include the information set out in regs. 2 and 4; and those advertisements etc. are obliged to exclude the material prohibited by reg. 3. Furthermore, the Regulations lay down, in considerable detail, the rights of participants in "trading schemes": those participants are entitled to written notice of the agreements under which the scheme operates; they are afforded certain rights of terminating their participation in the scheme; the obligation of participants to make repayments is limited and they have the statutory right to require the promoter to re-purchase goods supplied on the terms set out in the Regulations; the contractual, and other, liability of a participant is limited by the Regulations; and the fiscal liability which can be imposed on a participant under a scheme is similarly limited by the Regulations.

The Regulations also make provision for the civil liabilities of promoters and participants in "trading schemes". The detailed provisions are set out in reg. 10 and, broadly, give immunity to a participant against civil liability where the Regulations are contravened.

Contents of advertisements etc.

2. A person shall not issue, circulate or distribute any document, being an advertisement, prospectus, circular or notice, containing—

(*a*) any invitation to persons to become participants in a trading scheme; or

(*b*) any information calculated to lead directly or indirectly to persons becoming participants in such a scheme,

unless it—

(i) states the date from which the scheme first operated in the United Kingdom or, in the case of a proposed scheme, the date on which it is proposed to operate it;

(ii) states the name and address of the promoter or, in the case of a scheme promoted by more than one person, the names and addresses of all the promoters;

(iii) describes the goods or services which form the subject of the scheme;

(iv) states whether the transactions to be effected under the scheme by any persons who may participate are to be effected in the capacity of servant or agent of the promoter or promoters or one of the promoters or as a principal; and

(v) describes the role of participants, or if there are two or more classes of participants, the role of each class of participant and, if persons who may participate are expected to induce others to buy goods or acquire services, indicates that such persons are expected to sell. [**280**]

3. A person shall not issue, circulate or distribute any such document as is mentioned in Regulation 2 if it—

(*a*) includes any assertion or suggestion that the recruitment of participants is easy or that participants in the scheme will inevitably benefit financially from the scheme;

(*b*) includes any example or illustration of the operation of the scheme in which the benefits which may accrue to a participant are demonstrated by aggregating the particular benefits to which a participant is entitled in consequence of each of a series of similar transactions or other occurrences;

(*c*) indicates or suggests that a participant will as a result of participation derive during any period a specified financial benefit or a financial benefit which will be not less than or greater than a specified sum. [**281**]

4. A person shall not issue, circulate or distribute any such document as is mentioned in Regulation 2, being a prospectus or circular, unless—

(*a*) it states the date on which it was first published;

(*b*) it sets out the terms and conditions of the agreement on which persons invited to join the scheme are to participate;

(*c*) it states the total number of participants in the relevant scheme or, if the scheme involves different classes of participants, the total number of participants in each class, at the date of publication of the document or at a date specified therein, being a date not earlier than three months before the date of publication; and

(*d*) where the relevant scheme was in operation at the date twelve months prior to the date of publication of the document, it states the total number of participants, or if the scheme then involved different classes of participants, the total number of participants in each class, at that date. [**282**]

Written contracts and rights of participants

5. A promoter of, or a participant in, a trading scheme shall not do any of the following things, namely—

(*a*) supply goods or services to a participant in the scheme, or

(*b*) provide any goods or services under a transaction effected by such a participant, or

(*c*) be party to any arrangement under which goods or services are supplied or provided as aforesaid, or

(*d*) accept from any such participant any payment, or undertaking to make a payment, in respect of any goods or services supplied or provided as mentioned in any of the preceding paragraphs or in respect of any goods or services to be so supplied or provided,

unless—

(i) all the terms of the agreement under which the relevant participant is participating in the scheme are set out in an agreement in writing made between him and the promoter or, if more than one, each of the promoters;

(ii) a copy of that agreement has been furnished to that participant; and

(iii) that participant enjoys the rights mentioned in Regulation 6:

Provided that nothing in head (i) or (ii) of this Regulation shall apply to preclude the doing of anything mentioned in heads (*a*) to (*d*) if the relevant participant was participating in the scheme before the commencement of these Regulations. [**283**]

Participants' rights in connection with termination

6. The rights referred to in Regulation 5 are—

(*a*) a right to terminate participation at any time without penalty by giving seven days written notice of termination to the promoter or any of the promoters at an address in the United Kingdom which has been furnished to the participant in writing;

(*b*) where notice is so given not more than 7 days after the participant first agreed to participate in the scheme and the participant so agreed after the commencement of these Regulations, a right to require the promoter or any of the promoters to repay him within 7 days any monies which he had paid to or for the benefit of the promoter or any of the promoters in connection with his participation in the scheme or paid to any other participant in accordance with the provisions of the scheme less—

(i) any amount due from or paid by him in respect of goods which he has sold;

(ii) an amount equal to the value of any other goods which have been delivered to him under the scheme and which he has not re-delivered or despatched to the promoter or promoters or to a person nominated by the promoter or promoters to receive them;

(iii) where any goods so re-delivered or despatched have deteriorated and their deterioration was occasioned by an act or default on his part, an amount equal to the diminution in their value resulting from such deterioration;

(*c*) where notice to terminate participation is given by the participant in any other circumstances, a right to require the promoter or any of the promoters to buy—

(i) at a price which is not less than 90 per cent. of the price which the participant paid for them less, in the case of any goods the condition of which has deteriorated due to an act or default on his part, an amount equal to the diminution in their value resulting from such deterioration;

(ii) on terms whereby the price is payable upon delivery of the goods or, if the goods are already held by the promoter or any of the promoters, forthwith, and

(iii) for delivery within 21 days of the giving of the notice at any place which the participant may reasonably nominate,

any goods which he has purchased under the scheme after the commencement of these Regulations;

(*d*) a right to be discharged upon the termination of his participation from all contractual liabilities towards the promoter or any of the promoters in connection with the scheme except—

(i) liabilities relating to payments made to him under contracts which he has made as agent for the promoter or any of the promoters;

(ii) in a case where termination of participation does not give rise to the right described in head (*b*) of this Regulation, any liability to pay the price of goods already sold to him by the promoter or any of the promoters;

(*e*) if the promoter or any of the promoters determines his participation in the scheme in accordance with its provisions, a right to require the promoter or any of the promoters to buy—

(i) at the price which the participant paid for them less, in the case of any goods the condition of which has deteriorated due to an act or default on his part an amount equal to the diminution in their value attributable to such deterioration,

(ii) on terms whereby the purchase price is payable upon delivery of the goods or, if the goods are already held by the promoter or any of the promoters, forthwith, and

(iii) for delivery within 21 days of such determination at the promoter's expense at any place which the promoter may reasonably nominate,

any goods which the participant has purchased under the scheme after the commencement of these Regulations. [**284**]

£25 liability limit

7. A promoter of, or a participant in, a trading scheme shall not accept from a participant any payment or undertaking to make a payment in respect of goods supplied or to be supplied under the scheme after the commencement of these Regulations if—

(*a*) the amount of the payment in question exceeds £25; or

(*b*) the amount of that payment plus any amount which the participant has already paid or undertaken to pay for other such goods exceeds £25,

unless—

(i) the participant has requested in writing that the relevant goods be supplied; and

(ii) he agreed in writing to participate in the scheme at least 7 days before he made that request. [**285**]

"Non-returnable" deposits

8. A promoter or a participant in a trading scheme shall not accept from a participant—

(i) any payment by way of security for goods or the payment of the price of goods supplied or to be supplied to the participant for sale by him on behalf of the promoter or a promoter or another participant under the scheme; or

(ii) any undertaking to make such a payment,

unless the recipient has agreed in writing that the payment is refundable upon the participant returning the relevant goods in an undamaged condition to the promoter or a promoter or that other participant. **[286]**

Training facilities and services

9. A promoter of, or a participant in, a trading scheme shall not—

(*a*) supply any training facilities or other services to a participant in the scheme, or

(*b*) be party to any arrangement under which such facilities are supplied or are to be supplied to a participant

unless the facilities or services are supplied or are to be supplied without charge to the participant. **[287]**

Civil consequences of contraventions

10.—(1) When a participant makes any payment to or for the benefit of a promoter of, or to another participant in, a trading scheme and the accepting of that payment involves a contravention of Regulation 5, 7 or 8, the participant shall be entitled to recover that payment from the promoter or any of the promoters or where the payment is made to another participant, from that participant.

(2) No undertaking to make any payment given by a participant in a trading scheme in any circumstances involving a contravention of Regulation 5, 7 or 8 shall be enforceable against him in any civil proceedings.

(3) A participant in a trading scheme shall be under no liability to pay for goods supplied to him in circumstances involving a contravention of Regulation 5.

(4) A participant in a trading scheme shall be under no liability to pay for any training facilities or other services required by Regulation 9 to be supplied only without charge to him and shall be entitled to recover any payment made for such facilities or services. **[288]**

EXPLANATORY NOTE

(This Note is not part of the Regulations.)

These Regulations relate to pyramid selling schemes and other trading schemes falling within the ambit of Part XI of the Fair Trading Act 1973.

They apply in relation to all schemes regulated by the provisions of Part XI other than schemes having the characteristics mentioned in Regulation 1 (2) (a) *and* (b).

Regulations 2 *to* 4 *are concerned with the content of documents which may induce people to participate in such schemes. All such documents must include the information set out in Regulation* 2 *and must not include any suggestion or example mentioned in Regulation* 3. *Additional information is required to be included in prospectuses and circulars (Regulation* 4).

Regulation 5 *generally requires participants to be given written contracts and the rights set out in Regulation* 6, *which include a right to withdraw at any time and to recover all payments if withdrawal is effected within* 7 *days of first joining. Participants must also be given the right to sell back goods purchased under the scheme to the promoter or promoters.*

Regulation 7 *limits to* £25 *the payments and commitments of new participants for goods supplied or to be supplied. It similarly limits the payments and commitments of any participants for goods the supply of which has not been sought in writing.*

Regulation 8 *prohibits the taking of "non-returnable" security payments from participants selling as agents: Regulation* 9 *prohibits the supply of training facilities and other services to participants if charges are made for them.*

Regulation 10 *deals with the civil consequence of breaches of Regulations* 5 *to* 9. [**289**]

INDEX

References are to paragraph numbers. The letter "n" indicates a note following a paragraph.

References are to paragraph numbers

References are to paragraph numbers

References are to paragraph numbers

Index

References are to paragraph numbers

References are to paragraph numbers

References are to paragraph numbers